Dissenters and Mavericks

DISSENTERS AND MAVERICKS

WRITINGS ABOUT INDIA

IN ENGLISH,

1765–2000

Margery Sabin

UNIVERSITY PRESS

2002

OXFORD

UNIVERSITY PRESS

Oxford   New York
Auckland   Bangkok   Buenos Aires   Cape Town   Chennai
Dar es Salaam   Delhi   Hong Kong   Istanbul   Karachi   Kolkata
Kuala Lumpur   Madrid   Melbourne   Mexico City   Mumbai   Nairobi
São Paulo   Shanghai   Singapore   Taipei   Tokyo   Toronto

Copyright © 2002 by Oxford University Press, Inc.

Published by Oxford University Press, Inc.
198 Madison Avenue, New York, New York 10016

www.oup.com

Oxford is a registered trademark of Oxford University Press

Library of Congress Cataloging-in-Publication Data
Sabin, Margery, 1940–
Dissenters and mavericks : writings about India in English, 1765–2000 /
Margery Sabin.
p. cm.
Includes bibliographical references (p.) and index.
ISBN 0-19-515017-1
1. English literature—History and criticism. 2. India—In literature.
3. Anglo-Indian literature—History and criticism. 4. Indic literature (English)—History
and criticism. 5. India—Foreign public opinion, British. 6. Great Britain—Relations—India.
7. India—Relations—Great Britain. 8. Imperialism in literature. 9. Postcolonialism—India.
10. India—Historiography. I. Title.
PR129.I5 S33 2002
820.9'3254—dc21   2002066791

1 3 5 7 9 8 6 4 2

Printed in the United States of America
on acid-free paper

TO MICHAEL AND PAUL

ACKNOWLEDGMENTS

I am grateful to many colleagues, friends, and students whose expertise, responsiveness, and encouragement have helped me during the decade and more of work on the varied materials of this book. Richard Poirier, both as friend and as editor of *Raritan Quarterly*, gave invaluable editorial help as well as a steady welcome to my initial and subsequent ventures into the field of colonial and postcolonial studies. Stephen Wall and Christopher Ricks, of *Essays in Criticism*, also gave generous editorial assistance. The English Department at Wellesley College and James Maddox, director of the Bread Loaf School of English, encouraged my development of the courses "Fiction of Empire and the Breakup of Empire" and "Indian Writing in English," through which I came to explore much of the material now in the book. I am grateful to the thoughtful and provocative responsiveness of the many excellent students who took these courses and who wrote independent theses, among whom stand out Debie Titus Brown, Sonal Khullar, Rukhsar Sharif, Pamela Bandyopadhyay, and Mohsin Tejani, whose South Asian perspectives on our work taught me more than I could learn from books. Pankaj Mishra has generously responded to the queries of a stranger, introducing me to the special satisfactions of extending scholarly work to contemporary writers and events. My often critical relationship to the arguments of Edward Said in this book in no way diminishes my debt to his groundbreaking and provocative work and my appreciation for his friendship and encouragement over many years.

Of the many other individuals who have read or conversed and helpfully argued with me about parts or all of this work, I wish especially to thank David Bromwich, William E. Cain, Christopher Candland, the late Robert Garis, Michael Gorra, Ambreen Hai, Francis G. Hutchins, Judith Kates, Yoon Sun Lee, Peter J. Marshall, James Noggle, Jeff Nunokawa, Timothy Peltason, Lisa Rodensky, Lawrence Rosenwald, Vernon Shetley, Patricia Meyer Spacks, and Luther T. Tyler. Madeline McDonnell provided patient and painstaking help in preparation of the manuscript, and Linda White helped me through many computer crises. My husband, James E. Sabin, continues to keep up my spirits by his adventurous curiosity and his (almost) unflagging optimism. I also thank our sons, Michael Sabin and Paul Sabin, and our daughters-in-law, Deborah Paine Sabin and Emily Bazelon, for their interest and enthusiasm and for the inspiriting energy they stimulate through their own activities of reading, writing, and lively dissent.

An NEH Fellowship in spring 1992 allowed me to pursue research in London at the British Library, the Senate House Library, and the library at the School of Oriental and Asian Studies and to benefit from the hospitality of the Institute for Commonwealth Studies at the University of London, where I was a visiting fellow again in spring 1995, with sabbatical support from Wellesley College.

Earlier versions of chapters 3, 6, and 8 appeared in *Raritan Quarterly* (fall 1991; spring 1995; and spring 2002) and are reprinted by permission; an earlier version of chapter 5 appeared in *Essays in Criticism* (winter 1994) and is reprinted by permission; part of chapter 7 was developed for the Seminar on Commonwealth Literature at the Institute for Commonwealth Studies, University of London, and was printed in the institute's Collected Seminar Papers, no. 4, *Aspects of Commonwealth Literature* (1993). I am grateful to the Whitney Institute of Humanities, Yale University, for the opportunity to present my work on Naipaul, in April 1994, and to the English Department Colloquium at Tufts University for the opportunity to introduce my preliminary interpretation of Walpole's letters, in March 1999; parts of chapters 3 and 7 appeared in a paper, "Anecdote and Argument in British Writing about India," presented to the Association of Literary Scholars and Critics, in Toronto, in October 1998. I am also indebted to the Burke Faculty Study Group at Wellesley College for the opportunity to present and to receive responses to preliminary work for chapter 2, in 1999–2000. Some of my general concerns about reading and interpretation were presented in a paper delivered at the Presidential Forum, Modern Language Association meeting, December 1994, and subsequently published as "Literary Reading in Interdisciplinary Study," in *Profession 95,* and in the keynote address for the Northeast Annual Meeting of the Association of Departments of English in spring 1996, later published as "Starting from the Particular in Literary Reading," in *ADE Bulletin* (fall 1997).

CONTENTS

Dissenters and Mavericks

INTRODUCTION

Why Dissent Matters to Literature

I start with some explanation for what may appear an idiosyncratic selection of texts for analysis. This book is clearly not proposing a roll call of heroic dissenters in the history of British colonialism in India. As Edward Said and others have persuasively demonstrated, opposition to British rule in India (or elsewhere in the emerging empire) scarcely existed in England during the two centuries of British power.[1] There is no heroic textual tradition of anticolonial dissent. My final chapters about postcolonial Indian writing in English register the further point that, since Indian independence, the distinction between orthodoxy and dissent has shifted from decade to decade, depending also on where one stands and on whether one is male or female. The trauma of Partition and the rise of religious fundamentalism, state authority, and feminist protest, together with the mixed loyalties of Indians and Pakistanis living in what is now being called the Indian Diaspora, make any single honor role of postcolonial dissenters impossible to devise.

This collection of essays also differs from an inclusive survey of writings critical of the British–Indian relationship, valuable as such a study might be. Burke, who *is* featured here, would probably head such a survey at the far end; from the twentieth century there would be, of course, Gandhi and early twentieth-century English liberals, such as George Orwell and Leonard Woolf. The accomplishments of E. M. Forster and Salman Rushdie would merit entire chapters in a survey of dissent, rather than being left to come through in the form of pervasive points of reference. Finally, the complex and special place of women writers, conspicuously missing here, would certainly need to be addressed in such a survey. I mention my omissions more in the mode of invitation than apology. If others were to propose additional and even better examples of dissenters and mavericks, or to define the concept of dissent differently, that would be more than fine with me. I am left at this point in my own work with particular questions about how the collective challenge of postcolonial feminism to the subordination of women in both

3

colonial and anticolonial discourse multiplies difficulties for those women writers who are resistant to submerging their individual literary voices in any collective. The subject merits study beyond the scope of this book.

My goal here is to promote and participate in what is still a tentative opening of postcolonial studies to literary analysis and judgment. Some texts have been selected for their relative unfamiliarity; others for their importance to a range of concerns from different historical periods beginning with the mid-eighteenth century. The overfamiliar syllabus of canonical colonial and post-colonial texts tends to perpetuate fixed lines of interpretation and debate with scant regard to historical particularity. I also deliberately choose examples from a wide range of genres—personal letters, political speeches, novels, travel writing, autobiography, and journalism—because I argue that literary methods of reading need not be restricted to works of what used to be called "genius," nor even to conventional literary forms. Implicit in this broadening of the materials that literary reading may illuminate is the hope that both social scientists and literary professionals themselves may more clearly recognize what literary study offers to historical and other forms of social inquiry; in recent years, the field of literature has participated in inter-disciplinary work mainly as a needy recipient of theories and methods from other disciplines.

I call my standard of selection and method of analysis "literary" in that dissenters and mavericks are discussed here as *authors*, whose unorthodoxy manifests itself in distinctive qualities of language and design in their writing. How such a literary approach branches off from, say, sociology or anthropology recurs as a theme through the book, but a brief practical example here seems pertinent to the question of choosing texts. The social scientist who reads a ten-year run of a magazine such as *Quest*, the Bombay "Journal of Art and Ideas" from the 1950s discussed in chapter 6, or the Victorian archive of *sati* accounts discussed in chapter 3, legitimately looks for patterns and norms that constitute the collective discourse represented by this material; analysis of the discourse, in turn, yields further general insights into the culture reflected and expressed in this discourse. Most of the writing in *Quest*, or in any other magazine or cultural archive, will interest a later reader mainly for the ways it represents a classifiable cultural formation; in my own research, I in part follow the models and benefit from the methods developed in what has come to be called cultural studies. But only in part, because as a literary critic I am always also on the lookout for something special, something qualitatively better than the norm, and worth reading not primarily for more evidence of general discursive patterns but for its own value and as stimulus to further and different questions, such as "Look at this! Who wrote it? What makes it special? What else did this author write? How does this distinctive piece of writing help explain why so many of the others seem inert?"

The discovery of exceptional writings in unexpected places does not invalidate the concept of a colonial discourse; its value is to loosen the grip of cultural generalization by reintroducing evaluative literary distinctions as complicating factors. If no better than ordinary texts had emerged from my archival research, as a literary critic I probably would have lost interest in the chapters involving journalism and the *sati* discourse, even though analysis of mediocre writing is fun as well as informative. The fun of it comes from the mastery of the object that possession of a theory or method or set of hypotheses provides the interpreter. The exceptional text resists that mastery and, if the critic is willing, offers the different satisfaction of an experience that baffles and even contradicts expectations.

My chapters about famous writers similarly combine divergent lines of inquiry, exploring the tension between conformity to type and divergence from it—in terms of reading, the tension between discourse analysis and literary criticism. My sequence of argument, however, tends to reverse the order now dominant in postcolonial analysis, where the stature of an admired text usually comes at the start of an argument that, in the end, presses the author back into the general cultural pattern. I tend to put acknowledgment of a collective colonialist discourse first and then turn to what still remains distinctive and divergent in a particular text. My selection of examples was finally governed by where my interest was most attracted by that remainder.

But why, the uninitiated might ask, should these habits of literary curiosity and judgment, entirely familiar to editors, book reviewers, and nonacademic readers, need to knock at the door of interdisciplinary cultural studies in such beseeching terms? The simple answer goes back to the initial attraction of "discourse analysis" as a polemical theory and method of reading to set against earlier humanist tendencies to separate the aesthetic artifact from the cultural formation that shapes and limits its existence. Since my own American education in British literature and history managed to leave my ignorance of the British empire almost entirely undisturbed through both undergraduate and graduate study, I appreciate Edward Said's revelatory and profound arguments about the systematic neglect of Western imperial power as a dominant cultural formation. His *Orientalism* (1978) and *Culture and Imperialism* (1993) have greatly influenced my own turning of attention to this subject. But I have turned to it with enduring concern for literature and with continuing questions about how historical and aesthetic understanding can best be related to each other in the activity of reading.

Although Said has been the most forceful and influential advocate of colonial discourse analysis, he makes a peculiar prosecutor in the postcolonial case against literature and literary criticism because he is himself the most literary of postcolonial critics in his talents, training, and asserted tastes. Many sentences in *Culture and Imperialism*, and a few in *Orientalism*, caution that "novels are not reducible to a sociological current" (CI, 73); "one must always be at great pains to show that different imaginations, sensibilities, ideas, and philosophies were at work, and that each work of literature or art is special" (CI, 53). Said opens *Orientalism* by affirming: "I study Orientalism as a dynamic exchange between individual authors and . . . large political concerns" (O, 14–15). The problem with Said's two most influential books and, more specifically, with their influence is that, perhaps from exaggerating the strength of the literary side of this exchange, Said's formidable intellectual power has mainly gone into the attack, leaving the literary investigation of individual authors to others, who have been slow to muster equivalent energy and historical knowledge to keep the exchange alive. Very little dynamic exchange between the literary and the political occurs in current postcolonial studies or, for that matter, within Said's own writing, where the argument on behalf of different imaginations and particular works of literature usually appears as a concession in a subordinate clause: "And while one must always be at great pains. . . ." Said's sentences, paragraphs, and intellectual energy typically proceed from concession to massive attack on the homogeneous and unified quest for power throughout every activity of culture in the West: "There was virtual unity of purpose on this score: the empire must be maintained, and it *was* maintained" with "scarcely any dissent, any departure, any demurral" (CI, 53).[2]

My own term "dissent," in this context, carries a double reference: both to more unorthodox, if not revolutionary, qualities in certain individual colonial and postcolonial texts than Said and others actually concede and to the currently unorthodox procedures of reading I recommend to bring to the fore the whole range of literary qualities that are routinely subordinated if not extruded by prevailing academic terminology and methods.

Starting in the early 1990s, many of those who sought ways of advancing beyond what came to seem monotonous and predictable indictments of the literary past in postcolonial studies under the influence of *Orientalism* welcomed the theoretical and methodological revisions offered by critics such as Sara Suleri, in *The Rhetoric of English India* (1992), and Homi Bhabha, in his essays collected in *The Location of Culture* (1994). Bhabha, Suleri, and a new generation influenced by them have opened up the rigid oppositional structure of Orientalism by infusing into textual analysis indeterminacies derived from psychoanalytic and deconstructive hermeneutics. By turning to unconscious anxieties, ambivalences, fears, and displacements hinted at especially by elisions and contradictions in the writings, this new branch of postcolonial analysis focuses on disruptive currents of feeling across what are now perceived to be the more porous boundaries that separate colonizer from colonized. Colonial discourse, like other textual objects examined through the lens of these theories, becomes more dramatic, more intriguing, more neurotic and erotic (especially in Suleri's work).[3]

Stimulating as this new work is, problems for the exchange between literature and politics or history continue, because attention to the cultural unconscious of colonial relations offers new ways to withhold regard from the language and designs of individual writers and texts. Writing, like other acts of consciousness, is a way in which individuals differentiate themselves from each other—arguing, imagining, making and breaking relationships with the worlds they inhabit and even with their own unconscious. These negotiations, which for writers center in language, continue to get short shrift in this new phase of postcolonial criticism, not least because its dense, psychoanalytically inflected jargon so entirely displaces both the personal and the historical idiom of the texts being read. As in the worst professional psychoanalytic writing, a specialized, alien language asserts theoretical and scientific authority over voices rendered virtually inaudible in interpretive transcription. As a model followed by less original thinkers than Suleri and Bhabha, this "advance" of colonial discourse analysis has already reached an impasse of its own, installing its vocabulary and practices as professional requirements, while restricting its audience to a small group of academic initiates. Said, in his role as president of the Modern Language Association in 1999, forcefully criticized the confusion and isolation that have resulted from the dominance of these tendencies, not only in postcolonial criticism but throughout literary study: "All manner of fragmented, jargonized subjects of discussion now flourish in an ahistorical limbo. They are not completely anthropological or sociological or philosophical or psychological, although they seem to carry some of the marks of all those disciplines."[4] Said calls now for "a reinforced sense of intellectual responsibility" in literary studies: "responsibility to what in fact we ought to do, namely, the interpretation, analysis, and serious consideration of literature in its historical and social environment."

That there are not as yet very many models of current postcolonial criticism that fulfill Said's charge can be explained partly by the combination of theoretical, political, and professional prestige attached to what now constitutes the "discourse" of academic postcolonial criticism. Initially, the theoretical terminology of so-called counterhegemonic criticism had the explicit purpose of warding off contamination, compromises, or seductions that might seep through the common English idiom that carried the legacy of imperial power. Anti-imperialist critique, according to Ranajit Guha, founder of the Subaltern Studies Collective, must radically repudiate the very language, as well as the analytic methods and standards of evidence in the British colonialist tradition. Supported by citations from Hegel, Marx, Gramsci, and Hayden White, Guha asserts a position common also in other manifestos of Cultural Studies: "no discourse can oppose a genuinely uncompromising critique to a ruling culture so long as its ideological parameters are the same as those of that very culture" (DH, 11).[5] In order to reclaim "the purloined past" of conquered India, according to Guha, new forms of language were needed that could reverse the colonial sequence whereby the power of the "sword conferred a 'right' on the pen as well" (DH, xiv). Without actually discarding English in favor of native languages (as the Kenyan writer Ngugi wa Thiong'o boldly advocates),[6] Indo–English postcolonial critique has promoted a densely theoretical argot derived from Continental European terminology to signal dissociation (paradoxically) from the European colonial past.

But, as anti–imperial criticism has hardened into academic orthodoxy, a new generation of professors and students has accepted the jargon as a professional credential and taken for granted a limited method of analysis without any longer feeling pressed to defend or explain it—nothing so grand as a call for revolution, but more nearly what John Stuart Mill calls "dead dogma" in *On Liberty*, where he memorably outlines how even compelling and persuasive ideas lose their "living Power" in the absence of challenge and dissent:

> They [the doctrines or creeds] are all full of meaning and vitality to those who originate them, and to the direct disciples of the originators. . . . At last [the doctrine] either prevails, and becomes the general opinion, or its progress stops. . . . The doctrine has taken its place, if not as a received opinion, as one of the admitted sects or divisions of opinion: those who hold it have generally inherited, not adopted it. . . . Instead of being, as at first, constantly on the alert either to defend themselves against the world, or to bring the world over to them, they have subsided into acquiescence, and neither listen, when they can help it, to arguments against their creed, nor trouble dissentients (if there be such) with arguments in its favour. From this time may usually be dated the decline in the living power of the doctrine.[7]

Despite the current pertinence of Mill's account, some valuable examples of what he calls "dissentients" within postcolonial criticism do stand out. Bart Moore–Gilbert is one, not only in collecting work from a younger generation of literary critics in the volume *Writing India* but, more particularly, in his own excellent and suggestive interpretations of Kipling, which locate ambivalence and ideological tension in the ironic effects of Kipling's narrative technique and arrangements of detail in his art, rather than in a generalized, anonymous cultural unconsciousness.[8] An earlier important model is Dennis Porter, who has steadfastly insisted on characteristics of language that make certain texts more literary than others. "The literary," he argues, identifies "a qualitative distinction between texts that are characterized by a self-interrogating density of verbal texture and those that offer no internal resistance to the ideologies they reproduce."[9] In his evaluative emphasis, which also involves him in reattaching texts to individual authors and to particular historical contexts, Porter has been a strong critical voice in relation to what he calls "the relative coarseness of discourse theory when applied to the literary field."[10]

Porter's effort to reconstitute the category of the "literary" focuses on travel writing because he sees it as a genre exceptionally open to "powerful transgressive impulses."[11] The obscure energies that fuel the experience of travel generate verbal complexity, play, and the "internal ideological distanciation" Porter identifies as a "capacity" of literature as such and that is "usually absent from political tracts or statesmen's memoirs."[12] There is no essential reason, however, to deny "self-interrogating density" to the political speeches, memoirs, and journalism that I include here along with letters, novels, and travel writing. The distinction is qualitative, as Porter affirms.

In relation to political and historical writing, a valuable guide is the historian of political thought J. G. A. Pocock. In the introduction to *Virtue, Commerce, and History*, Pocock lucidly explains how every author "inhabits a historically given world that is apprehensible only in the ways rendered available by a number of historically given languages; the modes of speech available to him give him the intentions he can have."[13] Rather than use this version of discourse theory to efface the identity of authors or to freeze historical periods in rigid ideological molds, Pocock rejects the reductive methodologies commonly derived from discourse theory. So many idioms are available and interacting with each other at any particular historical moment, he argues, that individual authors may promote innovation and dissent by their ways of stretching or shifting the valence of received language. For Pocock, "the most powerful minds" in the history of political thought are "exploring the tension between established linguistic usages and the need to use words in new ways."[14]

It must be remarked, however, that although India engaged the attention of many powerful minds during the two hundred years of British rule, the whole phenomenon, with its astonishing profusion of writing, produced curiously little that fully meets Pocock's criteria, no less Said's. Even the most ambitious and exploratory writers in English, until well into the twentieth century, stumbled into a mental block at the seemingly unthinkable thought that the British should simply leave India (or never have gotten involved there in the first place). Debates center on *how* Britain should govern India but tend to back away into stereotyped formulae when defending the fundamental ethics of being there at all as a foreign ruling power. The "historically given world" during most of these two centuries presented India as an already fragmented field of contest for competing superpowers. In the middle of the eighteenth century the main rival to Britain was France; by the end of the nineteenth century, either Russia or the United States or both loomed as the British empire's major competitors for the future. The global reach of national interest was beyond debate: if Britain were not to be a global power, the argument went, then another ambitious nation would no doubt take its place. The unchallenged acceptance of this political and economic perspective makes the entire European discourse about India an easy prey to retrospective deprecation in our officially anti-imperialist age—not that Americans today actually inhabit a historically given world with fundamentally different assumptions about global power as an economic and political necessity for the nation.

The surprise is that, within the limits of the historically given, so much variety, dissent, and drama of thought do occur in writing about India in the English language; diverse idioms do clash within and between texts, and many individual writers in many genres do impressively confront the enormity of the British conquest as rule and legacy. If one substitutes English-language writers about India for the equally disparaged category of women singled out in the "Prelude" to *Middlemarch*, George Eliot's sympathetic irony offers attractive terms of appeal on behalf of individual variation, without claiming too much for it: "If there were one level of . . . incompetence as strict as the ability to count three and no more, [English-language writers about India] might be treated with scientific certitude. Meanwhile the indefiniteness remains, and the limits of variation are really much wider than any one would imagine."[15]

George Eliot helps to explain why the individual variations among writers about India respond better to literary than to scientific analysis. The indefinite relationship between the individual and the typical has long been a special interest of serious literature and the study of it. Pocock's own originality comes from his application to political theory of attitudes, skills, and idiom recognizable from the discipline of literary study. Close observation and qualitative judgment of the linguistic tensions in texts do not typically figure in political science. Pocock and other notable exceptions leave intact the generalization that the disciplines of the social sciences (in the century or so since they were invented) have differentiated themselves from the humanistic study of literature and history by focusing analysis on the representative case, rather than on individual variation. The anomalous scarcely affects the outcome in quantitative social science research, while other advanced methods of social science analysis often succeed in converting the apparently exceptional into a disguised form of the typical after all.

Prevailing postcolonial critique offers little space for literary reading as I am describing it because it denies individuation: every text is made to be representative of collective discourse, even when the point made concerns ambivalence or anxiety. Such reduced differentiation invites no exploration of the specific questionings and self-questionings that give distinction to particular voices, nor is it responsive to history in attending to the varying pressures of different historical moments. The molds of contemporary cultural analysis tend to coerce all of the past, and the present also, into its own often anachronistic categories. I am arguing for an approach to postcolonial reading that allows the voices heard in writing a chance to talk back, to exert pressure on the presuppositions and preferences that we, as readers, may bring.

Perhaps the greatest challenge to the inert categories of academic postcolonial criticism has come from the remarkable proliferation and success of current fiction in English by writers of South Asian location or origin. Book reviewers, prize committees, anonymous readers in Internet chat rooms, handwritten recommendations on index cards in bookshops report preferences in spontaneous, informal, evaluative terms, sometimes commending one part of a book over the rest or differentiating among works by a single author. The diverse accomplishments of this new generation of Indian authors, such as Vikram Seth, Rohinton Mistry, Amitov Ghosh, Arundhati Roy, Pankaj Mishra, Amit Chaudhuri, Shashi Tharoor, Jhumpa Lahiri, and others may eventually reshape the terms of postcolonial academic criticism to the extent of shifting interpretations of earlier writers, such as Nirad C. Chaudhuri, V. S. Naipaul, and Salman Rushdie. My choice of the young journalist, literary critic, and novelist Pankaj Mishra for the epilogue to this book expresses not so much a prediction of his future stature above the rest of his generation as my attraction to a young writer who brings an exceptional range of literary knowledge and skill to his writing about contemporary social and political events.

Because the essays that follow subordinate methodological dispute to the extended analysis of particular texts and writers, it seems useful to identify further in advance the crucial distinctions in reading practice that are at stake. I have chosen three examples of influential postcolonial analysis applied to texts not discussed elsewhere in this book but important to my own eighteenth-, nineteenth-, and twentieth-century selections. The examples serve the further purpose of introducing and differentiating among interpretive issues paramount in each of three distinct historical periods.

Ranajit Guha and Eighteenth-Century Historiography

Ranajit Guha, the eminent historian and founder of the group known as Subaltern Studies, offers a provocative first example, partly because his long-standing engagement with eighteenth-century colonial writing bears directly on my own readings of Horace Walpole and Edmund Burke, and partly because he has so explicitly confronted fundamental choices in the handling of textual evidence. The sequence of writings in Guha's own career displays a drama of self-repudiation not visible when his influential manifestos for Subaltern critique are taken alone.

Paradoxically, Guha's own compelling and original 1963 book, *A Rule of Property for Bengal*,[16] is an outstanding example of the liberal historiography that Subaltern Studies later rejects. What identifies Guha's lively and far-ranging monograph as liberal historiography is not the position of its argument, which harshly blames "neofeudal" mass poverty in India on the late eighteenth-century British land policy of granting permanent title and revenue collection privileges to the hereditary Indian class of *zamindars*.[17] Guha's central thesis, which remains the same through his thirty-five-year evolution into the leader of Subaltern Studies, directs particular animus against the Indian middle class that evolved from the landholding elite granted "permanent" privileges by the British at the end of the eighteenth century. According to Guha, the self-serving loyalty of this class to its British sponsors and its superficial affectation of Western culture mask an exploitative and alienated relationship with the Indian masses whom it illegitimately claims to represent. The fact that Guha reports, in the preface to *A Rule of Property*, his own lineage from this privileged class adds personal intensity to the abiding argument of his career.

For my purpose here, it is Guha's interpretive method, rather than his economic and political argument in *A Rule of Property*, that calls for further comment. The early book directs attention to the ideas behind the eighteenth-century land policy debates, exploring the intricate interplay between eighteenth-century political and economic theories and administrative policies. The fullness of textual demonstration is crucial to Guha's point that colonial land policy disputes must be broadly understood as manifestations of competing European conceptions of society and government. By analyzing the writings of five or six key figures, Guha traces the recommendations for Indian land policy to sources in a variety of advanced French, Scottish, and English writing on difficult political and economic questions not specifically related to colonialism: what forms of property ownership favor stable government? What systems of taxation promote prosperity and what kinds destroy it? How does wealth circulate through a society to encourage the most productive social distribution of wealth?

At every point in his argument, Guha draws on the widest possible range of references to show that what earlier historians had narrowly construed as quarrels about how the East India Company could best secure land revenues makes another, deeper kind of sense in terms of comprehensively different systems of thought as well as opposing interpretations of Indian history.

More in the spirit of Pocock than of later Subaltern critique, Guha, in *A Rule of Property*, identifies a variety of eighteenth-century idioms for arguing the relationship among virtue, commerce, and agricultural industry in India. Warren Hastings (through administrators such as James Grant) put forth the view that in India all land has always belonged to the "king"; this view supported the claim that the East India Company, as the successor to

Mughal rule in Bengal, was entitled to exercise all the royal privileges of land ownership throughout the conquered territory (RP, 101). Hastings's most severe opponent, Sir Philip Francis, denounced this idea of centralized royal power in India as a distortion of Indian history, which he interpreted to feature a class of noble hereditary landholders, more in line with advanced European (and Whig) thought on the conditions for agricultural prosperity in general. Francis's version of Indian history gave the sanction of Indian tradition to his alternative policy of promoting Bengali prosperity by further supporting this privileged Indian class. Alliances and divergences of thought are not so simply divided into two camps, however; Guha interestingly explains how the historiographer Alexander Dow could reach conclusions akin to Francis's but "drawn from . . . completely different economic premises" (RP, 32).

Insofar as a single powerful mind emerges from *A Rule of Property*, it belongs surprisingly to Francis, a figure not previously accorded much regard in British intellectual histories. According to Guha, nineteenth-century historians wrongly diminished Francis to the scandal-mongering manipulator of Burke's overzealous campaign against Hastings; Guha, by contrast, wishes to rehabilitate Francis by demonstrating the more comprehensive "spirit" of his moral as well as political and economic principles (RP, 93). Guha favors Francis over Burke for the idealistic radicalism that gave coherence to Francis's views of everything from Indian agriculture to slavery to the French Revolution to human nature itself. Burke admired Francis but broke off their close friendship in the 1790s after Francis severely criticized *Reflections on the French Revolution* and advised Burke not to publish it.[18]

The central paradox for Guha in *A Rule of Property* is how the "lucidity and power" of Francis's mind sponsored a land policy even more ruinous for India's future than the improvisatory *realpolitik* of Hastings would have been; the disastrous outcome of the "Permanent Settlement" was to stabilize an exploitative landholding elite.[19] The fatal flaw in Francis's plan, Guha explains, came from the excessively abstract idealism of a mind too unbending to adjust principles to the contradictory force of facts. Not least among the obstructive Indian facts that Francis did not accommodate in his scheme was the incompetence of the existing class of *zamindars* to perform the social and economic responsibilities assigned to them as landed proprietors in a Whig model of the English aristocracy. "The disparity between the ideal and the actual was nowhere more pronounced than in the condition of the Bengal zamindars. By the 1770s this ancient class had already lost its wealth, power and competence" (RP, 126). The error comes across as catastrophic but not ignominious. Guha lifts Francis into the honorable company of other victims of historical irony whose high intent seems virtually the cause of failure. Guha's view that Hastings's disregard for *zamindar* privileges would have in the long run produced a more egalitarian agricultural social structure in India further emphasizes the ironic discrepancy between intentions and consequences since Hastings's goal was the security of British power and not the social reorganization of India.

During the thirty-five years between *A Rule of Property* and his recent *Dominance without Hegemony*,[20] Guha discarded his earlier attentiveness to the differences between one thinker and another, as well as his sense of the ironic and tragic law of unintended outcomes in history. Whereas Guha in 1963 dissented from earlier liberal historians by more carefully differentiating the conceptual frameworks and idioms of writers and policymakers conventionally lumped together, Guha in his essay "Historiography and the Formation of a Colonial State" repudiates any kind of differentiation: "all" British historical writing in the last thirty-five years of the eighteenth century, he now asserts, was governed by the East India Company's drive to increase and more efficiently collect land revenue in Bengal (DH, 161). Following in the line of Said's argument that all the great projects of Orientalist scholarship were devised to serve the advancement of Western power, Guha unites the whole spectrum of British historical writers behind a single colonialist "purpose," which was to "aid a foreign power forcibly to exploit the resources of our land" (DH, 164). Two of the figures most thoroughly opposed to each other in *A Rule of Property*, Alexander Dow and James Grant, curiously reappear in the later work without differentiation, stripped down to a brief quotation or two that carry the total burden of evidence for Guha's generalization. Francis, the most admired writer in Guha's earlier book, receives no attention at all.

In displacing the idea of writing's "purpose" from individual authors to a single collective drive, Guha puts aside all signs of individual ambition or error. Differences of intellectual affiliation, the relationship of India to other major concerns within any individual mind, the complex of political, philosophical, and economic idioms that informed and even obsessed administrators as well as historians disappear in a newly dismissive view of eighteenth-century British historical writing as a "simple technical exercise" in the service of exploitation (DH, 165).

The same method used to deny complex, purposeful consciousness to individual colonial writers also turns into a strange way of bestowing consciousness on the peasant masses in Guha's 1983 monograph, *Elementary Aspects of Peasant Insurgency in Colonial India*. The drive to shift historical attention to previously neglected groups is an admirable and important goal of the Subaltern Studies Collective, as of other progressive movements in European and American history. Guha faces the severe problem of textual evidence common to this kind of study, however, since the illiterate Indian peasantry left virtually no written record of its thoughts and feelings. Guha's solution is to infer "rebel consciousness" through counterhegemonic reading of the same elite texts as before.[21] The extreme oppositional reading practice proposed in the preface to *Elementary Aspects of Peasant Insurgency* requires, quite simply, that the meanings of words in the dominant discourse be inverted so that the peasant consciousness suppressed by the hostility of the elite discourse may be deduced by contrast:

> The words, phrases and, indeed, whole chunks of prose . . . are de-signed primarily to indicate the immorality, illegality, undesirability, barbarity, etc. of insurgent practice and to announce by contrast the superiority of the elite on each count. . . . The antagonism is indeed so complete and so firmly structured that from the terms stated for one it should be possible, by reversing their values, to derive the implicit terms of the other. When, therefore, an official document speaks of badmashes as participants in rural disturbances, this does not mean (going by the normal sense of that Urdu word) any ordinary collection of rascals but peasants involved in a militant agrarian struggle. In the same context, a reference to any 'dacoit village' (as one comes across so often in the Mutiny narratives) would indicate the entire popula-tion of a village united in resistance to the armed forces of the state; 'contagion'—the enthusiasm and solidarity generated by an uprising among various rural groups within a region; 'fanatics'—rebels in-spired by some kinds of revivalist or puritanical doctrines; 'lawless-ness'—the defiance by the people of what they had come to regard as bad laws, and so on.[22]

Guha's drive to revolutionize reading appears nowhere more disturbing than in this recommendation to decode the meaning of texts by the system-atic inversion of words. Whereas earlier, Guha was arguably too deferential to the intellectual nuances in the prose of various colonial administrators, his corrective is now mechanical repudiation of colonial written language, ex-cept as a key to opposite meanings, as if there were no intermediary point be-tween excessive reverence and systematic inversion of language's stated meanings.

Homi Bhabha's Diagnosis of Colonial *Aporia* in John Stuart Mill

Although psychoanalytic revisions of the reading process involve quite com-plex verbal analyses, the authority of the interpretation's own complexity similarly distracts attention from what is actually happening within the lan-guage of individual texts. I take my second methodological example from Homi Bhabha's essay "Sly Civility" in *The Location of Culture*.[23] Instead of

Guha's subaltern militancy, Bhabha proposes sympathy for what he diagnoses as colonialist neurosis. According to Bhabha, "an ambivalence at the
very origins of colonial authority" generates collective pathology, "the paranoia of power," which converts frustrated authority into feelings of "im-
placable aggression" toward the self (95, 100). Bhabha's version of psychoanalytic method encourages the same confidence of generalization as
subaltern Marxism. Thus a rapid list of neurotic mechanisms sums up the
collective pathology of colonial discourse: "splitting, doubling, turning into
its opposite, projecting" (97). Although Bhabha does not go so far as to propose inverting the meanings of words in texts, the concepts of splitting and
projecting in psychoanalytic theory do also sanction the reversal of stated
meanings or, at the least, the unlocking of very diverse articulations with a
single master key.

A few sentences from Bhabha's use of John Stuart Mill can illustrate what
happens to an important nineteenth-century argument about the governing
of India when treated by Bhabha's adaptation of psychoanalytic technique.
Mill represents what Bhabha calls the *aporia* of English liberalism when
faced with the colonial question because, as Bhabha is not the first to observe,
Mill "divided his life between addressing the colonial sphere as an examiner
of correspondence for the East India Company, and preaching the principles
of postutilitarian liberalism to the English nation" (93).

Aporia was an obscure Greek philosophic term until deconstructionist
critics popularized it to name a host of allegedly unresolvable impasses in
thought and language.[24] Bhabha reaches for this technical philosophic term
in order to enforce the sense that no ordinary language of consciousness can
handle the contradiction between Mill's employment in the high ranks of the
East India Company and his intellectual career as philosopher of liberalism.
The impasse is representative, he argues, of colonial *aporia*, which he illustrates by juxtaposing two quotations from Mill: first, that "to govern one
country under responsibility to the people of another . . . is despotism"; then
this seeming contradiction: "The only choice the case admits is a choice of
despotisms. . . . There are, as we have already seen, conditions of society in
which a vigorous despotism is in itself the best mode of government for
training the people in what is specifically wanting to render them capable of a
higher civilization" (96).

Even taking these fragments of Mill's language as Bhabha offers them,
they hardly constitute *aporia*, in the sense of an unresolvable logical or
rhetorical contradiction. Mill seems to excuse the apparent violation of liberal principle in British rule of India by invoking a hierarchy of civilizations
and by adopting a notion of "Oriental despotism" already made conventional
in colonial discourse by the influence of Montesquieu in the eighteenth century.[25] If India were not under British rule, he seems to say in a routine Victorian formulation, it would surely suffer some other form of despotism, and

British despotism is at least preferable to Oriental forms in that it aims to train the subject people for a better future. That familiar argument may seem offensive to some twenty-first-century ears in its ranking of civilizations and its presumption to know what forms of government suit different conditions of society. But this colonialist arrogance is not in itself a symptom of *aporia*, paranoia, or even ambivalence.

Mill's specific argument in these pages, however, is far less conventional in context than it appears in what turns out to be Bhabha's quite extraordinary manipulation of quotations to support his general point about colonial contradiction. That Bhabha attributes the quoted sentences to *On Liberty*, rather than to their actual source in the final chapter of *Considerations on Representative Government*, might be mere carelessness (263 n. 15). The error favors Bhabha's emphasis on contradiction, however, since the *Considerations* do not so much "preach" liberty, in Bhabha's word, as take up a variety of consciously and explicitly difficult problems in government. The discrepancy between ideals and practical politics creates for Mill the difficulties in need of "consideration."

Bhabha further and more significantly distorts Mill's entire conception of "consideration" as a mental activity by actually rearranging the order of his sentences and eliminating through ellipsis those that would clarify Mill's train of argument. A reader needs to go back to Mill's original text independently to see that, in the pages cited, Mill is precisely *not* repeating but *dissenting* from the prevailing British view of Indian governance in the 1860s.[26]

The specific issue at stake for Mill is Parliament's vote of 1858 to take over direct rule of India from the East India Company. While from one point of view, this vote constituted only the last step in a progressive shift of political authority from Company to Crown, Mill thought the change sufficiently significant to refuse service in the new arrangement, thus terminating his thirty-five-year career in Indian affairs.[27] By depersonalizing Mill into a representative case study of colonial *aporia*, Bhabha simply erases the historical point that Mill, writing the *Considerations* in 1861, was explaining at some length why he still thought a seriously wrong choice had been made, with consequences he foresaw as disastrous.

Why dampen the thrill of *aporia* with these scrupulosities of context? The answer is simply that the context shows Mill to be suffering not from *aporia* but from the more mundane frustration of repeating and explaining judgments that seem obvious to him but that his contemporaries have rejected. The strained patience of tone as well as the considerable length of Mill's explanation belies Bhabha's melodramatic general point that colonial discourse "loses . . . its power of speech" when confronted with colonial contradiction (96). After asserting the difficulty of the colonial situation, which offers, he says, only a "choice of imperfections" and the need to distinguish practical possibilities from "ideal" governance, Mill raises his voice to urgency about the immorality of governors who do not act even in the direction of the ideal: "if they do not even aim at it, they are selfish usurpers, on a par in criminality with any of those whose ambition and rapacity have sported from age to age with the destiny of masses of mankind" (567–68).

It may still seem odd that Mill could in 1861 recommend the East India Company as a vehicle through which to approach ideal governance in India. The Indian Rebellion of 1857 and its ferocious aftermath testified loudly to the failure of East India Company rule; the trauma of 1857 was what precipitated the final takeover by Parliament that Mill so vehemently opposed. Mill, however, (accurately) foresaw a more punitive policy from the new parliamentary regime, while also imagining a worsening of hostility from Indian perception of that shift. Looking beyond these immediate political concerns, Mill also grounds his preference for the Company over the Crown in the principle of "expertise," a political idea still current, if still controversial, in foreign affairs today. Given the inevitable obstacles to any good form of foreign rule, Mill argues, only a body of professional experts independent of electoral or Crown politics has a chance of promoting the interests of a foreign people; the state, governing directly, will act first, if not exclusively, in the interests of its home constituency (568–71). Mill predicts doom from what had become and would remain official direct rule of the new British empire in India: "A free country which attempts to govern a distant dependency, inhabited by a dissimilar people, by means of a branch of its own executive, will almost inevitably fail" (573). These pessimistic pages conclude the entire book of *Considerations*.

Like Burke's the century before, Mill's tone is exhortatory; Burke and Mill are not representing public opinion as it exists but prophesying disaster from the country's refusal to heed their superior, expert insights. Mill's position and principle, however, entirely reverse Burke's vision of Parliament as the redemptive force in Indian affairs. Whereas Burke in the 1780s called Parliament to punish and control the East India Company, Mill seventy-five years later declares the fundamental *incapacity* of Parliament to rule India with any disinterested commitment at all. Each writer so eloquently foretells the doom of the opposed (and, in each case, prevailing) position that it may seem pathological to us that neither takes the obvious further step of simply denouncing the whole British colonial enterprise in India altogether. That boundary of thought, however, was not crossed by British writers until after World War I, when the terms of pessimism and warning in the writings of British dissenters such as Burke and Mill entered the discourse of Indian nationalism and (very gradually) circled back with new effect on English anti-imperialists, too.

Bhabha traces the contradictions and vacillations in British ideas of how to govern India to the unique *aporia* of colonialism: "Those substitutive objects of colonialist governmentality—be they systems of recordation, or 'interme-

diate bodies' of political and administrative control—are strategies of surveillance that cannot maintain their civil authority once the colonial supple-
mentarity, or excess of their address is revealed" (96). I interpret this oc-
cluded critical language to be making the same point that Bhabha insists on
elsewhere, namely that colonialism confronted the principles of British "civil
authority" with a unique challenge that defeated their very language for political thought. In *Considerations on Representative Government*, however, colonialism is only one among several difficult problems of governance addressed
by Mill with similar principles and equally arguable practical solutions.

The domestic issue of suffrage reform, for example, also shows Mill trying to move through some awkward vehicles in the direction of an ideal—in
this case, representative government within Britain. Although Mill in the
1860s was an activist advocate for extension of the suffrage to women and the
still disenfranchised working classes, his chapter "Extension of the Suffrage" comes up with the peculiar proposal of "plural voting," what he also
calls "graduated suffrage," whereby criteria of education and employment
would grant greater weight to some votes over others. Mill's faith in expertise (otherwise nameable as his elitism) pulls against his commitment to participation as the best form of political training. Mill might deny, however,
that there is real contradiction here at all. An unequally weighted vote, like a
grant of only limited civil authority to Indians, might have seemed to Mill a
practical resolution of the tension between the need for prior training and
the simultaneous need for participation as itself a form of training in self-
government.

Many of Mill's specific proposals for suffrage reform seem as fantastical
now as his faith in the civilizing value of East India Company rule. The notion that "a banker, merchant, or manufacturer, is likely to be more intelligent than a tradesman" (475), or that graduates of universities deserve double votes, look now like no more than vulgar snobbery. My point is not to
defend Mill's specific proposals but rather to identify the competing commitments, principles, and idioms that create tension and what we may regard
as limitations and errors in Mill's thought. Fuller textual and historical context dissipates the impression of *aporia*. The often strained interplay between principle and practice constitutes Mill's strength as well as his limitation as a political philosopher. His political writing about both India and
Britain explores, even if it does not satisfactorily resolve, the tension between
political ideals and practical governance, between progressive faith in liberty
and conservative fear of chaos from the collapse of hierarchy.[28]

A psychobiographical analysis of Mill's political preoccupation with the
tension between dependence and independence might go further to explore
its personal origins in the history of Mill's own self-documented struggle for
independence from his father, James Mill. India plays an intense role in this
personal drama, starting from Mill's childhood initiation into Indian history

at the age of twelve, reading proofs for James Mill's *History of India*, followed by his continuing apprenticeship at age seventeen as clerk to his father in the East India Company. Lynn Zastoupil and others have suggested Mill's increasing independence from his father's Utilitarian approach to understanding India in the course of his own colonial career. Zastoupil also notes that analysis of Mill's Indian writings has only just begun.[29] Bhabha's collective melodrama of colonialist psychopathology, along with his deconstructionist and psychoanalytic terminology, turns its back on this enterprise by depersonalizing Mill into a representative of collective colonial psychopathology. Coercing Mill's text into a generalized diagnosis of the unconscious of colonial discourse, Bhabha strips Mill's mind of its own personal unconscious, as well as blocking access to his purposeful conscious thought. In a caricature of psychoanalytic practice, the hapless author-patient has no authority to talk back.

Said's Two-Sided Argument and Edward Thompson

The schematizations of postcolonial critical practice often impose distorting grids on what the text offers, even when the critical goal is praise. My third example, to illustrate this more subtle form of coercion, appears in Said's choice to honor, in *Culture and Imperialism*, a small book published in 1925, *The Other Side of the Medal*,[30] by Edward Thompson (father of the distinguished British Marxist historian E. P. Thompson). An ex-Methodist missionary educator for thirteen years in Bengal, Edward Thompson left India in a mood of some disillusionment in 1923, returning to England to teach Bengali language and Indian history at Oxford and to write moderately successful novels based on his Indian experience. Thompson was also a regular on the liberal lecture circuit, where he joined E. M. Forster in telling unpopular truths about the Raj. *The Other Side of the Medal* is a quite shocking exposé of British atrocities during the Indian Rebellion of 1857. Said alludes to its title by calling his own big chapter on nationalist opposition "There Are Two Sides." An antithesis between imperialism and anti-imperial nationalism, drawn mainly from Frantz Fanon, organizes Said's interpretations in the chapter and his distribution of critical praise and blame. Thompson's merit as a "crusading opponent" is thus played off against E. M. Forster's weakness in *A Passage to India*. Said faults Forster for underrepresenting the force of anti-imperial nationalism in *A Passage to India*, while Thompson's recognition of the "other side" wins praise (CI, 203, 206–7).

The simple interpretive problem—again a question of whose terms shall control an argument—is that Thompson's text proposes its own two-sided structure that does not correspond to Said's opposition between imperialism and nationalist resistance. Indeed, Thompson's terms are manifestly at odds with Said's. If one begins with an open question—what does Thompson mean by his metaphor of a two-sided medal?—the answer is there on every page. Thompson's metaphoric medal (on its shiny side) honors Britain's imperial accomplishment in India, including the triumph of British power over the 1857 Indian Rebellion. That shiny side needs no polishing, in Thompson's view; it is the official British record on show. His book turns attention to "the other side of the medal," the dark and hidden side, which for him is not Indian nationalism but the suppressed history of British atrocity, British savagery, and British barbarism. The Mutiny legend had by the 1920s repressed this inglorious record from British consciousness and conscience. Thompson's book seeks to bring it back into the light and to do so by using documents that are unimpeachable because they come entirely from the British archive written at the time of the events. Thompson's two sides constitute an internal moral drama for the British, rather than the "contest between two warring nations" that is the only significant conflict in Said's interpretive structure.

Although Thompson recognizes the intensity of Indian hatred of the British, he plays down the nationalist political aspirations in anti-British Indian sentiment. His anxiety focuses on the implications of British more than Indian feeling. Thompson uses his language to make the British internal moral drama vivid. The suppressed record of British atrocity is like a ghostly shadow, haunting and poisoning all subsequent efforts at reform or reconciliation between British and Indians. He represents his British contemporaries as still morbidly obsessed with sensationalist visions of Indian barbarism in 1857. His documents, however, show equally lurid pictures of British deeds, and not only in retaliation. The British "mind," he exhorts, "should sit in judgment on its dream, unless the nerves of waking thought and action are to become diseased" (54). As for the Indians, like "men and women everywhere," they want their self-respect given back to them, and Thompson optimistically argues that the British can accomplish this by relinquishing the hysterical exaggeration of Indian savagery and atoning for the savage underside of British power. British atonement, for Thompson, has the goal of dissipating Indian hatred and ushering in a new attitude of "friendship and forgiveness" under political arrangements that it is not his main purpose to specify (75).

Once Thompson's quite explicit terms of argument are clear, what further interest does this text hold for postcolonial study? According to Said's interpretive antitheses, Thompson just gets demoted to yet another illustration of Western reluctance to recognize nationalist struggles against imperialism. His score plummets, and this little book may seem hardly worth reading.

The Indian historian Sumit Sarkar in a long afterword to an Indian reprint of *The Other Side of the Medal*, suggests some further possibilities.

Thompson's powerful imagery of haunted consciousness and diseased nerves acquires greater interest and sense as an individual drama in the light of Sarkar's description of Thompson's tortured years of ambivalence about Indian nationalism from 1925 to 1940. It was not easy for him to let go the commitments of his life's work as an educator in India. Only after the trauma of his older son's death while fighting with partisans against Nazi occupation in Bulgaria did he finally convert to the cause of Indian national independence.[31] Sarkar also complicates our historical understanding of the subtle tensions within particular subcultures, such as Bloomsbury, when he observes that, although Hogarth Press published Thompson's book in 1925, Thompson never really belonged to the Bloomsbury set; he notes that Forster is on record as having included Thompson on a list of "Public Bores."[32] Perhaps that marginality contributes to the audible strain in *The Other Side of the Medal*, as Thompson awkwardly exhorts a disaffected English audience to take a more intense moral interest in Indian affairs. No topic is more boring to an Oxford audience than India, Thompson remarks at the outset, anticipating only bitter and dismissive response to his exposé of British wrongdoing. Thompson is moralizing to a tired post–World War I audience, many of whom had already given up on the India adventure. "Very well, we will go," he imagines them saying (1). It is this callous and cynical indifference, as much as any jingoism, that Thompson wants to protest in his book.

It is true that Thompson indicts British immorality more severely and more earnestly than Forster does in his ironic novel. The accused rapist, Aziz, gets a full trial in *A Passage to India* and is acquitted when the English young woman gets over her hysteria. Thompson, by contrast, lays out documents from 1857 that attest to what he calls "government by gallows" and "government by massacre" (38), including British mass executions of both civilians and soldiers, carried out without trial and often without even accusations of crimes. It is upsetting, but not unimaginable, to think that Forster, and Bloomsbury generally, would condescend to Thompson's earnestness as boringly Methodist and lower middle class.

Forster's snub of Thompson, however, may reflect not only social snobbery but also critical judgment of earnestness as a moral tone that can cover up inconsistency and evasion. Forster puts the specific issue of British atonement in India into a tougher ironic structure through his novelistic art. I'm thinking of the moment in *A Passage to India* when Forster's liberal-minded schoolmaster, Fielding, comes to a final impasse with Aziz after the trial. Aziz is taking a hard line about reparations. He has personally suffered from false accusation, and he also wants to demonstrate solidarity with other Indian victims of British injustice. Fielding, despite being dressed up for the party in Indian costume, insists that Adela has already atoned, as it were, by so publicly and bravely admitting her mistake. Fielding's voice is full of the mild English idiom that the novel has from the beginning exposed as weak and meager. Fielding's colloquial idioms sound flat in the situation: "When she saw she was wrong, she pulled herself up with a jerk," or "In her place I should have funked it."[33] He also ineffectually flatters Aziz by extravagantly appealing to a myth of Mughal magnanimity: "Act like one of your six Mogul Emperors," he urges, "or all the six rolled into one." Aziz resists this manipulation by demanding impossible terms of apology from the English girl, namely that she admit she is an "old hag" and wished Aziz had come into the cave. Fielding is offended by what he sees as Aziz's excess, and the scene ends in melancholy separation.

Forster's irony in *A Passage to India* has the "self-interrogating density of verbal texture" that Dennis Porter identifies as the quality of literature. Through Forster's deployment of dialogue, English gestures of atonement come across as weakly mild; they cost too little. The language of regret is not insincere, but it lacks the power to bridge the distance between Englishman and Indian. Yet Fielding is not entirely wrong to insist that Adela has already paid heavily by being disgraced within her own community by a conscientiousness she didn't have to follow. The situation is morally ambiguous and irreparable.[34] Fielding leaves India soon after, and Aziz hardens further into a nationalist.

Although the moral earnestness of Thompson's writing compels attention, supported as it is by his display of shocking historical detail, comparison with Forster makes Thompson seem deaf to the weakness of his own moral rhetoric. "Atonement," Thompson says, "is the magnanimous gesture of a great nation, so great that it can afford to admit mistake and wrongdoing, and is too proud to distort facts" (75). "Mistake" seems far too weak a word for the crime and brutality Thompson has just finished disclosing, while "gesture" seems to confess the insubstantiality of what is being recommended as recompense. In addition, the appeal to British national pride shows Thompson turning the medal back to its shiny side. Whether trying to manipulate English public sentiment by gross flattery or else succumbing himself to stock self-congratulatory images of English honor, Thompson uses language that oddly ends by glorifying British power rather than humbling it. Is this hollow rhetoric the reason that Forster privately put him on his list of public bores? Forster, to be sure, gets into some rhetorical trouble of his own when he stages Fielding's return visit to India at the very end of his novel.

Here are evaluative issues that bring literary reading into connection with cultural and political judgments by way of the writers' own successes and failures of language. Does the ex-missionary educator, Thompson, succeed in recharging the Christian concept of atonement with the redemptive spiritual

force that he finds lacking in British imperial culture? Or does he evade conflict by retreating to a mild religious "gesture" of reconciliation on Western
terms? To expose collective wrongdoing to compatriots who deny it does take
boldness. In this sense, writers such as Burke and Mill, Thompson and
Forster are all dissenters and stand out from their contemporaries. Yet there is
also a deep commitment to English culture in this tradition of political criticism, which results in evasions, compromises, and constraints of language
and imagination, discernible especially in retrospect or from an outsider's position. No theory can finally decide how we should evaluate this bias, but since
Britain has had no global monopoly on two-sided medals, analysis of these
problems reaches beyond judgment of any single writer or national tradition
into hard, general questions about the status of moral discourse in the politics
of every nation. By what standards do we assess voices of dissent within particular nations or cultures? Once their limitations are recognized, in what
ways do they continue to matter at all? Does moral self-criticism in political
language inevitably reach an impasse if separated from more concrete economic and political reparations? How is just cultural or material reparation
for the crimes of history ever to be assessed? Postcolonial criticism has tended
to turn away from these difficult questions in its own assured mastery over
colonial discourse and in its preference for "interrogation" over questions.

In America, "dissent" went out as a vital term with the decline of the so-
called Old Left after 1968. Although the journal *Dissent* survives, its heyday
was the decade after its beginning in 1954. The first editors, including the literary critic and teacher Irving Howe, were not especially interested in "theo-
rizing" dissent; their concern was with the practice, valued by them in the
context of "the bleak atmosphere of conformism that pervades the political
and intellectual life of the United States."[35] They saw this conformism to the
Left (in Stalinism) and to the Right (in intellectual as well as political cold
warriors). *Dissent* affirmed, by contrast, humanist, independent, radical
thought and "the tradition of democratic socialism," while conceding that
the socialist part was unlikely to be realized soon. Unlike the Subaltern Studies Collective, *Dissent* was not shaping its critical insights to promote or to
prepare for revolution[36] but tried to separate the value of radical thought
from allegiance to any party or immediate political strategy. In England, the
history of religious sects colors the term "dissent" with a more doctrinal cast
than it carries in America, where, instead of an Established Church to oppose, there have been only more impalpable, pervasive pressures to conform
to one group opinion or another. As self-styled independent radicals, these
American dissenters wanted to come together while still preserving their differences from one another. The informal idiom of the writing in *Dissent* exemplifies and defines an Anglo-American style of criticism, on the alert for
humbug, whether in official or intellectual jargon.

In some radical Anglo-American circles, the concept of dissent is itself dead dogma, a throwback to the worn-out Old Left or the even older Victorian liberalism of Mill, now denigrated as complicit with imperialism and other forms of social injustice. Yet the contemporaneity of dissent as a contested value, specifically in relation to postcolonial literature, became dramatically manifest at the time of Rushdie's *The Satanic Verses*. His 1990 essay, "In Good Faith," written a year after the *fatwah*, puts the term "dissent" at the center of his plea for the allowance of creative freedom in literature: "*The Satanic Verses* is, I profoundly hope, a work of radical dissent and questioning and reimagining. It is not, however, the book it has been made out to be, that book containing 'nothing but filth and insults and abuse.' . . . What does the novel dissent from? Certainly not from people's right to faith, though I have none. It dissents most clearly from imposed orthodoxies *of all types*, from the view that the world is quite clearly This and not That. It dissents from the end of debate, of dispute, of dissent."[37]

Rushdie's self-defense was itself a matter of debate within the divided postcolonial community, which included many who simply placed the book within the offensive Western discourse of anti-Islamic abuse and insult. Rushdie's very reliance on the Western liberal word "dissent" seemed to reinforce this case against him, as did the pluralism of his praise for hybridity: "unexpected combinations of human beings, cultures, ideas, politics, movies, songs" (394). Without going so far as to endorse a death sentence, many detractors denied his claims for the autonomy of literature by consigning the claim itself to the aggressive assault by post-Enlightenment liberal orthodoxy against the equally legitimate orthodoxies it presumed to scorn.[38] In describing the pain of these accusations, Rushdie offered affirmations of his creative freedom in the essays of the early 1990s that start to sound rather wan, without the brash exuberance of his earlier images of dissent in literature as fun, as in his 1984 essay, "Outside the Whale," where he takes Orwell's late work to task for excessive pessimism: "[Orwell's] is a view which excludes comedy, satire, deflation; because of course the writer need not always be the servant of some beetle-browed ideology. He can also be its critic, its antagonist, its scourge."[39]

The *fatwah* deprived Rushdie not only of physical freedom but also of the exuberance that made his earlier reimaginings of history inspiriting to subcontinental as well as to Western readers. "In Good Faith" reasserts the artist's privilege of dissent with a plainness that would sound commonplace if it were not so fiercely contested: "I would like to say: do not ask your writers to create *typical* or *representative* fictions. Such books are almost invariably dead books. The liveliness of literature lies in its exceptionality, in being the individual, idiosyncratic vision of one human being, in which, to our delight and great surprise, we may find our own image reflected. A book is a version of the world. If you do not like it, ignore it; or offer your own version in return."[40]

I approach diverse writings about India in this book through the liveliness of their individual visions, while also exploring how this literature is constrained by history, "handcuffed to history," in a phrase Rushdie invented before he fully knew what it would mean for him.[41] As an image of writing itself, however, it is not entirely pessimistic. To be handcuffed to history is to be severely constrained, but it does not mean immobility or erasure, as Rushdie himself amply demonstrates in *Midnight's Children*.

I

THE COLONIAL PERIOD

I

Anti-Imperialist Wit in Horace Walpole's Letters

A by-stander often sees more of the game than those

that play.

—Horace Walpole, *The Castle of Otranto*

Horace Walpole's letters to his friend Horace Mann from the late 1760s to the 1780s follow the scandals of the British rise to power in India from the perspective of a bystander rather than a player.[1] As the son of Robert Walpole, the most powerful political figure in parliamentary politics for a generation in the middle of the eighteenth century, Horace Walpole had an insider's grasp of political machination, but without his father's relish or skill for it. Although a thirteen-year Member of Parliament in his own right, he chose the role of political dropout in 1768, when he let go his seat in the House of Commons and withdrew to his art collections, decorating projects at Strawberry Hill, and literary activity, mainly in the form of private correspondence. As public controversy about Indian (and other colonial) affairs picked up pace in the late 1760s, Walpole enjoyed emphasizing his new identity as the consummate outsider, a spectator who differed from others only in the sharpness of cynicism acquired from the experience of his former insider life. His friend Mann, mildly occupied in Florence with the diplomatic task of keeping track of the Jacobite Pretender (a position Walpole had helped him acquire), was sufficiently far away to receive Walpole's reports from the English metropolis as news: "We have another scene coming to light," "new horrors coming out every day," "I . . . can scarcely believe what I hear and see," "Do you believe me?" Such dramatic phrases animate Walpole's invitations for Mann (and any future reader) to share Walpole's own sensations of dismay and incredulity.

More than a decade before Burke developed his oratory of indignation at the misbehavior of the East India Company, Walpole was using the more intimate, informal genre of the personal letter for laments and protests against what he gleaned from the news to be greed, recklessness, and national disgrace: "Oh! my dear Sir, we have outdone the Spaniards in Peru!" he laments in a letter of 1772 about the Bengali famine (5 March 1772, 23:387). A year later, when the parliamentary motion to censure Clive was rejected, Walpole extended his indictment to include the politicians who sponsored, exonerated, and even applauded English conquistadors: "I told you the attack on Lord Clive was begun—oh! he is as white as snow. He has owned all, and Machiavel would be the first to acquit him—for he has pleaded supreme policy as his motive. The House of Commons have been of Machiavel's opinion. The censure was rejected, and even a vote of applause passed. Cortez and his captains were not more spotless heroes" (29 May 1773, 23:484–85).

British appropriation of territory in India and British behavior as a ruling power became the shocking news of the day in England around 1770, when allegations of excesses in Bengal under Robert Clive's governorship (from 1765 to 1767) began to circulate in the London press. After Parliament's investigation (and ultimate rejection) of a motion to censure Clive in 1772–1773, the crisis in the American colonies diverted English public attention from India. But by the 1780s, the traumatic loss of America had fueled new anxiety about alleged misdeeds in the nation's still unstable possessions in the East. Walpole's letters chronicle the controversies that accompanied Britain's shift from trade to dominion in India during the two decades when British conquest and rule there was still an ongoing event and only arguably a fait accompli.[2]

Walpole was not unique in his opposition to what was widely publicized in the 1770s as plunder and usurpation by the servants of the East India Company in Bengal. His running commentary stands out, nevertheless, for the unusual dramatic immediacy it gives to the oppositional side of public debate. Equally interesting, Walpole's brilliant, witty style in the letters stimulates general consideration of wit as in itself a particular style of critique, with both strengths and limitations. Although Walpole's private correspondence had negligible influence on affairs of state and was even judged by eighteenth-century and later detractors to be beneath serious political consideration, our postcolonial perspective allows us to see Walpole's wit curiously deconstructing imperialist discourse *avant la lettre*.[3] His verbal play, surprising juxtapositions, and tonal disjunctions undercut justifications for British power in India a generation before the rhetorical molds in defense of empire were fully set.

In the 1760s, Clive's military victories in both South India and Bengal had been hailed with patriotic satisfaction as important triumphs in Britain's Seven Year War with France. Walpole registers Clive's celebrity in a letter of 1763, for example, where his tongue-in-cheek tribute to a fashionable new actor suggests that Clive's triumphs had made him a byword for stardom; the actor "had an impulse for the stage—was a *heaven-born hero*, as Mr Pitt called my Lord Clive" (17 October 1763, 22:176).[4] By 1772, rumors of Company misdeeds and economic problems, combined with the alarming influx of new Indian wealth into England, provoked parliamentary investigation. Walpole's letter of 1772 measures the fall by ironically evoking Pitt's earlier hyperbole to recast Clive as a fallen angel: "The groans of India have mounted to heaven, where *the heaven-born* general Lord Clive will certainly be disavowed" (5 March 1772, 23:387).

Burke was among the majority who voted for Clive's acquittal, at that time supporting the Rockingham Whig opposition to Crown interference in the affairs of a chartered company. It was not until a decade later that Burke, first as Chair of a Select Committee of investigation, then as chief designer of Fox's East India Bill, emerged as chief advocate for parliamentary regulation of Indian affairs. Burke's reputation as the leading voice of British imperial conscience in the eighteenth century has overshadowed the intensity of opposition that took shape a decade before he had taken up his relentless, not to say obsessive, prosecution of imperial crimes.

The anti-Company critique of the 1770s relied more on the public circulation of news than on the mountains of data that Burke mastered to become one of the first in a long line of British India experts. Allegations of East India Company involvement in the Bengali famine of 1769 published in the *Gentleman's Magazine* of 1771, for example, provide some of the wording as well as the charge relayed in the 1772 letter already cited: "nay, what think you of the famine in Bengal, in which three millions perished, being caused by a monopoly of the provisions by the servants of the East India Company? All this is come out, is coming out—unless the gold that inspired these horrors, can quash them" (5 March 1772, 23:387).[5]

Walpole never presents himself as among the first to know what was going on in India. There is, to begin with, the six-month boat journey of the mail that in the eighteenth century made all Indian news "old" by the time it reached England. The India scandal of the day in London generally referred to events of a year or more earlier in India, while the events themselves often involved the kind of freelance activities ventured by men conscious that by the time they request and receive either authorization (or counterorders) from home, their activities will have already become hard-to-reverse facts on the ground. Deliberate blockage in the flow of information in itself created notable scandals and conflicts: between the Company's men in India and the Directors in London, and between the London Company and the Select and Secret committees of Parliament. And finally there were blockages created by rival political factions attempting to control public perception and opinion through opposing pamphlets and public letters of advocacy and indictment.

Walpole locates himself at the low end of this tangled chain of communication. He does not pretend to be an expert; insofar as he affects a role, it is that of unillusioned observer. Like a dandyfied Thersites, Walpole issues a cynical commentary from the sidelines that sardonically undercuts the emerging script on both sides of the debate about emerging British power in India. Distinctions, for example, between the "bad" Company and the potentially "good" government—later so important to Burke—become mockable from the perspective of Walpole's presumption of intimate collusion between private business and the House of Commons. The greed and gold that shape events in Bengal are for him the same greed and gold that determine votes in Parliament. Nor does Walpole revere the constitutional autonomy of the chartered company. East India Company exploits in Walpole's language always appear as *national* events. The Company and the nation are entirely entwined in Walpole's use of "We," as in "We have outdone the Spaniards in Peru" or "We have murdered, deposed, plundered, usurped." Walpole is therefore less inclined than other anti-Company critics of the day to scapegoat either the Company or individuals but presumes them to be agents and instruments of national "policy."[6]

In the same spirit, Walpole forgoes the rationalization (dominant in British historiography from the eighteenth century until recently) that military engagement and then political control followed as a necessity to protect the benign activity of trade. Walpole goes straight to the morally dubious word "conquest." While not entirely devoid of patriotic satisfaction at British victories against the French in India and elsewhere, by 1762 Walpole already shrinks with wry, if fatalistic, distaste from the triumphal expansionist momentum of British conquest: "Well! I wish we had conquered the world and had done! I think we were full as happy, when we were a peaceable quiet set of tradesfolks, as now we are heirs apparent to the Romans, and overrunning East and West Indies" (22 March 1762, 22:16).

Walpole's comparisons of Britain in the second half of the eighteenth century to imperialist Rome and Spain, his perception of conquest and territorial expansion as national policy rather than accident or an imperative of trade, his refusal to scapegoat one or two isolated villains all establish odd connections between his eighteenth-century skepticism and late twentieth-century critique of Britain's nascent imperialist culture. Walpole's letters reach across Britain's two hundred years of glory to address us in tones that often seem strangely close to our own harshest judgments of the past.

The seeming modernity of Walpole's anti-imperial cynicism should not, however, be exaggerated. In part, his eighteenth-century anti-imperialism participates in the bias of a propertied class threatened by the fantastical new wealth being acquired in Indian adventures. The alliance of twentieth-century anti-imperialism with Left politics and the struggles of other "subaltern" groups can confuse historical understanding of the eighteenth century. Walpole's anti-imperialism reflects the revulsion of a gentleman for the new order (or disorder) of money that was accompanying the combined triumphs of military and commercial power in the second half of the eighteenth century. With no evident desire to identify intimately with any set of tradesfolks, except perhaps those who could aid his artistic collections, his nostalgia for a simpler England belongs to a conservative eighteenth-century discourse, what Pocock and others call classical civic virtue.[7] The corruption of imperial Rome, in this discourse, reinforces distaste for the aggressive energy of new monied tradesfolks: in its Indian form the vulgar nabob, invading English society with bad manners as well as ill-gotten Indian gold.[8]

Nostalgia, however, never becomes Walpole's dominant note, any more than classical simplicity is his aesthetic ideal. Like his eclectic Gothic contrivance, Strawberry Hill, Walpole's political ideas and formulations collect and arrange pieces from a variety of sources. The value of the idiosyncratic result involves assessments that remain open to dispute. The very choice of private withdrawal, while dignified by Horatian precedent, went against the neoclassical ideal of civic virtue, as formulated, for example, in Adam Ferguson's 1767 *Essay on the History of Civil Society*. In terms with pointed relevance to Walpole at this date, Ferguson invokes Cato the Censor to strengthen his insistence on the responsibility of active civic participation; the liberty of all is threatened, writes Ferguson, citing Cato, when men choose "to value their houses, their villas, their statues, and their pictures, at a higher rate than they do the republic."[9]

Direct denigration of Walpole's political irresponsibility receives its definitive Victorian statement in Thomas Macaulay's review of an 1833 edition of Walpole's letters to Horace Mann.[10] In a long essay in the *Edinburgh Review*, Macaulay portrays Walpole as poseur and dilettante, incapable of serious opinion on any political subject: "About politics, in the high sense of the word, he knew nothing, and cared nothing" (229). According to Macaulay, Walpole was no more than a gossip and an aesthete before, during, and after his active political career. Macaulay much prefers the father, Robert Walpole—a real politician, however corrupt. The second half of Macaulay's review abandons Horace altogether for the sake of reassessing what is to Macaulay the more interestingly controversial career and character of Robert.

Insofar as Macaulay grants Horace Walpole any character at all, he sees him as only "a bundle of inconsistent whims and affectations" (227), a kind of freakish, unmanly chameleon, like a figure out of Pope's satire on women. Walpole's lack of character receives Macaulay's fullest disdain in relation to his frivolous performance in Parliament: "After the labours of the print-shop and the auction-room, he unbent his mind in the House of Commons. And, having indulged in the recreation of making laws and voting millions, he returned to more important pursuits,—to researches after Queen Mary's comb, Wolsey's red hat, the pipe which Van Tromp smoked during his last sea-fight" (228).[11] This caricature doesn't so much deny all consistency to Walpole as indict him for violating by inversion the fundamental decorums separating labor from leisure, responsibility from recreation.

Macaulay's 1833 review offers a representative Victorian judgment of Walpole,[12] with particular animus fueled by Macaulay's own political ambitions at this time when, as a young M.P., he was already demonstrating a different model of labor, specifically in relation to India. In addition to publishing essays and reviews, Macaulay had by 1832 already attained appointment as secretary of the parliamentary Board of Control of the East India Company. He was soon to depart for four years of what the *Dictionary of National Biography* calls "prodigious work" in India on the Supreme Council.[13] In 1835, Macaulay issued from India his influential "Minute on Indian Education," recommending the establishment of English as the language of instruction in Indian schools; in 1837, he published his sweeping reform and regularization of the Indian penal code. By the time of his long, widely read essays about Clive (1839) and Hastings (1841), Macaulay had become an important "player" in British India, and his judgments of Indian figures and events carried the authority of thorough expertise. In his writing about India, as in his *History of England*, Macaulay not only turned Victorian Whig orthodoxy into clear, popular prose, but went far to shape that orthodoxy. By Macaulay's standards of responsible participation, Walpole's comments on India would have seemed beneath notice; in actuality, no reference to India appears in Macaulay's review of the letters to Mann. Walpole could have no opinion worth comment about what was already to Macaulay in 1833 such an important subject: "The conformation of his mind was such, that whatever was little, seemed to him great, and whatever was great, seemed to him little. Serious business was a trifle to him, and trifles were his serious business" (228).

The only talent Macaulay concedes to Walpole is a certain engaging, if rather insignificant, order of wit. Echoing Samuel Johnson's famous definition of metaphysical wit,[14] Macaulay emphasizes the oddity and affectation, the peculiar grotesqueries of Walpole's wit, which remind him specifically of the metaphysical poets: "He coins new words . . . and twists sentences into forms which make grammarians stare. . . . His wit was, in its essential properties, of the same kind with that of Cowley and Donne. Like theirs, it consisted in an exquisite perception of points of analogy, and points of contrast too subtle for common observation. Like them, Walpole perpetually startles us by the ease with which he yokes together ideas between which there would seem, at first sight, to be no connexion" (239).

Johnson's definition of metaphysical wit provides Macaulay terms for a grudging concession to Walpole's eccentric, trivial charm as entertainer. Modern judgment, of course, is accustomed to turning the same Johnsonian terms into more serious praise—in this case, the praise can name qualities of mind as well as style regrettably missing from Macaulay's balanced commonplaces and complacencies. From a postcolonial perspective, Walpole's wit in the letters challenges in advance Macaulay's self-satisfied contempt for subtleties beyond "common observation" and his recourse to the notion of "serious business" as a way of disqualifying ethical objection. Walpole himself wittily takes up the word "trifling" as an important critique of the way the business of British expansion was being conducted in the late 1770s: "it just got abroad, that about a year ago we took possession of a trifling district in India, called the Province of Oude [*sic*], which contains four millions of inhabitants, produces between three and four millions of revenue, and has an army of 30,000 men—it was scarce thought of consequence enough to deserve an article in the newspapers" (6 February 1780, 25:12–13).

Walpole insinuates that the politics of conquest has either lost all measure of its own scope or is deliberately hiding it from public view by delaying, downplaying, and perhaps even withholding news. As Robert Walpole's son, and from his own insider's experience, Walpole knows to distrust the political community's way of working; in his self-styled detachment, he looks beyond the content of the news to the suspect partiality of its dissemination.

For Johnson, detachment was a limited virtue. He remarks that because the metaphysicals wrote "rather as beholders than partakers of human nature," their wit tended to stop at novelty, rather than advancing to "great thoughts." Yet Johnson is willing to concede that metaphysical wit "sometimes struck out unexpected truth." The surprising effects of metaphysical wit, at the least, exercise the mind, "either something already learned is to be retrieved, or something new is to be examined."[15]

Johnson aimed his own wit toward great thoughts and anticipates Victorian disparagement of Walpole's mind as "little."[16] Johnson's critical terms nevertheless illuminate what an un-Johnsonian style of wit like Walpole's could achieve in a political domain where great-sounding thoughts more than ordinarily served to cover and rationalize ignominious deeds. Walpole's wit does, at its best, strike out unexpected truths by the very novelty of its surprising conjunctions, analogies, and framing of particulars. He can give even sheer numbers—the millions of people and pounds under British control in Oudh,[17] for example—a startling actuality missing from the style, if not entirely from the content, of official reportage. His wit calls attention not only to the events of conquest but also to the language through which the significance of events is being muffled or disguised.

Among the emergent items that caught Walpole's attention in the Clive investigation of 1772 was a tax on Indian subjects imposed for the private use of company administrators:

We have no public news, but new horrors coming out every day against our East India Company and their servants. The latter laid a tax on our Indian subjects, without the knowledge of the former. One article was £24,000 a year—yes—to Mr Sykes for his table—yes, yes—and this appeared at the bar of the House of Commons from a witness he brought thither himself—*ex uno disce omnes*.[18] Poor Indians! I fear they will be *disaffected*—Would you believe I read that epithet t'other day in a Portuguese relation of a mutiny among their negroes in the Brazils. Hacked, hewed, lamed, maimed, tortured, worked to death, poor Africans do not *love* their masters! O, Tyranny, thy name should henceforth be Impudence! (22 December 1772, 23:451–52)

Walpole relies on a variety of daring analogies, grammatical play, and abrupt shifts of tone to break open the rationalizing order of formal argument, as practiced, for example, at the bar of the House of Commons. Walpole's colloquial dashes and exclamations "—yes—" and "—yes, yes—" deftly break rhythm and syntax to set off the exorbitance of the sheer sum, £24,000, for one Englishman's food, while also turning the sentence aside to the further impudence of the swindler's own witness's having evidently reported this excess without shame. Then the Latin tag from Virgil (slightly misquoted) brings classical authority for making an exemplum out of the single case: "from one, learn them all."

Supported by Virgil, the next, bigger leap to Portuguese slave mutiny transfers horror from the case of Mr. Sykes to the more general impudence of euphemism used to mask the relations of power in colonial situations. British historians and statesmen might list a dozen objections to Walpole's analogy between Britain's Indian subjects and Portuguese slaves, but Walpole's seemingly outrageous conjunction is part of his wit's power. Considerably less farfetched is his italicizing of "*disaffected*" as an epithet. Whatever the equivalent in Portuguese, the decorous English word "disaffected" (recurrent in British colonial discourse well into the modern period of Indian nationalism) is a good target for Walpole's irony for reasons of both etymology and usage. In its root meaning, "disaffected" signifies an anomalous falling off from a norm of loyalty and love. Walpole's astonished "Would you believe . . ." underlines the impudence of presuming such a norm in relation to colonial subjects as well as slaves. The passage comes to a brilliant climax through Walpole's contrasting style of blunt monosyllables for the reality of slavery. Recited almost as a rhyming refrain, Walpole's language makes present both the physical savagery of the master/slave relationship and the brutality of power masked by official euphemism: "Hacked, hewed, lamed, maimed, tortured, worked to death, poor Africans do not *love* their masters!"

Walpole does not debate the legitimacy of his leaps and analogies between England and Portugal, Indian subjects and African slaves. British and Portuguese impudence become "strangely yoked," to use Johnson's phrase, in the swift movement of Walpole's associations. If the leaps shock English sensibility, that is the point of Walpole's expostulations. The linkage depends not on literal parity between the treatment of African slaves and Indian subjects but on the root meaning of "impudence" as immodesty, shamelessness. British rule in India need not descend to the full barbarity of Portuguese or (for that matter) British slavery to be shameless in evading the human consequences of plunder and exploitation. "Disaffected" becomes an impudent word in situations where the fundamental relationship of brute power makes love and loyalty beside the point.

Perhaps only the long historical retrospect from the 1857 Indian Rebellion makes Walpole's reckless insinuations seem to strike out "unexpected truth," to invoke Johnson's phrasing again. The "disaffection" of large numbers of Indians for their British rulers in 1857 shocked Victorians who had convinced themselves of their benevolence through their own rhetoric, but it would not have surprised the Walpole of the 1772 letter. While opposing factions in the eighteenth-century East India Company controversies were already beginning to compete with each other for status as the true protectors of Indian peoples, and thus entitled to their loyalty and love, Walpole brashly cuts through the self-consoling distinctions between high and low, honorable and brutal, British and Portuguese styles of tyranny and rule by force.

Yet well-aimed wit alone does not constitute a political philosophy or policy. Even if we grant Walpole's rhetorical effectiveness, he still remains less a political thinker than a collector and arranger of opinions in common circulation. Among Walpole's cosmopolitan readings, the most obvious source for his links between imperial Portugal and Britain is the widely circulated French work (translated into English two years after its French publication in 1770) *A Philosophical and Political History of the Settlements and Trade of the Europeans in the East and West Indies*, with authorship ascribed to the Abbé Raynal (though it is now demonstrated that Diderot wrote at least a third of it).[19]

In multiple volumes, Raynal's *History* traces the mutability of empire, starting with the Phoenicians; extensive chapters are then devoted to the rise and fall of empire in Portugal, then Spain, then Holland, then England. In addition to themes common in Western historical writing since the classical era—the destructive processes of time, the dangers of luxury, the misdeeds of despots—the *History* features contemporary eighteenth-century concern for the treacherous relationship between commercial trade and political expansion. Commerce is not intrinsically opposed to political virtue, in Raynal's argument, since commerce is recognized as a primary engine of civilization. But a seemingly inescapable dynamic seems to make colonization follow as the consequence of trade, and the ruin of both the colonized society and the colonizer follows as the consequence of the shift from trade to dominion. "Commerce is finally destroyed by the riches it accumulates, as power is by its own conquests" (Bk. 1.3).

Walpole supplements the British tradition of historical reflection on the mutability of empires with the French *philosophes'* more cosmopolitan perspective on Britain's still indeterminate place in history. Macaulay, labeling Walpole the most "Frenchified" of English writers, criticizes him for attending only to the most frivolous "gossip of the old court," rather than to the eminent French writers who were, in the mid-eighteenth century, "studying with enthusiastic delight English politics and English philosophy" (234).[20] But Diderot and Raynal (neither mentioned by Macaulay) were exhorting English readers to regard their own condition with as much anxiety as enthusiasm. For Walpole in the early 1770s, French humanitarianism is one important influence encouraging less than wholehearted satisfaction in Britain's increasing glory.

Walpole's critique of British imperial aggression goes beyond Raynal/Diderot[21] in that Walpole predicts a British collapse sooner rather than later, while the French book entertains at least the possibility that the British, specifically in India, might succeed in escaping the destructive and self-destructive dynamic of other commercial empires. If only Britain can exercise an orderly self-restraint, control individual and collective avarice, and enter as a state into an alliance of mutual benefit with its Indian subjects, then no nation offers better promise than Britain of such an accomplishment. This tribute perhaps explains why *A Philosophical and Political History* was popular in England, while being banned and burned by authorities of the ancien régime in France.[22]

It is worth noting that Raynal/Diderot's *History* displays none of the concern for the cultural or political autonomy of subject peoples so prominent in modern anti-imperialism. The philosophical question posed at the start is whether new worldwide commercial activity will prove to "add to the tranquillity, the happiness, and the pleasures of mankind" (Bk.1.1). Twentieth-century retrospective judgment is inclined to rank both political and cultural self-determination higher than did the French Enlightenment on any list of human rights. The American Declaration of Independence proposes liberty from colonial dependency as an important basis of happiness. But for Diderot/Raynal, as for Walpole and other eighteenth-century European cosmopolitans, human happiness was first of all threatened by despots, by extortionary and tyrannical rulers, whether foreign or domestic. Racial and cultural identity between ruler and ruled did not, in this line of argument, necessarily promote human well-being.

Enlightenment discourse recognizes no intrinsic barrier to the idea of a foreign rule that respects the rights of humanity. Diderot/Raynal's *History* thus pauses to differentiate slavery from colonization. Slavery by definition violates human rights because it degrades human beings, whatever the race or nationality of the slave trader or owner. The condition of subjection to foreign rule differs from slavery in having at least the potential to provide for the "general satisfaction of the natives." The French book does spell out, however, the way that colonial rule can and easily does lead to enslavement, by describing how the "ties of commerce" that should promote mutual alliances between peoples so easily tighten into "the yoke of subordination," as when the Romans "ravaged the globe" and "their despotism and military government oppressed the people, extinguished the powers of genius, and degraded the human race" (Bk.1.7). In a rhetorical twist that makes the book seem directed specifically to readers across the Channel, Diderot/Raynal calls upon "august legislators" in England to "restore mankind their rights" in India by reforming the imperial relationship (Bk.3.401).

In the total historical argument of *A Philosophical and Political History*, the likelihood of Britain's achieving a just and mutually beneficial commercial empire in India (or anywhere else) is undercut by the stronger historical perception of how that ideal has already repeatedly succumbed to the human realities of greed and brutality. Chief among the impediments to ethical foreign commerce is the evidence that base passions are released more easily on foreign ground: "At a distance from their country, men are no longer restrained by the fear of blushing before their countrymen" (Bk.3.388).[23] The book's leading example of such self-abandon comes from British behavior in India. Apparently drawing on some of the same scandalous reports that Walpole would have read in the English press, the French book draws out the implications of current misdeeds to make a general reproach to the English national character. In the very midst of envisioning the British as a possible exception to the ruinous dynamic of empire, the book's strongest language goes to denouncing the secret shame of the British in India. In the light of actual British behavior in India, the very argument that English principles of liberty and justice favor the British exception inverts to single out the British as the epitome of hypocrisy, presented as one of the worst manifestations of human wickedness: "Strange indignity, to wish to exercise oppression, without appearing unjust; to be desirous of reaping the fruits of one's rapine, and to throw the odium of it upon another. Not to blush at acts of tyranny, and yet to blush at the name of a tyrant. How wicked is man, and how much more flagitious would he be, if he could be convinced that his crimes would remain unknown, and that the punishment or ignominy of them would fall upon an innocent person" (Bk.3.388).

Walpole's preoccupation with the impudence and hypocrisy of British imperial rule in India has a clear counterpart, if not a specific antecedent, in Diderot/Raynal. Walpole comes into his own voice in the letters, however, when he ironically marks instances of hypocritical language and then self-consciously questions what language, what tone, what genre of writing can adequately register the kind of tyranny that refuses to acknowledge what it is. Diderot's contribution notwithstanding, *A Philosophical and Political History* does not make lively reading, at least not in English translation; the style keeps to a middle and often pedestrian pace, occasionally rising to eloquence or sinking to lament and invective, almost never calling attention to its own rhetorical instruments.

Walpole, by contrast, shows himself acutely aware of the rhetorical as well as ethical challenge of writing about empire. The letter of 1772 that reports the Bengali famine introduces an epigram italicized as if Walpole were already quoting himself in a bit of wit intended to last—as *Bartlett's Quotations* suggests it has: "Recollect what I have said to you, that *'this world is a comedy to those who think, a tragedy to those who feel.'*" Shifts of tone in the letters make more subtle choices and combinations. Walpole's self-consciousness about style, together with his own rapid shifts of rhetorical posture, creates the impression in these letters of a voice trying on styles, no one of which adequately suits the character of Indian events:[24]

> Do you believe me, my good Sir, when I tell you all these strange tales? Do you think me distracted, or that your country is so? Does not this letter seem an olio composed of ingredients picked out of the history of Charles I of Clodius and Sesostris, and the Arabian Nights?—yet I could have coloured it higher without trespassing on truth—but when I, inured to the climate of my own country, can scarce believe what I hear and see; how should you, who converse only with the ordinary race of men and women, give credit to what I have ventured to relate, merely because in forty years I have constantly endeavoured to tell you nothing but truth? Moreover, I commonly reserve passages that are not of public notoriety, not having the smallest inclination to put the credulity of foreign post offices to the test. I would have them think that we are only mad with valour, and that Lord Chatham's cloak has been divided into shreds no bigger than a silver penny amongst our soldiers and sailors. Adieu! (6 February 1780, 25:15)

Events in India collapse the boundary between dream and reality, romance and reportage, exotic tale and historical chronicle, outrage and mockery. Imperial conquest has made the English regress to superstition, worshipping false angels and making relics out of politicians' cloaks. The assured philosophic tone of Enlightenment political principle is itself a style that, by 1780, becomes as subject as any other to Walpole's increasingly cynical wit. That the righteous orations of parliamentary prosecutors do not impress Walpole more than other political performances is made clear in a letter of 1783, the year of the Fox East India Bill:

> The newspapers intimate that you was in the right when you judged that the two ambitious Imperials [Austria and Russia] were determined to treat the Turkish Empire as they did Poland, and share it between them. . . . Formerly an emperor and empress, with no more reli-

gion than these two, would have christened it a holy war: modern rapine is more barefaced. Our nabobs do not plunder the Indies under the
banners of piety like the old Spaniards and Portuguese. I call Man *an
aurivorous animal*. We pretend just now to condemn our own excesses,
which are shocking indeed—*sed quis custodiet ipsos custodes?*[25] a Parliament is a fine court of correction! The Lord Advocate of Scotland,
who has sold himself over and over, is prosecuting Sir Thomas Rum-
bold for corruption at Madras! . . . We talk and write of liberty, and
plunder the property of the Indies. The Emperor destroys convents
and humbles the Pope; the Czarina preaches toleration, but protects
the Jesuits; and these two philosophic sovereigns intend to divide
Constantinople after sacrificing half a million of lives! In one age religion commits massacres, in another philosophy—oh! what a farce are
human affairs! (30 April 1783, 25:399–400)

Walpole's jibes at political philosophy in the 1780s noticeably set him
apart from Burke, who was just then working up his impassioned campaign
on behalf of imperial regulation and reform in India. Burke's famous speech
on behalf of Fox's East India Bill in 1783 accepts the Diderot/Raynal challenge to the "august legislators" of Britain to regulate empire according to
principles of fair commerce and just rule. As I discuss further in chapter 2,
Burke elevated the responsibility of imperial regulation to a high mission,
whose outcome would either redeem or doom Britain in the eyes of God and
posterity. Walpole in the letters never praises Burke's vision of Parliament,
invoking Juvenal to support his cynicism: "*sed quis custodiet ipsos custodes?*"

Burke's campaign, and indeed his entire concept of a moral empire, de-
pended on faith in Parliament's potential if not actual independence from
other social and economic forces. Walpole's consistent disbelief in this vision
contributes to his labeling the Hastings impeachment a "farce" from the
start. By the time of the impeachment, Burke's Roman model was Cicero,
with Hastings cast as Verres, the despot of Roman Sicily.[26] Burke's Roman
model singles out individual despotism; Walpole stays with Juvenal to identify an entire system of corruption, in which there are no impartial guardians
of liberty, at home or abroad.

Walpole likes to parody as well as cite Latin authority, cleverly coining
his own pseudo-Latin words and epigrams. He first wrote down the quip
"I call Man an *aurivorous animal*" in a pocket book and preserved it in his
"Detached thoughts."[27] Walpole makes no exception for august British
legislators in his cynical epigram. With some pleasure in political blas-
phemy, he implicates his countrymen, from Henry VIII to George III, in
the same Machiavellian politics that characterize regimes most antipathetic
to Britain's emerging sense of national identity. Nor does political philosophy distinguish English culture; to Walpole, "philosophy" in this era of

enlightenment covers the same aggressive drives previously masked by
principles of piety and law:

> I suppose Mr Hastings will be honourably acquitted. In fact, who but
> Machiavel can pretend that we have a shadow of title to a foot of land
> in India; unless as our law deems that what is done extra-parochially,
> is deemed to have happened in the parish of St Martin's in the Fields,
> India must in course belong to the crown of Great Britain. Alexander
> distrained the goods and chattels of Porus upon a similar plea; and the
> Popes thought all the world belonged to them as heirs at law to one
> who had not an acre upon earth. We condemned and attainted the
> Popes without trial, which was not in fashion in the reign of Henry
> VIII and by the law of forfeiture, confiscated all their injustice to our
> own use; and thus till we shall be ejected, have we a right to exercise all
> the tyranny and rapine that ever was practised by any of our predeces-
> sors anywhere—As it was in the beginning, is now, and ever shall be
> world without end. (30 April 1786, 25:642)

In Walpole's abbreviated history of the world, what the British are doing
in Bengal is basically the same as what the popes did all over Europe, what
Henry VIII did to papal property, and what the Czarina will do in Constantinople. While Walpole shows no special interest in or respect for existing Indian civilizations, neither does he propose that Britain (or any nation in
Christendom) has been providentially selected to bring civilization to other
lands. Walpole's radical skepticism thus repudiates not only East India Company legalism but also divine endorsement for British imperial rule.[28] Walpole is dry-eyed and earthbound: "Who but Machiavel can pretend that we
have a shadow of title to a foot of land in India."

Walpole's colloquial sharpness cuts into a discourse already stuffed in the
eighteenth century with dubious legal and pious rationalizations for territorial usurpation. If his litany of tyranny and rapine is more invigorating than
depressing, that is perhaps because the agile motion of his wit sweeps past
the barely intelligible laws of forfeiture and inheritance, treaties and alliances
that clog the arguments of the India experts who justified the appropriation
of Indian lands. History as farce calls upon a different kind of stylistic expertise: rapid exits and entrances, shocking revelations and juxtapositions,
caricatures of dignitaries caught hiding their impudence behind painted
screens of words.

The trial of Hastings lasted seven exhausting years beyond Walpole's
1786 letter, which accurately predicted his acquittal. By the time of its conclusion, the public had largely lost interest in the entire event, and later commentators have come closer to Walpole's emphasis on the theatrical, if not
farcical, character of even its best moments. Over the course of its nine-year

run, the impeachment not surprisingly wore down its star prosecutor; Burke liberated himself from what had become a repetitive and obsessive role only when the French Revolution displaced India from the center of his imagination. Following the public flow of news, Walpole, too, trades Indian for French "horrors" at the end of the 1780s, but ill health, fatigue, and sentiments of old age drain the letters of his final years of their earlier spirit.

Even at his most alert, Walpole offers less perspective than we might wish on the political limitations of his bystander's wit. For intimations of his own ambivalence about detachment as a political stance, one needs to go back to the gothic novel of 1764, *The Castle of Otranto*, written while Walpole was still an active parliamentary player but despondent, frustrated, and "very glad to think of anything rather than politics."[29]

In its concentration on a situation of tyrannical usurpation, *The Castle of Otranto* may seem a peculiar distraction from politics. But the medieval Italian setting and the initial pretense of a "found" Italian manuscript from the sixteenth century sets up expectations of a romance plot in which usurpation will involve mainly familial and sexual struggles. Insofar as Walpole claims Shakespeare as his model,[30] the relevant plays are not the Henriad, which investigates the political consequences of usurpation, so much as the often Italian-based comedies and tragedies of familial betrayal and revenge: *As You Like It, Measure for Measure, Hamlet*. In *The Castle of Otranto*, Manfred's drive to keep his illegitimate power seems to arise less from any political ambition than from his sexual drive to discard his wife and force himself on young Isabella, the intended bride for his now deceased son. His "reasons of state" (47) are his need for a son, but no community outside the household seems affected by the problem. The stated "moral" of the romance, that the *"the sins of fathers are visited on their children to the third and fourth generation"* (5, 91), has the potential to become a rich political theme, as it does in the cycle of recurrent civil disturbances represented by Shakespeare in the English history plays. But retributive justice in *The Castle of Otranto* terminates with Manfred's son and daughter, both dead at the end.

The almost unintelligible tangle of blood lineage in the novel further trivializes the significance of usurpation, since the whole machinery of secret marriages, abandoned children, and miraculous rescues reduces the entire issue of "rightful title" to a virtual pastiche of blood entitlement as a political theme. While the narrative language invokes the distinction between wrongful usurpation and "lawful," "rightful," "just" title, the entangled marital and filial relationships in the novel seem only a more lurid version of the court gossip notorious from Walpole's letters about the intrigues of contemporary royal families.

The most interesting figure in the novel for my concerns is Father Jerome, a priest who first seems only to preside over the book's holy spaces of retreat from political mayhem but who ultimately turns out to be at the center of the novel's political plot as the father of the rightful heir, Theodore.[31] Father Jerome turns out in the end to be the only character in the situation who has known all along the secret and confused lineage of the family.

Walpole's rendering of Father Jerome brings to the fore basic ambiguities about the position of political bystander. For Father Jerome, priestly detachment is a role, a guise. His doubleness as both religious and worldly "father" casts doubt on the motive behind all his ostensibly disinterested speech and behavior; as the novel proceeds, he becomes as involved in strategy and disguise as are all the other characters, villains and victims alike.

Even more perplexing is the question of Father Jerome's inefficacy as the possessor of "true" history. At several moments, he proposes to reveal the secrets he knows. But Walpole curiously arranges interruptions for the friar's every effort to make public his truths. "Is this a season for explanations?" (107) impatiently cries his own son, Theodore, at one dramatic moment near the end when Father Jerome, "assuming an air of command," begins a public narrative of the family history. Melodrama turns to farce as the other characters are too busy with their absorbing activities of marrying, dying, cursing, and grieving to listen to Jerome's tale. They finally come to know, if not to understand, Theodore's rightful claim to power at the moment when thunder roars, the castle walls collapse, and the ancestral apparition of Prince Alfonso, "dilated to an immense magnitude" (108), appears to declare: "Behold in Theodore, the true heir of Alfonso!" No speech beyond the simple pronouncement is needed: "having pronounced those words, accompanied by a clap of thunder, [the form of Alfonso] ascended solemnly towards heaven."

The Castle of Otranto is important in the genre of gothic fiction precisely because theatrical and supernatural scenic effects take the place of narrative explanation to create horror and wonder. In the book's concluding scene, after the main villain and victims have emoted their guilt and grief, Father Jerome abortively tries one last time to explain events. "What remains is my part to declare" (109), he begins, only to be interrupted again, this time by the tyrant, Manfred, who prefers expressing his remorse to listening to an historical narrative. Jerome consequently abbreviates his account to a few barely intelligible sentences, while acknowledging the superfluity of a more protracted story: "I shall not dwell on what is needless" (110). Since none of the main characters is particularly interested in knowing the full details of how the usurpation came about and how the true lineage has been so hidden, the friar appears to have no role at all in the novel's conclusion. He has now become a true bystander, with no political, spiritual, or explanatory authority. The novel's narrator winds up the business of the plot succinctly, with Father Jerome absent from the final scene altogether.

The spirit of Shakespeare's Prince Hamlet may be hovering somewhere behind Walpole's image of a chaotic denouement to a tangled story that the public never gets to hear fully. Like Shakespeare's hero, Father Jerome has as

his chief talent all along a capacity for quick-changing, enigmatic performance. But neither the psychological nor the strategic motives for these
changes seem deeply motivated in the case of Father Jerome. At one moment
he sides with the tyrant's betrayed wife, appealing to Heaven as the protector
of injured innocence in terms similar to Walpole's lament about British cruelty in the Bengali famine: "The injuries of the virtuous Hippolita have
mounted to the throne of pity" (48). On the same page, he confuses even the
tyrant, Manfred, by agreeing to help him gain the church's sanction for dis-
solving his marriage. One page after he joyously discovers Theodore to be his
son, he pronounces to Manfred a piety that nullifies all human bonds: "But
alas! my lord, what is blood? . . . We are all reptiles, miserable sinful creatures.
It is piety alone that can distinguish us from the dust" (55). Walpole makes it
impossible to ascertain when Father Jerome is strategically dissembling. But
unlike *Hamlet, The Castle of Otranto* fails to make this uncertainty deeply interesting, perhaps because the friar's verbal gestures in each role seem so
stereotyped and shallow.

The Walpole of the letters is more interesting than the fictive Father
Jerome, partly because Walpole's language is livelier; the rapid shifts of voice
create the immediacy and spontaneity so attractive in personal letters. In addition, Walpole's inconstancy of style is less bewildering in the letters because, by the 1770s and 1780s, he had truly withdrawn from the political
stage, in contrast to Father Jerome, who travels constantly back and forth between chapel and castle through the subterranean passages Walpole designs
for his novel's architecture. As a true bystander to Indian politics, Walpole's
"olio" of a style becomes in itself a distinctive form of critique. In relation to
India, Walpole's self-conscious instability of tone becomes a provocative response to fantastical "news" that no single style can adequately represent.

The serious "work" of empire in the nineteenth century had no more
place for Walpole's rhetorical play than the monarchy of Shakespeare's
Henry IV and V had place for Falstaff. "What, is it a time to jest and dally
now?" scolds the Prince on the battlefield when, instead of a pistol, Falstaff
tries to give him a bottle of sack: "there's that will sack a city."[32] Although in
every sense thin by the standard of Falstaff, Walpole's sallies do similarly cut
through a political discourse whose goal is to get on with the urgent business
of power. But Walpole as knowing bystander can no more gain a hearing than
could Father Jerome at the end of *The Castle of Otranto*.

Although the appropriation by Britain of vast territories in India in the
eighteenth century is as vulnerable to the undercutting of cynical wit as is
Bolingbroke's usurpation of Richard's crown in Shakespeare's play, Walpole's wit remains vulnerable to the contrary judgment that Shakespeare also
invites in relation to Falstaff. However brilliant in exposing pretense and evasion, this kind of wit neither promotes nor envisions any alternative course of
political action; it offers no alternative vision of government or national

behavior in the competitive, potentially chaotic public world. Walpole quotes Roman satirists and French philosophers with a melancholy fatalism, but his epigrammatic irony sidesteps the responsibility of articulating the choices and principles that political action requires.

Walpole's wit, therefore, does not constitute an "oppositional" political position any more satisfactorily than Falstaff's does. At its best, what the style of wit offers may be thought of as forms of play that are alternatives to politics, rather than positions within the spectrum of political choice. A letter of 1783 comes closest to articulating Walpole's longing for the privileged freedom of play in the context of eighteenth-century Europe's *aurivorous* aggression. The "wonders" of new French flying balloons lead Walpole to prophetic imaginings of future dangerous inventions—the sky's the limit: "I hope these new mechanic meteors will prove only playthings for the learned and the idle, and not be converted into new engines of destruction to the human race, as is so often the case of refinements or discoveries in science. . . . Could we reach the moon, we should think of reducing it to a province of some European kingdom" (2 December 1783, 25:451).

It took longer than Walpole expected for toy balloons to evolve into engines of destruction from the air, just as Britain's Indian empire evolved into a longer lasting phenomenon than he anticipated. Yet the ingenuities of Walpole's skeptical wit also have acquired more potency than might have seemed perceptible in the heady early days of conquest. Banished by the political community of British imperialism, Walpole's ironic commentary on the emerging empire survives as an astringent newscast on Britain's headlong imperial success through an era when events of great long-term consequence were hardly better understood by the active players.

2

Burke's India Campaign:
Goliath, Scourge, Redeemer

Although Walpole and Burke both represent the critical side of eighteenth-century British debate about India, in other ways they stand at opposite ends of the spectrum of writing on the subject. Instead of Walpole's cynical wit mixed with observations on other items of the daily news, Burke offers impassioned exhortations in speeches and writings through a parliamentary campaign of fifteen years, from 1781 to 1795; instead of the bits and pieces gleaned by Walpole from rumor and newspapers, Burke's research and analytic mastery of what was already the massive British Indian archive constitute a feat of herculean energy and sustained concentration. By the time of the "Speech on Fox's India Bill," at the end of 1783, Burke had already asserted his authority as Parliament's India expert—the very opposite of a bystander, even though he had to rely on secondhand evidence and testimony, since (like Walpole) he had no direct experience of this faraway place.[1]

The legacy of Burke's India writings to the nineteenth century was also the inverse of Walpole's; instead of a dismissible hodgepodge of trifles, Burke's published speeches and writings bequeathed to the Victorians lustrous rhetorical jewels for the crown of empire: valuable words such as "duty," "trust," "justice," "Providence," and aphorisms to cast ever-expanding imperial power in the mold of ethical responsibility. "The situation of man is the preceptor of his duty," he said in the "Speech on Fox's India Bill"(5:404),[2] and the Victorians adopted the maxim as the moralizing banner for their rule of India and vast other portions of the world.

In these same India texts, however, Burke also produced the most sustained and far-reaching indictment of the British Indian enterprise to appear in England during the entire period of empire. Burke marks the outer limit of serious dissent on the question of India for the following 125 years of British commentary. His writings about India thus form a seemingly anomalous chapter in his career, for they probe deeply the ethical as well as the pragmatic failings of the English nation he became so famous for extolling.[3]

Although the Victorians absorbed Burke's anomalies through notions of the English genius for practical wisdom (another Burkean teaching, drawn especially from his critique of abstract theory in the anti-Jacobin writings), modern and postcolonial commentators have reopened the controversy about how to interpret and judge the apparent doubleness of his colonial position—at once chief prosecutor and eloquent advocate. At the high end of praise, Conor Cruise O'Brien places the great Indian speeches in "the Great Melody" of Burke's best political writing;[4] at the low end, Burke's whole India campaign is denigrated as political opportunism or, at best, only a long, loud amplification of anxieties and ambivalences already commonplace in eighteenth-century discourse before Burke even acknowledged an India problem.[5]

The difficulty for those seeking to judge Burke's India writings is made overwhelming, however, by the sheer volume and density of its detail. Burke states the problem for his own political advocacy of parliamentary reform near the start of the Fox Bill speech, when he remarks, "we are in general . . . so little acquainted with Indian details; the instruments of oppression under which the people suffer are so hard to be understood; and even the very names of the sufferers are so uncouth and strange to our ears, that it is very difficult for our sympathy to fix upon these objects" (5:403–4). Burke's own ability to combine densely detailed narrative and analysis with compelling exhortations to sympathy reaches its greatest expression, I think, in the Fox Bill speech, which lays out at the start the magnitude of the challenge it so vigorously goes on to meet. Any commentator who attempts to convey the scope of this accomplishment to a latter-day general audience can only gasp in wonder at Burke's skill.

I propose here to cut a path into this dense textual thicket by focusing on the relatively short but traumatic four-year period framed by the "Speech on Fox's India Bill" at the end of 1783 and the beginning of the Warren Hastings impeachment trial in February 1788. The trauma was the defeat of the Bill in the House of Lords at the beginning of 1784, despite Burke's rhetorical and political success in the Commons a few weeks earlier;[6] the aftermath of that defeat included the dissolution of Parliament and the loss of ministerial power by the Whig Party and by Burke himself for the remainder of his career. Burke undertook and sustained the Hastings impeachment from a position of ever-increasing isolation, even within his own party. After surprising initial success in the Commons, given the factional political bitterness of the time, the impeachment campaign of seven years also terminated with defeat in the Lords, in 1795, an outcome that had been predicted as virtually inevitable from the start.[7] The end of the trial had the virtue of finally releasing Burke from what many, by 1795, had come to regard as a fifteen-year monomania. In actuality, Burke had already turned enough attention to "horrors" closer to home, in Jacobin France, to produce his most famous book, *Reflections on the Revolution in France*, in 1790. Among other consequences for

Burke's political imagination and legacy, the French Revolution and its aftermath offered him the opportunity to recast England and its governing institutions as the guardians of true liberty, rather than the rapacious force of destruction that had become embodied for him not only in Hastings but also in the parliamentary rejection of his India vision.

Concentrated attention on the four-year crisis of hope, failure, and renewed energy in the middle of this chronology has the advantage of bringing to the fore competing political and imaginative visions within Burke's India writings and a shift in Burke's own conception of his role. Even though a prosecutorial air gives coherence to the whole, there is also a discernible difference between indictment in the service of reform and prosecution as a largely symbolic performance. The year 1783 marks the culmination of a period when Burke was writing and speaking with the intent and the realistic possibility of persuading Parliament and the contemporary public to accept his analysis of the nation's ruinous India policy and the consequent need for fundamental reform. After defeat at the beginning of 1784, Burke turned more to posterity as audience, with himself in the role of scourge and minister of God.[8] In his new isolation, Burke not only intensified his invective but also changed its target; after defeat, he sought not only redress for suffering Indians but also revenge and self-justification against his own countrymen for their earlier and ongoing rebuffs.

This competition between roles and audiences goes on within what O'Brien praises as the "complete consistency" of Burke's position on India from 1781 to 1795:[9] O'Brien is accurate up to a point in interpreting the Hastings impeachment as an extension of the parliamentary drama begun in Burke's reports for the Select Committee in the early 1780s;[10] the shifts are not sharp turnabouts of the sort that some detractors regard as a Burkean specialty.[11] What we can see in Burke's prose during this period is a change of orientation, a different internal ordering of imaginative and rhetorical forces in contention in his India writings from 1781 on.[12]

The shape of the Burkean drama shows most vividly at its point of greatest personal crisis and in writings interesting mainly for their intimacy of confusion, anger, and pain. Burke's letters after the electoral debacle in the spring of 1784, for example, display his frustration and disgust with public indifference to what he thought he had exposed as national disgrace in India:

> The havock [sic] and destruction of the species made in the East Indies does by no means touch the humanity of our countrymen, who, if the whole Gentoo race had but one neck, would see it cut with the most perfect indifference. To their own interest they have sensibility enough, but then it is only in the moment of suffering.[13]
>
> I consider the House of Commons as something worse than extinguished. . . . all the Tyranny, robbery, and destruction of mankind

practised by the Company and their servants in the East, is popular
and pleasing in this Country; and . . . the Court and Ministry who evidently abet that iniquitous System, are somewhat the better liked on
that account.[14]

Unassuaged by the rapid introduction of a more moderate East India Act
by the new administration of Pitt, Burke's angry despair boils over in what is
known as the "Speech of Almas Ali Khan," delivered in July 1784. One of
the most oddly dramatic of Burke's India performances, the speech barely
survives as a written text at all, since Burke never published it. All we have is
a transcription of uncertain provenance (printed in the Parliamentary Register)[15] of a raucous confrontation between an isolated, embittered Burke and
a hostile House of Commons, not averse to baiting him. Burke's recent biog-
rapher, F. P. Lock, cites the Almas Ali Khan speech as one of several "self-
induced humiliation[s]"[16] of this bad season, though other commentators
admire the moving immediacy of distress registered by the unlaundered
transcript.[17] Recorded disruptions from the floor, along with the third-
person convention of transcript style, inadvertently create an effect of comico-
pathetic nightmare in which Burke performs to no avail a defense of himself
in the face of catcalls and insults. In uncharacteristic clichés, he appeals to
posterity and to God, who will eventually recognize that "he had fought the
battle of humanity; and that as a British subject, he had laboured, though in
vain, to rescue from ignominy and abhorrence the British name" (5:476).
Mockery and the Chair's gavel enforce Burke's own point that the time of his
justification is yet to come.

Burke's beleaguered tribute to himself in the "Speech on Almas Ali
Khan" is humiliating not only because the audience rejects it but also because Burke himself seems confused as to the main battles and list of casual-
ties at issue. The titular victim is Almas Ali Khan, the most important administrator of revenue in the province of Oudh. He had incurred the
punitive wrath of the Hastings administration two years earlier by appearing
to withdraw his allegiance to the Wazir, the British-sponsored local ruler of
the province.[18] For Burke, Almas typifies the once-prosperous, self-suffi-
cient Indian whose futile resistance to British control warrants particular
sympathy. The punishment for Almas's resistance to extortionate revenue
demands, Burke alleges, was a death sentence in the form of an assassination
plot ordered by Hastings. Burke has the evidence in the form of a letter by
Hastings that rather openly recommends murder to the English Resident in
Oudh, while also advising and insisting on ways that the Resident must dissociate Hastings (and the Company) from the crime. It is Burke's motion to
introduce this letter among other "papers" into the parliamentary record
that occasions the Almas Ali Khan speech.

But only one page of the speech transcript actually pertains to Almas Ali Khan, who, after having intercepted Hastings's letter himself, settled his revenue conflict by paying up and thus managed to live in complex and not unprofitable relations with the British for another twenty-five years.[19] Whatever Almas's hardships or later successes, he figures here more as an emblem of Hastings's treachery than of Indian suffering. Murderous conspiracy and a cover-up—here is the same sinister combination that Burke alleged but could not definitively prove in the notorious Nandakumar case of "judicial murder."[20] More than any other Indian examples, however, Burke's most conspicuous association here is between Almas's plight and his own, with Parliament as much a scene of treachery as any Indian province.

Repudiation of Burke's evidence makes him more than an advocate for Indians; he has become a fellow victim, even the very embodiment of their own victimization, as he perceives a conspiracy of British interests determined to "kill" his proof of atrocities and oppression. The British nation has dismissed Indian grievances as "chimerical," "groundless and absurd" (5:463), he bitterly laments. Every new rebuff to him becomes conflated with new evidence of abandoning Indian peoples. Their fate, "absolutely without friends or resource" (5:463), mirrors his own. Parliament's complicity with tyranny in the guise of ordinary political procedures of debates, elections, and rules becomes a version of the sham legalism of Hastings's Indian rule.

Burke's self-preoccupation veers out of control, but it is not insane. Lord Chancellor Thurlow, who had acted as conveyor of the King's mind to the Lords before the Fox Bill vote, had publicly quipped that he would pay as much attention to Burke's Select Committee reports as he "would do to the history of Robinson Crusoe."[21] Hastings's agent in England, one Major John Scott, struck the same note of contempt for Burke's overimaginative sensibility in a pamphlet addressed as a public letter to Burke: "Your feelings are so tremblingly acute, your nerves are so strung to compassion . . . that forms of horror and distress, scenes of destruction and desolation, seem to arise *spontaneously* in your mind, and to occupy that portion of the sensorium, which, in men of irritable habits, is the province of reason, of judgment, and of common sense."[22] Now Scott sat in the Commons as a newly elected M.P.

In the "Speech on Almas Ali Khan," evidence of Hastings's denial of responsibility enrages Burke almost as much as the murder recommendation itself. "No matter what is done, provided the manner of doing it be properly managed," Burke sneers. He denounces Hastings's "flagitious rapacity" (5:467) in language that echoes Raynal/Diderot on the "flagitious" wickedness of British hypocrisy;[23] "this gentleman-like business must be done in the most gentleman-like manner. The Chief must be taken, and he must also be *put to death*; but all this must be so contrived as to imply no *treachery*. . . . Plunder, peculation, and even assassination, without treachery!" (5:464).

Burke then directly challenges the Company's "friends" in the Commons to answer his charges, singling out Hastings's agent, Scott, who duly takes up the gauntlet. Burke brushes past his remarks because Scott matters to Burke here only as the emblem of a Parliament now *collectively* seen as the agent of Company servants. Scott, he concedes sarcastically, at least has the excuse of being known as the paid agent of Hastings. What about the others?

The hostile mockery provoked by Burke's own sarcasm has the effect of raising his invective to a fearsome prophecy of divine vengeance: "Millions of innocent individuals had been made the victims of our indiscretion, and what reason had he to complain being made the butt of juvenile statesmen. . . . Much innocent blood had been shed, and he doubted was still shedding—But an avenger would certainly appear and plead the cause of the wronged. . . . Yes, the arm of God was abroad—His righteous visitation was already begun, and who could tell where it might end? He knew with accuracy how to discriminate the good from the bad, those who had, from those who had not, imbrued their hands in the blood of their fellow creatures" (5:471–72).

Burke as prophet of divine wrath, already the avenging "arm of God," slides into a virtual identification of himself *with* God. "He knew with accuracy how to discriminate the good from the bad." The ambiguity of the pronoun only partly comes from the transcript style. "Accuracy" ordinarily names a human rather than a divine quality—the exactness, for example, of a good investigator. Burke endows divinity with the same virtue he is most eager to defend in himself: accuracy with the evidence becomes not only Burke's human virtue but also an attribute that joins him to God.

When Pitt's gavel interrupts the ensuing clamor by calling for the "*order of the day*," Burke instantly incorporates the venerable rituals of parliamentary procedure into his higher drama: "Indeed the *order of the day* had its effect within these walls; but would the *order of the day* satisfy the world? Would the *order of the day* wipe away the disgrace which branded the character of the nation?" (5:473–74).

By the end of the speech, "the insensibility of government," as enacted in the here and now of the parliamentary scene, has all but merged with the false order that covers "foul enormities" of British tyranny in faraway India. In a final, superbly theatrical gesture, Burke takes an oath on a volume of his own Select Committee reports, as if his book of evidence held more secure promise of divine justice than the Scriptures appropriated by corrupt authority: "I swear, said he, by this book, that the wrongs done to humanity in the eastern world, shall be avenged on those who have inflicted them: They will find, when the measure of their iniquity is full, that Providence was not asleep. The wrath of Heaven would sooner or later fall upon a nation, that suffers, with impunity, its rulers thus to oppress the weak and innocent" (5:477).

Burke's grandiosity arouses more laughter than fear from his audience in the Commons, partly because his adversaries hold power and surely also because his self-aggrandizing substitutions and inversions topple over into the ludicrous that I have already noted in Walpole's version of the political sublime in *The Castle of Otranto,* and in the letters by Walpole where he regards Burke's parliamentary pursuit of Hastings as farce.[24]

Sublimity in the "Speech on Almas Ali Khan" turns especially bizarre, if not farcical, when Burke peculiarly identifies himself with one of the least attractive (and least successful) figures in Scripture, the giant Goliath. In his invocation of the David story, one might expect Burke to cast himself as David, venturing alone to challenge the gigantic combined power of the Company, the Government, and special Indian interests. But instead of identifying his inspired courage and intelligence with the Israelite hero, Burke chooses Philistine gigantism as the image of his own role: his eleven volumes of Reports, his additional "papers," his countless hours and years of investigation constitute the Goliath, unaccountably vulnerable to paltry "insinuation and surmise, which, like a stone in the hand of a David, might demolish the greatest giant on earth. It was a weapon, which, as any one might wield with success, no man—no reasoning could repel" (5:477).

Burke's identification with Goliath seems to epitomize the confused passion that drives the Almas Ali Khan speech. In addition to making himself represent a gigantic hostile threat to the Chosen People, the activity of "reasoning" itself paradoxically moves into the position of the monstrous, thereby losing reason's more familiar power to reduce and deflate.[25] Perhaps some underlying ambivalence impels Burke to degrade his own Indian advocacy by identifying it with the efforts of the doomed Philistine giant. Burke here recalls Hamlet not only in the way he confuses his personal rage with divine wrath but also in the feeling he conveys of unbearable alienation from self and community created by his avenger's role. "O cursed spite / That ever I was born to set it right": "He deprecated the day the knowledge of [the crimes] had ever come to his mind. The miserable objects it exhibited, countries extirpated, provinces depopulated, cities and nations all overwhelmed in one mass of destruction, constantly preyed upon his peace, and by night and day dwelt on his imagination" (5:471).

I have stayed so long with the Almas Ali Kahn speech not only for the fascination of its excesses but also because its drama sets off the very different kind of intensity manifest in the "Speech on Fox's India Bill" of the preceding year. In the published version that has become the text for posterity, no disruptions from the floor distract attention from the controlled strain of the speech's argumentative effort.[26] The political goal of winning support for the Fox Bill required concession and conciliation, as well as a demonstration of leadership within the community of legislators. In particular, Burke had to build a case for government intrusion into the business of a chartered company, the constitutionally protected independence of which he had himself defended within this same House of Commons a decade earlier, when he had joined the Rockingham Whigs in opposing the Regulatory Act of 1773.[27] Intervention could be justified, he now argued, by persuasive evidence of enormous crimes and abuses. Yet while the evocation of this "horror" would be his principal task, he also had to concede the aversive effect of sentiments too harsh to be intelligible, not to say persuasive, in the circumstances: "I am sure that some of us have come down stairs from the committee-room, with impressions on our minds, which to us were the inevitable results of our discoveries, yet if we should venture to express ourselves in the proper language of our sentiments, to other gentlemen not at all prepared to enter into the cause of them, nothing could appear more harsh and dissonant, more violent and unaccountable, than our language and behaviour" (5:404).

Emphasizing the distance that separates the upstairs committee room stuffed with sinister documents from the downstairs assembly of English "gentlemen," Burke announces his choice of a deliberately "cold" style (5:403). The necessity to choose a controlled style for argument introduces a drama of willed self-restraint into the rhetoric of the Fox Bill speech, with Burke's intermittent outbreaks of passion gaining additional force by appearing to have forced their way through the constructed barriers of his decorum. He wants the audience to feel and know that he feels the solemnity of bringing charges against one's own country: "But it is an arduous thing to plead against abuses of a power which originates from your own country, and affects those whom we are used to consider as strangers" (5:403).[28]

The tension in Burke's style between "cold" analysis and sentiments of "detestation and horror" animates many of the sentences and also the method of alternation between detailed specific examples and sweeping generalizations, between what Burke calls "proof" and what he calls "assertion." The general charge of vast government abuse depends on the accumulation of detailed examples, yet his "infinite mass of materials" requires a method of selection, which is to say that its detail works as what literary criticism now calls metonymy, as distinguished from metaphor. The narrative language does not rely on metaphors nor on the conversion of the individual case into emblem. Particular cases are presented as samples selected from the mass of documentation that could be produced but for practical impediment. Since an avalanche of detail would only crush the argument, political practicality requires the skillful balancing of proof and assertion.

At the outset, Burke prefers to lead with striking assertions, in a rhetoric that combines variety and repetition to build a burningly cold effect of intense but rational emotion: "First . . . there is not a *single* prince, state, or potentate, great or small, in India, with whom they have come into contact, whom they have not sold. I say *sold*, though sometimes they have not been able to deliver according to their bargain.—Secondly, I say, that there is not a *single treaty* they have ever made, which they have not broken.—Thirdly, I say, that there is not a single prince or state, who ever put any trust in the

Company, who is not utterly ruined; and that none are in any degree secure or flourishing, but in the exact proportion to their settled distrust and irreconcileable [*sic*] enmity to this nation" (5:391).

"These assertions are universal," Burke goes on to insist (pointing at the further detail in his appendixes), "in the full sense *universal*." The insistence may seem odd because Burke at first seems to mean "universal" only in the limited sense of a generalization supported by a host of particulars. But he also needs to invoke meanings of "universal" that go beyond the merely additive. After all, no parliamentary committee could police all "281, 412 square miles" that Burke precisely calculates to be the current British dominion, "a territory larger," he remarks, "than any European dominion, Russia and Turkey excepted" (5:389). Just as the sheer quantity of evidence defeats an exhaustive presentation of proof, geographical magnitude undermines the rational possibility of total surveillance. No matter how vigilant, a panel of commissioners in England cannot supervise every transaction in India, any more than Burke can narrate every instance of misgovernment. Burke's political argument therefore requires further strategies to enforce the universality of abuse as a pattern: systematic, logical, predictable. Some of Burke's strongest analytic writing in the Fox Bill speech uses the specific case to illustrate a characteristic pattern within a system.

The desolate situation in the province of Oudh is one such case. The demonstration begins as a highly specific historical narrative: "In the year 1779 the Nabob of Oudh represented, through the British Resident at his court, that the number of Company's troops stationed in his dominions was a main cause of his distress . . ." (5:404). The specific story goes on for three densely detailed pages, starting with how the excessive number of Company troops drove up the revenue demands. Moving through a sequence of causes and consequences, Burke ends with the complete domination and desolation of the province four years later. "Proof" of the policies involved in this sequence include letters by Hastings disclosing his goal of securing British power as well as further revenue in Oudh.

Burke moves from proof to assertion, and from the specific to the universal, by identifying in the particulars of Oudh "the invariable course of the Company's policy" as a system. The argumentative force of the general assertion does without striking images or tropes:

Either they set up some prince too odious to maintain himself without the necessity of their assistance; or they soon render him odious, by making him the instrument of their government. In that case troops are bountifully sent to him to maintain his authority. That he should have no want of assistance, a civil gentleman, called a Resident, is kept at his court, who, under pretence of providing duly for the pay of these troops, gets assignments on the revenue into his hands. Under his provident management, debts soon accumulate; new assignments are made for these debts; until, step by step, the whole revenue, and with it the whole power of the country, is delivered into his hands. The military do not behold without a virtuous emulation the moderate gains of the civil department. They feel that, in a country driven to habitual rebellion by the civil government, the military is necessary; and they will not permit their services to go unrewarded. Tracts of country are delivered over to their discretion. Then it is found proper to convert their commanding officers into farmers of revenue. Thus, between the well paid civil, and well rewarded military establishment, the situation of the natives may be easily conjectured. The authority of the regular and lawful government is every where and in every point extinguished. Disorders and violences arise; they are repressed by other disorders and other violences. Wherever the collectors of the revenue, and the farming colonels and majors move, ruin is about them, rebellion before and behind them. The people in crowds fly out of the country; and the frontier is guarded by lines of troops, not to exclude an enemy, but to prevent the escape of the inhabitants. (5:407)

This remarkably lucid as well as sardonic analysis of Company "policy" identifies the participation of every sector of the British presence: the civil department, the Resident, the troops, the Colonel, the bankers, the collectors, and, of course, the local ruler, either "odious" already or made so by British alliance. Syntax and diction enforce the impression of systematic ruination. Anonymous subjects and passive verbs ("troops are . . . sent," "tracts of country are delivered over," "lawful government is . . . extinguished") depersonalize the process of economic and political usurpation into a "step-by-step" sequence of causes and effects.

A similar method of analysis represents sequences involving not so much extortion or other criminal activity as more fundamental and arguably illegal intrusions into a social order that then disintegrates under the British influence. Critics of Burke who have objected to his scapegoating of Hastings's alleged villainy and his excessively "imaginative, romantic, theatrical" rhetoric[29] neglect the powerful passages in the Select Committee reports and in the Fox Bill speech where Burke coolly analyzes the aggression against a complex social order in India that had over time developed its own workable *system* for meeting its own needs, in its own natural space, and in accord with its own religious and social institutions.

Burke's account of how British usurpation undermined the system of water supply in the Carnatic is another good example. In one sense, the image of water might figuratively (and romantically) stand for any and every source of indigenous fertility and wealth in India. In another important sense, however, the Carnatic reservoirs belong to a very particularized configuration of climatic, economic, political, and social relationships. The universality of the example comes from the reservoirs' place in a characteristic pattern rather than from the emblematic meaning of these structures or any other single item. The particularity within the pattern matters a great deal for Burke's argument, because interventions that cut crudely through the interrelated structures of Indian society are precisely what Burke is identifying as destructive in Company policy. Again, only a fairly long excerpt can convey the important relationship between narrative and analysis that Burke patiently constructs:

> This country [of the Carnatic], in all its denominations, is about 46,000 square miles. . . . In that country the moisture, the bounty of Heaven, is given but at a certain season. Before the aera of our influence, the industry of man carefully husbanded that gift of God. The Gentûs preserved, with a provident and religious care, the precious deposit of the periodical rain in reservoirs, many of them works of royal grandeur; and from these, as occasion demanded, they fructified the whole country. To maintain these reservoirs, and to keep up an annual advance to the cultivators, for seed and cattle, formed a principal object of the piety and policy of the priests and rulers of the Gentû religion. . . . In all the cities were multitudes of merchants and bankers, for all occasions of monied assistance; and on the other hand, the native princes were in condition to obtain credit from them. The manufacturer was paid by the return of commodities, or by imported money, and not, as at present, in the taxes that had been originally exacted from his industry. In aid of casual distress, the country was full of choultries, which were inns and hospitals, where the traveller and the poor were relieved. All ranks of people had their place in the public concern, and their share in the common stock and common prosperity; but *the chartered rights of men*, and the right which it was thought proper to set up in the Nabob of Arcot, introduced a new system. It was their policy to consider hoards of money as crimes; to regard moderate rents as frauds on the sovereign; and to view, in the lesser princes, any claim of exemption from more than settled tribute, as an act of rebellion. Accordingly all the castles were, one after the other, plundered and destroyed. The native princes were expelled; the hospitals fell to ruin; the reservoirs of water went to decay; the merchants, bankers, and manufacturers disappeared; and sterility, indigence, and depopulation, overspread the face of these once flourishing provinces. (5:422–23)

Again, it is a "system" that Burke attacks, and not individual villainy. The reservoirs in Burke's Carnatic belong to a functioning traditional society with complex interlocking dependencies and responsibilities that evolved over a long period of time before the British arrival. This is not the nineteenth-century British vision of a decadent India in the last stages of social, economic, and political disintegration that James Mill offered in his multivolume textbook history for the Utilitarian generation of Indian civil servants. To be sure, Burke idealizes the Indian ancien régime, in somewhat the same way as he will in the following decade exaggerate the social harmony in European traditional social orders. The Edenic harmony he projects onto the pre-British Carnatic renders invisible the exploitation, poverty, local warfare, and injustice no less rampant in traditional rural India than in other feudal societies.[30] Burke may also be charged with a kind of perverse Western vanity in blaming (or crediting) British intervention alone for a situation that, according to recent historians, was already itself in the process of change, with new dynamic commercial Indian classes welcoming and profiting from the British presence and not merely victimized by it.[31] It is beyond my purpose or expertise to adjudicate these controversial historical judgments or to assess exactly where Burke may exaggerate both post–British Indian ruin and pre–British Indian well-being. What remains striking and impressive, whatever corrections later historical knowledge brings, is Burke's lucid understanding of the many-faceted assault on an intricate social and economic system brought by aggressive, foreign, profit-seeking intervention. Current historians of modern India modify Burke's analyses and particular narrative accounts without fundamentally refuting the patterns he discerned. The West is still in the process of learning (and ignoring) what our own versions of aggressive interventions in foreign societies entail. Triumphal global capitalism at the turn of the millennium repeats and extends the processes analyzed by Burke more than two centuries ago.

Further examples could reinforce the impressiveness of Burke's analytic clarity about the devastating changes wrought by early capitalist imperialism. My focus now shifts, however, to the difficulties created for Burke's own argument by the very force of his analysis. His tight sequences of cause and consequence have the effect of leaving little room for the redirection that reform supposedly promises. If the logic of these sequences is endemic to the dynamic of profit-seeking foreign dominion, how much difference could any reform make that did not relinquish the fundamental ambition of the whole enterprise? Burke brilliantly formulates the futility of superficial reform when he dismisses the prospect that the Company's own Court of Directors could more forcefully regulate itself: "controuled depravity is not innocence," he pronounces pithily, "it is not the labour of delinquency in chains, that will correct abuses" (5:440).

By entrusting reform to Parliament, Burke envisions a separation between legislature and Company that is, however, belied by his own language everywhere. As in Walpole, Burke's regular usage of the plural "we" presumes the national identity of the Indian imperial enterprise as a whole. The territories designated as "the British dominion" are in "our hands"; they have become "our possession," without distinction between nation and Company. Nor can Parliament, as an elected government institution, be insulated from Company interests, as Walpole had so clearly remarked a decade before. Not only were Indian investors among the interests represented in Parliament, but the financial problems of the Company in the 1770s and 1780s had become significant economic facts in England, just as military victories and defeats in India had become crucial facts in Britain's protracted struggle for global power with France. What if oppression in India derived not only from criminal misbehavior but from the destructive sequences of competitive capitalist imperialism itself? How could even the wisest and most honorable group of parliamentary commissioners control that dynamic?

The extent of damage already done to Indian society, in Burke's vision, creates further difficulties for his own reform proposal. In language that foreshadows *Reflections on the Revolution in France*, Burke identifies the East India Company as no less than a force of "revolution" in India. Not only systems of water supply, but also law, land tenancy, inheritance, and domestic relationships are all displayed as past and ongoing victims of the Company's revolutionary recklessness. The scale and the seemingly irresistible momentum of the British revolution in India overwhelm Burke's "cold" style in the Fox Bill speech with emotions and rhetoric associated in the eighteenth century with the uncontrollable disasters of the sublime: "I was in a manner stupified by the desperate boldness of a few obscure young men, who having obtained, by ways which they could not comprehend, a power of which they saw neither the purposes nor the limits, tossed about, subverted, and tore to pieces, as if it were in the gambols of a boyish unluckiness and malice, the most established rights, and the most ancient and most revered institutions, of ages and nations. . . . The country sustains, almost every year, the miseries of a revolution" (5:427).

Suleri, in her provocative interpretation of Burke's "Indian sublime," uses this and other striking passages of stupefaction and astonishment in the Fox Bill speech to cast Burke's entire performance in that mode of the sublime that disempowers reason and language itself. In her reading, Burke's "Indian sublime becomes indistinguishable from the intimacy of colonial terror."[32] Burke's own early treatise on the sublime provides theoretical support for the idea that reason collapses in the face of the sublime: "Hence arises the great power of the sublime, that far from being produced by them, it anticipates our reasonings, and hurries us on by an irresistible force" (57).[33] By using such sentences from the *Enquiry* as an "incipient map" for the Fox Bill speech, Suleri works to rescue Burke from postcolonial charges of Orientalist arrogance: for her, the salient point about the rhetoric of the speech is not its analytic force but its implicit confession of inadequacy. This interpretation underlies Suleri's admiration for Burke's India writings; postmodern literary criticism likes the writers and even the politicians of the past best when they seem closest to deconstructing their own competence.

The Burke I have been presenting through the analytic passages of the Fox Bill speech would resist the embrace of posterity on these terms. Even his own *Enquiry* offers alternative, less disempowering dynamics of the sublime. For example, Burke traces the psychological, almost biological dynamic by which up to a certain point terror arouses the mind from depressive indolence to "the exercise of the finer parts of the system," an activity that (so long as there is no immediate threat of personal destruction) invigorates and dignifies the mind (134–36). In a line of thought common to Burke's contemporaries, the sublime thus does serve ethical and political argument.[34]

As a skillful orator, Burke strategically punctuates his argument with sublime pauses to move auditors out of what he scorns as their "low and mean" preoccupations and the sloth into which the mind is always prone to sink, according to his psychology. The sublime passages in addition attest to Burke's own awakened mental energies. In the section of the *Enquiry* titled "Ambition," Burke cites Longinus in support of the "satisfaction" accessible to the mind when it swells to claim for itself "some part of the dignity and importance of the things which it contemplates" (50–51). This language returns more explicitly in the "Speech on the Nabob of Arcot's Debts," where the capacity for sublime arousal becomes for Burke a virtual test of national character: "if . . . we do not stretch and expand our minds to the compass of their object, be well assured, that every thing about us will dwindle by degrees, until at length our concerns are shrunk to the dimensions of our minds" (5:488). Astonishment and horror do not in any simple way incapacitate the mind for Burke; the alternation of styles in his India writings exhorts his audience to follow his movement through and beyond the sublime to argument.[35]

Yet Suleri is right to identify a crux in the relationship of the sublime to the political argument in the Fox Bill speech. For while sublime horror may invigorate the analysis of destruction, its value for the purpose of proposing alternative courses of action is much more uncertain. It is in the passages where Burke turns from analysis to the proposed reform that the "burden of inadequacy" identified by Suleri becomes conspicuous—not a small weakness, to be sure, since the project of reform ostensibly motivates the whole occasion.

The troubled relationship between sublimity and reform appears sometimes within a single paragraph in the Fox Bill speech. For example, in the very midst of Burke's "stupified" vision of ancient Indian institutions "tossed about, subverted, and tor[n] to pieces" appears a corrective sentence whose mild reasonableness seems entirely inadequate to meet the horror: "nor will any thing give stability to the property of the natives, but an administration in England at once protecting and stable" (5:427), he says, in the voice of a future commissioner (as Burke expected to be). But if Burke's own vision of ruin in this very paragraph is to be believed, what remains for a commissioner to stabilize and protect? Burke's own sublime language itself erases the Indian object of protection. Elsewhere, Burke similarly pictures "total revolution" having already occurred in the Bengali legal system: "at one stroke, the whole constitution of Bengal, civil and criminal, was swept away" (5:429). What, then, will a stable administration stabilize? Only the imposed British system? Burke's sublime language defeats in advance even the efficacy of surveillance because it bestows impenetrable obscurity on the Company's methods of concealment and obfuscation: "In the obscure and silent gulph . . . every thing is now buried. The thickest shades of night surround all their transactions" (5:429–30). How can ordinary political instruments or ordinary political virtues control and redirect forces that Burke's own language compares to mysterious and overwhelming natural or even supernatural catastrophes?

Burke's contemporary opponents were quick to seize on this disproportion between his terms of indictment and reform. Major Scott's pamphlet snidely taunts Burke for failure of cogency: if Burke's allegations are true, Scott argues, "nothing short of restitution can repair the mischief."[36] To be sure, Hastings's agent is not himself proposing any kind of restitution, even if the total destruction of institutions and social systems in Burke's vision made such a concept imaginable.[37] Scott is simply discrediting the reform proposal so that the charge of criminality lands on the would-be reformers, pictured as a new band of thieves and revolutionaries: "Is it less rapacious, or treacherous, or barbarous, for a Government to seize the property of its own subjects . . . than for those subjects to have originally seized it in the same manner from the then lawful owners?" Political cynicism, as I have discussed in relation to Walpole, in a sense accepts the irresistibility of the sublime. Scott represents India's entire history as a succession of horrors. Parliamentary intervention can claim no superior ethical standing; the Fox Bill merely transfers power from the Company to a parliamentary faction, without fundamentally interrupting the dynamic by which Indian wealth and power have been usurped, lost, and stolen again by one aggressor after another.

Burke in the Fox Bill speech struggles to overcome cynical fatalism, while at the same time acknowledging the dynamic of British activity. What alternatives other than reform hover at the margins of the imaginable? The American colonies had separated only a few years before. Why should not the Indian territories do the same? The Fox Bill speech glances only a few times in the direction of the possibility that separation, rather than reform, might be the eventual just outcome of the British-Indian relationship.

The best-known and most interesting passage comes directly after Burke has explained that his "cold" style should not be mistaken for absence of "horror and detestation" but that a fuller language of sentiment would seem too "harsh and dissonant" for such an audience and occasion. In accord with the point, his own voice drops to a milder sociable idiom: "All these circumstances are not, I confess, very favourable to the idea of our attempting to govern India at all. But there we are; there we are placed by the Sovereign Disposer; and we must do the best we can in our situation. The situation of man is the preceptor of his duty" (5:404).

As suggested at the outset, these famous sentences enjoyed more than their due reverence from nineteenth-century imperialists who took them as Burke's paternal blessing and ethical guide for imperial power. In the context of the Fox Bill speech, the maxim and the whole passage seem more perplexing and evasive than in their formulaic familiarity. What Burke elsewhere characterizes as universal catastrophes here shrink, as he drops into the idiom of manageable problems: "circumstances are not . . . very favourable." Some more than human force, here awkwardly termed the "Sovereign Disposer," gets called in to minimize further the degree of human choice and will in politics, as Burke transfers responsibility to some providential "Disposer" for a situation that he is simultaneously tracing to human vices of greed and lust for power. In addition, the very word "situation" bestows a factitious stability on a dynamic that he elsewhere describes as ongoing or, at least, very recent. "But there we are; there we are placed." Since when? Burke elsewhere in the speech remarks with wonder that the whole British dominion in India is hardly twenty years old (5:402). This is no venerable, ancient institution, such as Carnatic reservoirs or French royalty. At the very moment of the Fox Bill debate, as he also observes, wars against Indian resistance and rebellion were being fought by the British in the Carnatic and elsewhere (5:395–97). British victory would ensure further expansion and further "revolution," according to the patterns he describes. How much or little time converts revolutionary aggression into an established "situation"?

"But there we are" almost makes better sense as a colloquial designation of Burke's place, really his impasse, in argument. I still prefer an idea of blockage rather than *aporia* because the limit to argument here is set not by logical contradiction but by willed choice to stop short at a certain point. This indictment, Burke affirms (or concedes), will not go back to first principles of entitlement in conquest; it will not go forward to envision radical restitution or probe the legitimacy of ongoing wars. The aphorism of duty converts a chosen limit of inquiry into a precept of practical ethics. The form of aphorism strains at a rhetorical level to achieve an ethical stability belied by Burke's more powerful language of indictment elsewhere.

Aphorisms of duty, however, do not dominate the style of the Fox Bill speech any more than do pauses of stupefaction. Burke's movement of language in the speech is dramatic, in the sense that different idioms—homily, narrative, analysis, sublime vision, concession—yield to one another but also compete without entire resolution. The sublime visions that seem designed to infuse the political argument with urgency sometimes acquire a contrary finality of their own, just as the precepts, when extracted from context, sound like more decisive ethical formulations than the narrative supports.

At moments, the sublime does seem to operate as a kind of disempowerment, a pause that anticipates the defeat of Burke's entire campaign for reform: "It is impossible . . . not to pause here for a moment, to reflect on the inconstancy of human greatness, and the stupendous revolutions that have happened in our age of wonders. Could it be believed . . . that on this day, in this House, we should be employed in discussing the conduct of those British subjects who had disposed of the power and person of the Grand Mogul? This is no idle speculation. Awful lessons are taught by it, and by other events, of which it is not yet too late to profit" (5:392). Burke's own performance on this day already begins to recede along with other "stupendous" recent events into a "monument to astonish the imagination" (5:426), like other ruins that arrest the mind in eighteenth-century poetry and art. That it is "not too late to profit" from "awful" truths of history seems a feeble trailer tacked onto the end of a wobbly sentence. What reassuring political lesson, after all, follows from the fall of the Grand Mogul or other instances of power's mutability? Here is a pause of astonishment that, instead of invigorating the mind, seems to draw it away into depressing reflections on futility.

I emphasize the unstable and dramatic tensions among idioms in the Fox Bill speech because they reflect the competing rhetorical and intellectual energies that together convey the full dimensions of India's challenge to one of the strongest English political minds in the eighteenth century. Whatever Burke's failures as a legislator, it is to his credit as a writer that his language never settles into either simplistic endorsement of an inadequate reform proposal or the artificial clarity of moral precept.

After 1783, the excessively immediate threat to his career and reputation at first collapsed Burke into the more confused pain seen in the "Speech on Almas Ali Khan," where personal rage overwhelms all other forms of vision and language. By the time of the Hastings impeachment, and surely in part through its demands and surprising initial success in the Commons, Burke regained an impressive rhetorical and emotional self-control. Once again, the formidable arsenal of evidence called forth Burke's own formidable analytic, narrative, and oratorical brilliance. But this recuperation of energy works within a narrower range of imaginative and intellectual ambition than the earlier work. To be sure, the structure of a single man's trial constricts the scope of argument. But Burke's obsession with the action of impeachment also corresponds to a deliberately more limited conception of how to present

the nation's relationship to Indian conquest, and a deliberately more self-aggrandizing conception of his own role.

The task of converting Parliament, and England itself, into worthy collaborators in what he presents as a great act of national justice stands out as
Burke's most novel ambition in the impeachment trial's "Opening," a
speech of four days (more than eleven hours). Since the impeachment
charges and most of the Indian detail had already been presented by Burke
on other occasions, and in at least as cogent form, what makes the trial
"Opening" distinctive is Burke's reshaping of his own role and purpose.[38]
Even though Burke is obviously there to prosecute, he also works to shed his
adversarial posture as scourge of the nation in favor of an even loftier role as
healer and redeemer.

The pyrotechnics required by this new priestly role show in the historical
narrative of British imperial beginnings on the second day of the speech,
when Burke rhetorically absolves the nation of any collective guilt. Starting
with the same events in Bengal so scandalous to earlier critics of Clive's ad-
venturing, Burke curiously announces that he is passing over squalid details.
Instead, he will fill the space where such an historical narrative would appear
with an alternative, hypothetical version of events that *would have* done
honor to Britain as a nation "*if* it had shewn its virtue upon that occasion to
be altogether equal to its fortune" (6:314; italics mine). Burke acknowledges
that "it has happened otherwise," but his substitution of a fictive history for
the actual has the effect of instating an ideal version of Britain in a space deliberately emptied of the historical actuality. A string of counterfactual con-
ditionals virtually cleanses history, instead of narrating or analyzing it. Ide-
ally, history should show Britain having brought peace, happiness, and
security to the people of India:

> And indeed some thing might have been expected of the kind. For
> when it was to come from a learned and enlightened part of Europe,
> in the most enlightened period of its time; when it was to come from a
> Nation the most enlightened of the enlightened part of Europe, it
> would have been a great deal to say that they came from the bosom of
> a free Country, which carried with it at least to a Country who had not
> the benefit of its forms, all the advantage of the liberty and spirit of a
> British constitution. It would have been glorious to this Country and
> would have saved the trouble of this day, in some measure at least. It
> would have been glorious to us too, that in an enlightened state of the
> world, possessing a religion an improved part of the religion of the
> World—I mean the reformed religion—that we had done honor to
> Europe, to our Cause, to our religion, done honor to all the circum-
> stances of which we boast and pride ourselves at the moment of that
> revolution. (6:315)

In this unedited flow of oratory,[39] Burke's repetitions of "glorious," "enlightened," and "honor" float free from the syntax so that the sentences paradoxically glorify Britain for what "would have been" as if it were a reality. Burke chooses not to look back in detail at the controversial events of the 1750s and 1760s that Continental as well as some British critics had at the time observed with dismay. In language that recalls how Burke's "duty" in the Fox Bill speech came into play only in relation to an arbitrarily stabilized "situation," Burke now more elaborately shields the early episodes of British territorial conquest in India with images of mystery and danger:

> Many circumstances of this acquisition I pass by. There is a secret veil to be drawn over the beginnings of all governments. They had their origin, as the beginning of all such things have had, in some matters that had as good be covered by obscurity. Time in the origin of most governments has thrown this mysterious veil over them. Prudence and discretion make it necessary to throw something of that veil over a business in which otherwise the fortune, the genius, the talents and military virtue of this Nation never shone more conspicuously. But a wise nation, when it has made a revolution itself, and upon its own principles, there rests. The first step is revolution to give it power; the next is good laws, good order, to give it stability. (6:316–17)

This famous passage remarkably combines evasion and candor. Burke justifies his rhetorical strategies of evasion even as he performs them. More openly than in the Fox Bill speech, he here acknowledges the first conquests as a *human* quest for power, without reference to any "Sovereign Disposer." Territorial dominion resulted from the nation's entirely human genius, talents, and military virtue—along with whatever other less noble qualities remain unnamed beneath the mysterious veil. Like "duty" in the Fox Bill speech, justice comes into play only belatedly, in order to stabilize a postrevolutionary situation through "good laws, good order."

The concealment of early crimes of conquest serves the prosecution's effort to disarm Hastings's defense that he inherited a situation of intrinsic instability and injustice to Indians when he assumed his position as governor general in 1772. Burke urges the concealment of earlier crimes, as though to peer under the veil would be sacrilegious. The trope of the veil mystifies the ignominy of imperial genesis by recasting it into yet another version of the Indian sublime. But the image has its own rhetorical impenetrability. Does the veil cover a sacred mystery or simply the nation's human sins? Does its warrant come from divinity or only from a strategic weighing of political dangers and advantages?[40]

By distracting attention from the sins of conquest, the imagery of the veil contributes to Burke's substitution of imaginary for actual history in the

"Opening": "Prudence and discretion make it necessary to throw something of that veil over a business in which otherwise the fortune, the genius, the talents and military virtue of this Nation never shone more conspicuously." "Otherwise" replaces what actually occurred with what would have been— except that it did not happen that way!

A different, equally mystifying fiction dominates the famous peroration on the fourth and final day of the "Opening." Burke precedes his final summation by offering posterity as well as his contemporaries an ideal vision of the England capable of staging this trial.[41] A radiant celebration of English society and government stunningly erases his own preceding four years of combat and isolation. Whereas in a stark letter of 1785 he had remarked: "We know that we bring before a bribed tribunal a prejudged cause,"[42] this same tribunal now surpasses in its glorious commitment to justice anything that "the range of human imagination can supply" (6:458). Seemingly lost in awe at what his own imagination is supplying, Burke goes on to pay tributes: first, to the Crown: "that sacred majesty . . . what we all feel in reality and life, the beneficent powers and protecting justice of His Majesty"; then, to the "great hereditary Peerage . . . who will justify, as they have always justified, that provision in the constitution by which justice is made an hereditary office." Burke even extends his imaginative embrace to the "new nobility, who have risen and exalted themselves by various merits." As for the House of Commons, that same institution that he had so recently threatened with the wrath of God has now become the wondrous center of the universe: "and I believe, my Lords, that the sun in his beneficent progress round the world does not behold a more glorious sight than that of men, separated from a remote people by the material bounds and barriers of nature, united by the bond of social and moral community, all the Commons of England resenting as their own, the indignities and cruelties that are offered to all the people of India" (6:457–58).

These hyperboles, which surely surpass custom even in a ceremonial age, raise difficult problems of interpretation. Burke had in no way transcended his hostile conflict with every object of his tribute. Indeed, the same Lords who had defeated the Fox Bill were busy deciding procedures for the trial that would ensure the defeat of the impeachment even while Burke was performing his "Opening."[43] It is true that the Commons (including Pitt) did vote favorably on at least some of his impeachment charges. But no revolution of national sentiment had transformed the "perfect indifference" to Indian suffering remarked by Burke in 1784 into the humanitarian solidarity Burke invokes. It is Burke himself who has decided to transform his own demeanor: no longer a doomed Goliath but a more priestly, more redemptive figure, more thoroughly at one with the nation's ideal identity as Burke would soon elaborate it in the memorable tribute to English character, tradition, and liberty in *Reflections on the Revolution in France*. To be sure, the weeks and years of Burke's oratory in the trial would continue to make use of every form of his rhetoric of indictment. But the trial at the very start promises to exalt the prosecutor, elevate him from scourge to priest of a collective sacred ritual in the spirit of the English nation's Christian redeemer: "knowing that He who is called first among them, and first among us all, both of the flock that is fed and of those who feed it, made Himself The Servant of all" (6:459).

Thus sanctified and inspired, Burke prepares in the impeachment "Opening" to transcend the difficulties of the Fox Bill speech, where, as legislator, he struggles through argument to awaken the drowsy imperium. The peroration instead creates the soothing fiction of a new and perfect harmony joining the order of the trial to the order of human nature, under the higher order of "those eternal laws of justice" that Hastings alone must be punished for having "cruelly outraged" in India.

The fictive harmony of the peroration comes across as a quite explicit, deliberate strategy by Burke and not an unconscious denial or evasion visible only to the eye of retrospective criticism. The sense of choice appears explicit near the beginning of the first day: "We are to decide by the case of this gentleman [Hastings] whether the crimes of individuals are to be turned into public guilt and national ignominy, or whether this nation will convert these offences, which have thrown a transient shade on its glory, into a judgment that will reflect a permanent lustre on the honour, justice and humanity of this Kingdom" (6:271). From the veil to the shade, Burke's tropes of darkness set off a contrasting artifice of "lustre" to be created by the trial itself. Hastings alone remains cast into darkness, the personification of Indian crime: "one in whom all the frauds, all the peculations, all the violence, all the tyranny in India are embodied, disciplined and arrayed" (6:275–76).

The cleansing of Britain through the impeachment trial becomes for Burke a symbolic ritual, directed partly to the public but even more to posterity. With no realistic expectation of political or legal action against Hastings, the whole impeachment trial becomes something of a fictive construct for the edification of Britain in the future. The ideal of English justice in an English Parliament seems to speak past the actual (unworthy) judges in the case to a superior audience—to an idealized future Parliament and public and, ultimately, to God.

Burke's performance initially enthralled the public as theater. Here was a version of the sublime that beautifully conformed to one of Burke's own criteria for success in drama, as explained in the *Enquiry* (38): the audience must feel its own safety. The Fox Bill speech risks violating this dictum, as it scourges the whole nation for complicity in the systematic ruination of India. That performance created drama out of the difficulty of converting horror to political argument and action. The rhetoric of the "Opening," by contrast, encloses both audience and speaker in a high glow of divinely sanctioned righteous power. From this position, speaker and audience can together tremble, weep, collapse in sorrow at the personification of Indian horror in Hastings, with no more jeopardy to their own safety as a nation than is felt by an audience at a play. Whatever evil of empire cannot be embodied in Hastings is consigned to invisibility under the "mysterious veil." Reviews of the "Opening" enthusiastically praise Burke's speaking as "one of the most sublime achievements of eloquence we ever witnessed," in the words of one newspaper.[44] This enthusiasm was entirely congruent with the widespread consensus that Hastings neither would nor should actually be punished for his actions in the real world of law. His eventual acquittal was generally greeted with satisfaction as a just outcome.

In a sad paradox, Burke's most protracted Indian campaign in relation to British crimes opens with a retreat from his earlier struggles of political dissent. The priestly role he adopts in the "Opening" protects rather than challenges the nation's comfort by sanctifying a redeemed empire for posterity. Although the reform proposal of the Fox Bill may seem weak, the shifting and partially inconsistent styles of Burke's speech survive as an extraordinary work of argument, analysis, and exhortation, different in its sublimity from the impeachment "Opening" in Burke's ardor to confront and grapple with the cruelties and crimes of modern history.

Victorians preferred the more reassuring Burke of the mysterious veil. In celebrating what he regarded as Britain's reformed and redeemed Indian governance of the nineteenth century, Macaulay relegated Clive and Hastings to the remote, lawless, but also generative past. Macaulay's complacency ignores the degree to which grandiose nineteenth-century projects such as his own Penal Code promoted stability of British rule only through further destruction of institutions and traditions that Burke respected.[45] Victorian culture was content to bask in the luster of Britain's enlightened empire, as if this area of light were a real phenomenon and not the artifice that Burke shows himself creating. Even in the impeachment "Opening," the veil that Burke offers the nation to protect its moral comfort only partially hides Burke's own tumultuous and unresolved struggle with competing values and insights. Despite all the limitations, evasions, and historical errors that can be charged to Burke's India writings, the best of them survive the tarnishing of British imperial luster because his own mind never settled into even his own formulae or fictions. His calls on our attention feel daunting, not only by their volume and detail but by the complexity, depth, and intensity of engagement he both offers and demands.

3

William Henry Sleeman and the Suttee Romance

The revival of scholarly attention to the vexed subject of Hindu widow burning comes partly from its long, conspicuous, and now suspect role in British imperial self-justification, starting in the nineteenth century.[1] Historical interest is reinforced by current widespread public uncertainty about how to think and what, if anything, to do about continuing social practices such as female circumcision, female infanticide, and other violent behaviors against women that retain cultural sanction in some parts of the world. Even without the lawmaking power that the British exercised in the Indian territories under their control in 1829, when *sati*[2] was officially banned, current practical and sometimes legal dilemmas about political asylum, court intervention in relation to immigrants, and the legitimacy of foreign protest in the name of "human rights" make the issues involved in the history of Hindu widow burning more than an academic or simply textual matter, even in the West.

Precisely because *sati* belongs to a category of social practices that remain profoundly disturbing to both modern South Asians and Westerners, new anticolonial certainties have been slower to take hold in relation to texts concerning *sati* than for those having to do, say, with the organization of land revenues. Rebukes to the cultural arrogance or venal motives in British colonial policies typically stumble over critics' own desire to state their opposition to the practice of *sati,* without falling into colonialist terms. No anticolonial "alternate discourse" against *sati* has so far been able to replace discredited colonial positions.[3]

The problem became conspicuous when the 1987 *sati* in Rajasthan of Roop Kanwar, an affluent, educated eighteen-year-old, generated new controversy and scandal: 300,000 pilgrims flocking within a fortnight to her village near the major city of Jaipur, a profit-making traffic in "holy" souvenirs by local priests and entrepreneurs, legalistic and political evasions of responsibility by officials, and the fracturing of tenuous intellectual alliances—for example, between Westernized academic theorists and activist feminist reformers. Opponents of *sati* who shrink from colonialist language of rescue and reform became caught in a rhetorical impasse, what Rajeswari Sunder Rajan calls a "methodological crisis."[4]

This atmosphere of uncertainty has the merit of supporting the more tentative, differentiated responses to colonial texts that I am recommending in this book. I divide my discussion here into two parts, using the example of *sati* to argue that two equally crucial kinds of reading need to coexist, not only in some loose pluralism of separate disciplines, courses, journals, and coteries but together—within the same reader—in sequence, perhaps, and admittedly in tension with each other, possibly without final resolution. In the first part of this essay, I lay out in my own terms the collective British discourse of suttee, emphasizing how it rigidified in the nineteenth century in response to shifting historical circumstances and pressures within domestic as well as colonial culture. Sheer repetition in the writing about *sati* reflects the hardening into stereotype of even "sympathetic" emotions like pity, horror, and outrage. The focus of Indian feminists such as Lata Mani on the "official" documents of parliamentary papers and their missionary informants exaggerates, I think, British indifference to the human suffering of *sati* victims, but the effect of depersonalization certainly does result from the formulaic expression of horror and pity that characterizes even eyewitness accounts and autobiographical narrative.[5] In most of the writing about *sati*, overlay from earlier texts causes the writing to feel inhumane, no matter what its genre and explicit emotion.

But some writings stand out against this pattern, and the second part of the essay probes the distinction between stereotyped and individualized writing within the suttee discourse by looking at the unusual suttee story in *Rambles and Recollections of an Indian Official*,[6] the best-selling Victorian memoir by Sir William Henry Sleeman, reporting in the 1840s in the midst of his forty-five-year career as military officer and administrator in the East India Company.

Since Sleeman is so firmly situated in the colonial enterprise, it may be asked why it is worth arguing for his distinctiveness now. Said has shown that even Karl Marx or the boldly eccentric Victorian traveler and writer Sir Richard Burton "in the end" remain within colonialist structures of thought.[7] The writings of a loyal colonial official like Sleeman will much more easily yield to a strategy of analysis that either seizes on selected details that make apparent exceptions conform to type or more simply ignores anomalies.[8]

Theoretical and methodological choices here may seem irreconcilable,[9] although readers and teachers do in actuality move among a greater variety of reading practices than discourse analysis validates. Empirical testing of what method produces more interest for which texts may be the best guide for choosing one critical approach over another in the particular case. Most accounts of suttee do yield most when read for their participation in a collective colonial discourse. Indeed, except as data and illustrations of this discourse, there is no reason to read very many of these suttee texts, and none of them very many times; once the discourse has been defined, the value of such cultural texts has been exhausted. Sleeman, I argue, belongs to that smaller class of writers who seem worth reading and rereading, precisely because of their departures from stereotype in form, tone, and detail. One response may be "Why bother?" An anonymous negative reader of an earlier version of this chapter did impatiently challenge the value of attending to "exceptions to the rule": "exactly why are they significant? Is there any particular reason the author thinks they lead to an important or new conclusion about British attitudes to *sati*?" I quote the wording of this reader's challenge because it has been such a stimulating irritant throughout the writing of all the chapters in this book.

One answer has to be that Sleeman, and other dissenters and mavericks, do *not* clearly produce new generalizations or conclusions about *sati* or British attitudes toward it. The interest for the reader of a writer such as Sleeman leads in different directions, to further considerations about the possibility and difficulty of unorthodox thought and expression at any particular historical moment, for example, and about the importance of that quality as a stimulus to further thoughts of our own about difficult subjects, and to fuller interest in an author's whole work. Of the little anthology of suttee accounts appended to Edward Thompson's interesting historical essay *Suttee*,[10] all but Sleeman's seem anonymously uniform; his is the only one that arouses curiosity to read more of his writing: "What else does this interesting man have to say on other topics? Does his suttee narrative belong to some larger pattern in his work?" Having followed that line of curiosity into a full reading of *Rambles and Recollections*, I think that Sleeman's suttee story is not anomalous for him; interestingly, the same characteristics that distinguish his writing on this topic make his total memoir distinctive and worth reading, even if (or perhaps especially if) *sati* is not your exclusive concern. Sleeman's memoir, in other words, offers a variety of literary as well as historical satisfactions; its literary interest depends on the author's fresh and flexible registering of many situations that are typically fixed in predictable molds for most of his contemporaries. Since these distinctions may be more elusive in principle than in practice, I turn first to the collective suttee discourse, an intricate and fascinating story in its own way.

The Suttee Plot

The British suttee plot follows an old pattern of romance: the Hindu widow is the touching female victim of enchantment; the British rescuer has the heart, if not always the power, of a chivalric hero. This is the note struck at the close of the polemical compendium *The Suttees' Cry to Britain* (1827): "If all *the Knights* of the present day could be persuaded to undertake the rescuing of Bengalee widows from the flames, they would attempt a nobler deed than was ever achieved since the order was instituted; and, should they be successful, would transmit to posterity a name more honourable than any or all of their brethren."[11] More honor than burden, the mission of civilization in the early nineteenth century offered a modern arena for noble deeds.

The suttee romance took hold as a cultural myth because it organized a variety of values and fantasies promoted by the reformed and reorganized East India Company of the new century.[12] Burke, to be sure, had his own chivalric imagination, which tended to fix on the distresses of royal ladies— Marie Antoinette or the Begums of Oudh so lamentably reduced to beggary by the machinations of Warren Hastings, working on the ladies' weak and greedy male relative.[13] As colonial rule extended into the everyday administration of Indian society (a direction that Burke opposed), British colonial chivalry became less exclusively regal in its rescue missions and more structured to divide heroes from villains on racial lines. Burke lamented the plight of the Begums as part of his impeachment proceeding against the governor general of the East India Company; for nineteenth-century Indian colonial reformers, the foes were Hindu priests, brothers, fathers, sons, and sometimes the woman victim herself.

The Evangelicals exploited the plight of Hindu widows to support the crusade for Christian conversion; the Utilitarians used it to demonstrate the sinister effect of any barbarous superstition on the rational ordering of society. James Mill, in his influential *History of British India* (1816), gathers missionary corroboration for "the immoral influence of the Hindu religion and . . . the deep depravity which it is calculated to produce."[14] While other Hindu practices, like child marriage and untouchability, were as shocking to the British as *sati*, widow burning had more sensational and sentimental power even than other forms of human sacrifice, as James Mill remarks: "none however has more excited the scornful attention of the Europeans, than the burning of the wives on the funeral piles of their husbands. To this cruel sacrifice the highest virtues are ascribed."[15]

Deeper interventions into Indian private life also extended opportunities for British self-congratulation on its own "advanced" civilization. In nineteenth-century Britain, to be sure, not everyone agreed on how much sacrifice was desirable for women, and specifically for widows. Still, British sentiment cohered around its reassuring distance from Hinduism. In *Middlemarch*, for example, Casaubon has a copious imagination regarding wifely sacrifice after his death. But as Mrs. Cadwallader remarks about the rules for mourning and remarriage: "It is lawful to marry again, I suppose; else we might as well be Hindoos instead of Christians."[16]

George Eliot, like other Victorian novelists, expresses considerable ambivalence about female self-sacrifice. *Middlemarch* comes close to being a suttee plot in English terms: the enchanted girl, the moribund husband demanding worship, the valorous rescuer from afar. In the climactic chapter
before Casaubon's death, the narrator extends Dorothea's virtue of self-sacrifice beyond the boundary of Victorian common sense, soliciting admiration for what the community would reject as weakness or folly. At the same
time, she intensifies Dorothea's desire for self-preservation beyond Victorian
standards of feminine virtue. It is really the intensity of Dorothea's inner
conflict that Eliot asks us to admire, but she backs away from resolving the
conflict in exclusively inward terms. By striking Casaubon dead just before
Dorothea makes her pledge of postmortem obedience, Eliot as author rescues the heroine from the consequences of extreme spirituality. The novel
thus "saves" Dorothea from self-destruction, though Eliot still admires the
spiritual aspiration that she arranges for the plot to interrupt. In the end,
Eliot endorses more than she ridicules Mrs. Cadwallader's worldliness about
Christian as distinct from Hindu widows. The impulse to self-sacrifice en-
nobles female character in Victorian eyes, but only "up to a point," as Mr.
Brooke would say.

With regard to *sati*, the British more simply resolved the problem of judging female self-sacrifice by denying the Hindu victims any semblance of
Dorothea's spiritual stature. Although the calm bravery of certain warrior
wives in the princely states merited amazement, no representation of inner
struggle spiritualizes their sacrifice, according to the Western tradition of
heroines, saints, and martyrs. In the language of feminist analysis, Indian
women did not acquire "complex subject status" or "agency" in the suttee
discourse, even when their apparently steadfast faith was remarked.[17] The
"heroic" death remains merely conventional, a matter of costume and ceremony in which the individual woman loses spiritual distinction, sometimes
quite literally because she is only one in a crowd of five, ten, or even a hundred other wives and concubines. More commonly, British accounts deny the
spiritual authenticity of *sati* by emphasizing physical coercion of the woman.
The British discourse develops mainly in relation to the inglorious appear-
ances of *sati* in Bengal. There, the coercion of the family was often visible and
seemed to stem as much from economic as from religious motives.[18] With the
woman pictured as no more than a helpless victim of male greed, active virtue
belongs entirely to the British rescuer. Male dominance splits along racial
lines: the base cruelty of Hindu husbands, fathers, and priests, opposed by
the noble, protective generosity of the British would-be rescuer. To be sure,
the act of looking, as in pornography, involves as well as dissociates the spectator. In eye-witness accounts, sensual imagery obscurely interacts with humanitarian, patriotic, and Christian self-assertion. Here is how the scene appears in a report of the General Baptist Missionary Society in 1825:

Her jet-black hair was smeared with ghee and other greasy substances, and decorated with flowers and gaudy ornamented paper: round her neck was a large rope nearly as thick as my wrist, and one or two smaller ones: thus attired, she looked the picture of all that is degraded and wretched. . . . Altogether, I never saw any thing so infernal. The barbarous indifference of the multitude to every feeling of humanity—the thoughts of an awful eternity—the idea that the poor creature before me would soon rush, thus polluted with Idolatry, into the presence of an awful God, who hates sin and abominates Idolatry . . . altogether so pressed upon my mind that the feeling beggars description. . . . I got off my horse and the two Europeans came near with their elephant; I made my way to the woman, and found she was quite intoxicated; there was a strange wildness in her appearance. I looked at her eyes, turned up the eyelids and found them very blood-shot and heavy: the woman could not utter a syllable distinctly, all that could be understood was "Juggernaut" and "koosee," meaning, I suppose, Juggernaut is my pleasure. A thrill of horror ran through my veins. . . . We thought the law protected us under such circumstances, and determined to rescue her.[19]

This fairly typical personal report is shocking in several ways. The "thrill of horror" sensationalizes British dismay, while also masking political complications. One reason the British witnessed so much widow burning was that the Bengal Presidency in 1813 instituted supervisory "Directions" that required an administrative presence at the ceremony. The British were attempting to control the practice, supposedly according to the rules of the sacred Hindu texts: no involuntary suttee, no drugs, no pregnant women, no girls under age sixteen, no mothers of small children unless custodial care was ensured.[20] Suspicion of intoxication explains the bold eye-examination of the Baptist missionary, and then his belief that the law sanctioned his intervention. And he was right. After bodily removing the woman from the scene, he was able to get the court to prohibit her *sati* the following day.

But British intervention had the paradoxical effect of vastly increasing the incidence of *sati* in Bengal, whether by bestowing official imprimatur or, conversely, by stirring up zeal for seemingly threatened religious autonomy. Whatever the reason, by far the greatest number of *satis* in British India after 1813 occurred in Bengal, particularly around Calcutta, the center of British rule.[21] Far from figuring as unique rescuers, as the myth proposes, the British in Bengal exemplify the more problematical situation of reformers who somehow incite the very horrors they deplore.

The British suttee myth collapses the complicated, mixed record of Indian history into the romance of Britain's civilizing mission. Outside Bengal and the independent regions of Rajasthan and the Punjab, where the funeral ritual was part of the warrior code of honor, the practice of *sati* had greatly declined in India well before the nineteenth century, and for a variety of reasons other than British outrage.[22] Muslims did not practice *sati* at all; lower-caste Hindus did rarely. The Mughal rulers had discouraged the practice and had effectively suppressed it in their territory in the seventeenth century. In the powerful independent Hindu states of Central India, many princes opposed *sati* for political, if not moral, reasons. The widows of Mahratta princes often had to act as regents to the royal successors and heirs. John Stuart Mill curiously invokes these powerful Hindu widows in *The Subjection of Women* when he adds examples even from "Hindoostan" to show that women are more capable of political responsibility than British law and public opinion recognize.[23] The most famous Mahratta queen, Ahalya Bai, revered as a saint in parts of India, ruled Indore virtuously for thirty years after being dissuaded from *sati* by her father-in-law in 1765.[24] The priests of Bengal went farthest in maintaining the holiness of widow sacrifice, both as a marital duty and as a means to conjugal reunion after death. But even in Bengal, Hindu reformists, such as Rammohun Roy, opposed *sati*, questioning whether the sacrifice was really required or even recommended by the sacred texts.[25]

In British reformist myth, Indian controversies and the complexities of caste, region, and economics yield to a simpler structure: only civilized Britain offers hope for Hindu widows, while suttee represents the helpless depravity of the subcontinent as a whole. The slow, complex movement away from *sati* within India, reported by older, conservative administrators, was ignored in the 1820s by the British faction that urged quicker, more thorough reform. The myth frames *The Suttees' Cry to Britain*, which sanctimoniously begins: "It is a melancholy reflection, that the religion which influences the population of the vast regions of India, is totally unfavourable to the exercise of every principle either of humanity or virtue."[26] Concern for political security simultaneously supports the contrary argument that suttee has so little connection to Hinduism that it can be eradicated without arousing native protest. The Reformists saw no contradiction in representing suttee as both the proof of depravity at the heart of India and a superficial excrescence that British action could easily remove.

Legal abolition of *sati* was accomplished, with surprising ease of enforcement, in 1829 under the Reform administration of Governor General William Bentinck. In certain independent territories, such as the Bundelcund, mentioned by Jules Verne in *Around the World in Eighty Days*, the "proof" of Indian degradation remained. Moreover, the rhetoric of depravity persisted throughout British India and England, independent of the political settlement of policy. In the later nineteenth century, and even in the twentieth, the *frissons* aroused by *sati* did not so much diminish as stiffen into a reflex, a kind of moral spasm, unsoftened by the decline of the practice, or even of the Empire itself.

After 1829, the moral logic of the suttee myth adapted to shifting British needs; the necessity for a continuing moral justification of power was both reflexive and conscious. As John Stuart Mill explains in *The Subjection of Women*, civilized nations advance from "the primitive condition of humanity" by abandoning "the law of the strongest" as the "regulating principle" of their affairs: "nobody professes it, and, as regards most of the relations between human beings, nobody is permitted to practise it. When any one succeeds in doing so, it is under cover of some pretext which gives him the semblance of having some general social interest on his side."[27]

If Mill sounds cynical about the "pretext" that veils power in social decency, the reason is that he wants to expose the primitive bases of women's subjection to male power in modern English society, where "right founded on might" survives without jarring civilized sensibilities. Mill does not apply his point to colonialism, although his long career in the East India Company surely taught him how power is covered with moralism in foreign as well as domestic affairs.

Mill's point applies with interesting ambiguity to the suttee romance. Insofar as widow burning enacts a more primitive subjection of women to men than any visible in England, British opposition to it extends civilization into distant regions. But insofar as English society disguises its own subjection of women, outrage at suttee serves to "cover" male abuses of power at home. The issue in England was legal as well as cultural; the Women's Property Bill, which secured widows (and other married women) in England control of their own property, was passed only in 1882, though its provisions had been debated over the three preceding decades.[28] In earlier English Common Law, a husband could dispose by will of most of his wife's property as well as his own.[29] Good English husbands did not behave in such dastardly ways, but a sacrificial ideal of widowhood was piously endorsed in the English cultural tradition even by a feminist such as Mary Wollstonecraft, who urged fuller education for women partly on the grounds that it provided the training necessary to become more heroic widows. Brought up to "comprehend the moral duties of life, and in what human virtue and dignity consist," the well-trained woman afflicted by the misfortune of widowhood "forgets her sex— . . . She no longer thinks of pleasing. . . . Her children have her love, and her brightest hopes are beyond the grave, where her imagination often strays."[30] The reinforcement (or covering) of male economic power by spiritual imperatives can be seen in the English as well as the Indian attitude toward widows, but the suttee romance muffles Victorian ambiguities with indignation at Indian barbarity. As the rescuer of Hindu widows, the colonial administrator exalts the virtue and dignity of English womankind by casting Hindu women in the ignominiously dependent role of helpless or mystified victim.

With rather less complexity, the suttee myth supported British power abroad by moralizing every extension and consolidation of Empire. After the outlawing of *sati* in 1829, urgency about saving victimized Hindu widows yielded to arguments that justified British domination of unworthy Indian men, and of the whole subcontinent. This shift illustrates the often noted movement from reform to control in British attitudes toward India generally in the course of the Victorian period.[31] The suttee myth came to serve a remarkable range of policies and prejudices. On the subject of language in the 1830s: English is the right language for higher education in India because Sanskrit, aside from its scientific, historical, and literary uselessness, promotes "monstrous superstitions" such as suttee.[32] On the drive to annex further territory in the 1840s: how else could the British eradicate suttee in the independent kingdoms? On the postponement of Indian self-government: a population that believes in suttee could not exercise the responsibilities of citizenship. "Imagine," sneers the *Calcutta Review* in 1867, "native Justices of the Peace for the town of Calcutta stating their inability to attend a discussion on the waterworks of the metropolis because they wished to follow the widow of one of their number to her husband's pile at Chitpore or Garden Reach."[33] A tone of contempt, and even brutality, replaces earlier Reformist enthusiasm following the Rebellion of 1857: the same natives who attacked British women at Cawnpore drove their own wives and mothers into the fire.[34] In the later nineteenth century it is British women who are seen to need protection, while the latent erotic charge in the language of power covertly shifts to excited disgust toward Indian men.

The casual racism of *Around the World in Eighty Days* (1873) identifies it with a late stage of nineteenth-century imperialism, but Verne reverts to the earlier suttee romance for his plot. As a Frenchman ridiculing British sangfroid, Verne also enjoys making Phileas Fogg a national caricature: habitué of the Reform Club, scholar of Bradshawe's Rail and Steamship Guide, master of a French servant and carpetbags full of British pounds, Fogg has the features of a Victorian imperialist, even to the joke that he is not the bank robber he so closely resembles. Verne keeps just enough of the sentimental suttee romance to please rather than discomfit a British audience. As in the actual expansion of British rule in India, the episode of chivalric rescue in the novel gives needed heart to what might otherwise seem a monstrous or merely mechanical conquest of space.

Verne's manipulation of convention—and verisimilitude—underscores key features of the suttee romance. He fantastically adds to the iconography of coercion by making his heroine not a Hindu at all but a Parsi, unwillingly married to a disgusting old Hindu rajah. Parsis enjoyed most-favored status among Britain's Indian subjects, being seen as ambitious, light skinned, and quick to master English customs and language. Verne combines this stereotype with others. The high-caste association of suttee encouraged romantic idealization of the victims, even if the ceremony itself degraded them: the pity of it, laments *The Suttees' Cry,* is that the doomed widows are the most "amiable" part of the population. To make her compliant, Verne's heroine requires enough opiate to keep her unconscious for a whole day. When she awakens, she speaks perfect English, and her "thoroughly English education" prepares her even to play a good hand of whist.

Verne's mild sentimental plot, with its suppression of both sexuality and cultural conflict, mimics the censorship in nineteenth-century British myth-making. In an earlier period, suttee evoked wilder imaginings. Eighteenth-century British memoirs preserve unsettling alternate plots. One anecdote is a kind of parable about the dangers of spectatorship at suttee for any "gentleman" who has betrayed a Hindu lady (as many eighteenth-century British traders did). The story tells of a jilted woman who has gone on to marry someone else. Upon the death of this husband, and at the very scene of her suttee, she "espie[d] her former Admirer, and beckned him to come to her. When he came she took him in her Arms, as if she had a Mind to embrace him; but being stronger than he, she carried him into the Flames in her Arms, where they were both consumed, with the Corpse of her Husband."[35] Strong rather than helpless, vengeful as well as self-sacrificing, this Hindu widow inverts the sexual design of Hindu polygamy by going with *two* husbands to the fire. While civilized Britain pitied Hindu women for their subjection to polygamy as well as to suttee, eighteenth-century British men in India were not above enjoying male privileges less easily available at home.[36] The anecdote gets its charge from the opportunity it offers to glimpse some exaction of payment by Hindu women, even at the most dramatic moment of self-abnegation.

The same reversal of power appears in another, better-known story, from the end of the seventeenth century, which features the founder of Calcutta, a roughhewn agent-soldier of the East India Company named Job Charnock. A kind of "founding legend," this story also constructs suttee into a plot about the power of Eastern enchantment to bind strong British men. The eighteenth-century memoirist brings to mind Shakespeare's Enobarbus recounting Antony's fall into Eastern dotage:[37]

> Before the *Mogul's* War, Mr *Channock* [sic] went one time with his Ordinary Guard of Soldiers, to see a young Widow act that tragical Catastrophe, but he was so smitten with the Widow's Beauty, that he sent his Guards to take her by Force from her Executioners, and conducted her to his own Lodgings. They lived lovingly many Years, and had several Children; at length she died, after he had settled in *Calcuttta,* but instead of converting her to *Christianity*, she made him a Proselyte to *Paganism,* and the only part of *Christianity* that was remarkable in him, was burying her decently, and he built a Tomb over her, where all his Life after her Death, he kept the anniversary Day of her Death by sacrificing a Cock on her Tomb, after the *Pagan* Manner.[38]

The business of nineteenth-century empire bred disdain for such Eastern dallying. The earlier anecdotes survive as spicy tidbits from wilder, bygone days, reminders that nineteenth-century colonial moralism was narrowed out of an earlier, more variegated British response to India. Verne caricatures the Victorian narrowness in Phileas Fogg. Sticking to the straight rails of British transport, a determined Victorian Englishman could handle India in a matter of days. True, a fifty-mile break in the track puts Fogg in the jungle of Bundelcund. But no pagan dalliance complicates his adventure of rescue. When he hears that the procession going by is for a suttee, he handles the situation with the humanitarian efficiency of a true British reformer:

> "Is it possible," resumed Phileas Fogg, his voice betraying not the least emotion, "that these barbarous customs still exist in India, and that the English have been unable to put a stop to them". . .
>
> The guide now led the elephant out of the thicket. . . . Mr. Fogg stopped him, and, turning to Sir Francis Cromarty, said, "Suppose we save this woman."
>
> "Save the woman, Mr. Fogg!"
>
> "I have yet twelve hours to spare; I can devote them to that."
>
> "Why, you are a man of heart!"
>
> "Sometimes," replied Phileas Fogg, quietly, "when I have the time."[39]

Rambles and Recollections of William Henry Sleeman

Sir William Henry Sleeman's suttee story follows neither the rescue plot of nineteenth-century romance nor the darker fantasies of seduction and danger in eighteenth-century legend. He recounts a more exceptional, if also more mundane, episode of administrative uncertainty in a long Indian career, lasting from 1810 (when he was twenty-one) to 1856, when he died at sea while homeward bound. The chapter of Sleeman's memoir called "Suttee on the Nerbudda" [40] describes his revisiting the site of suttee shrines in a district where he had governed in the 1820s, and especially his memories of the "subject" of one shrine, a woman whose suttee he had reluctantly allowed in 1829, a month before Bentinck's edict. Several conversations about suttee with other Indian acquaintances in the 1840s end the chapter on an ambiguous and inconclusive note.

Sleeman is far from obsessed by suttee, even though his anomalous sanctioning of one became well enough known to be mentioned in the entry for him in the *DNB*;[41] Thompson includes a long extract from Sleeman in his own book about suttee, and the popular historian Philip Woodruff also cites the incident as a curiosity in *The Men Who Ruled India*.[42] But I have come across no one who reflects on the implications of Sleeman's story; although it is one of the longest suttee texts in Victorian literature and comes from a best-selling book of the time, it is mentioned in no postcolonial discourse analysis of *sati*, as far as I know.

Sleeman's reputation as an energetic agent of Reform was secured by his effective campaign against thuggee, the cult of highway robbery and murder that rivaled suttee in horrifying British minds. Neither his own reputation nor the dominant suttee discourse was much affected by Sleeman's story. Yet it fits with other quirks in his career (also reported in the *DNB*), such as his turning down an important promotion because a bankrupt colleague needed the income more. Read now, his story is notable as much for its quality as narrative as for the unusual action it reports. Placed early in the book, it sets a low key by describing a dilemma rather than a success and a decision to withhold rather than exercise authority. In its absence of heroics, the story prefigures the unimposing character of Sleeman's whole memoir, even to its title: *Rambles and Recollections of an Indian Official*. I do not mean to glamorize a self-effacement that may accurately register limited accomplishments. While Sleeman's modesty makes him unusual among memoirists, in India or elsewhere, his is no case of neglected political or literary genius. Yet he was special enough, in his daily work and in his writing, to challenge a line of interpretation based on stereotypes of the anonymous Indian official. Although Sleeman does not boldly oppose received attitudes, he does "ramble" quite far from the official line in both his behavior and his style.

"Suttee on the Nerbudda" departs from the conventional suttee plot in virtually every detail. This woman is old, not young; her family does not coerce her but is itself torn between her resolve and official orders to prevent the suttee. This is not a "voluntary" suttee of the sort permitted and regulated between 1813 and 1829, because Sleeman had himself banned the ritual in his own territory the previous year.[43] Sleeman becomes flustered and frustrated by the woman's stubbornness, but not indignant or contemptuous. Finally, when the suttee does take place, there are no drugs, no howling spectators, no signs of agony, no rescue fantasies. The woman wants to be united with her husband "under the bridal canopy in paradise" (1:28). Her family regards her desire as an honor to them, as well as to her husband and herself, and they share her faith in the Hindu promise of marital reunion after death. Sleeman speaks from outside this faith, seeing the woman and her family as bound to mere illusion. Yet in retrospect at least, he recognizes the analogy to sacrifices no less fervently honored in his own Christian civilization: "Soon after the battle of Trafalgar I heard a young lady exclaim, 'I could really wish to have had a brother killed in that action.' There is no doubt that a family in which a suttee takes place feels a good deal exalted in its own esteem and that of the community by the sacrifice" (1:31). In the suttee romance, every detail enforces the difference between Hindu superstition and honorable Western sacrifice—in Christian martyrdom, say, or war. Sleeman, by contrast, touches the not very solid ground beneath Western heroic postures by observing how honor is not an objective or absolute value but works as part of a local code in particular communities.

Thompson, writing *Suttee* in the shadow of the "voluntary" self-sacrifices of World War I, extends this troubling analogy in response to the 1918 challenge to British moral self-assurance by Ananda Coomaraswamy, an early twentieth-century Hindu spiritual apologist to the West, who endorsed the prohibition of *sati* because it had become "to some degree" a coercive social convention. But no more than war: "pressure was put on unwilling individuals, precisely as conscripts are even now forced to suffer or die for other people's ideas."[44] Although Thompson chastises Coomaraswamy for "absurdly" minimizing the evil of suttee, the analogy to war destabilizes his own perspective: "the history of every country has shown—that men and women, not only separately, but in the mass, can be disciplined and trained to an extent to which no limit can be set. . . . It is but a few years since men of almost every nation in Europe were disciplined to the point that they would accept a command to go to inevitable death with resignation or even joy."[45]

Sleeman anticipates Coomaraswamy and Thompson in collapsing the distinction between male heroism and female mystification so prominent in the suttee romance. But Sleeman's relativistic view of honor stops short of Thompson's anguished post–World War I meditation on the dangerous power of social training. For Sleeman, the truth that all honor is rooted in communal codes does not necessarily invalidate honor as a value. His perception of cultural relativism leads him to respect the old Hindu woman more, whereas Thompson looks darkly into the abyss of human vulnerability to fatal disciplines.

There are other qualities in Sleeman's account that also anticipate modern perception and that would even recommend him to James Clifford's new program for a more dialogic ethnography.[46] Sleeman tells his story, for example, almost entirely through reported dialogue between himself and the woman. A rhetorical decentering of authority subverts the monovocal convention of the suttee romance, where the victim's voice typically cannot be heard, whether because it is drugged, or drowned out by a howling mob, or because it is lost in nearly unintelligible incantations, or because the narrator is too far away to hear. The scene of human sacrifice hardly conduces to conversation, anyway, and the suttee romance conventionally attends to the spectacle, rather than to any conversational preliminaries, or aftermaths, if there is a rescue.[47] Sleeman, by contrast, unobtrusively recasts the entire drama by focusing on the five days of verbal negotiation that preceded the suttee, when he shuttled between the family and the woman, as she sat upon a bare rock in the riverbed, fasting and awaiting his permission. Even after describing the burning, Sleeman turns back to his earlier talks with the woman, as if this memory of conversation was more vivid than the scene of death: "I asked the old lady when she had first resolved upon becoming a suttee, and she told me, that about thirteen years before . . ." (1:32).

By giving the woman a voice of her own, Sleeman grants her a separate subjectivity and also reduces his control over the shape of the plot. The temporal dimension opens up not just to five days but to thirteen years. The woman's speech composes a separate story, even a counterplot, in which Sleeman figures more as tormentor than hero. He torments her by his very effort to save her, and she appeals to his gallantry to make him desist: "My soul has been for five days with my husband's near that sun—nothing but my earthly frame is left; and this I know you will in time suffer to be mixed with the ashes of his in yonder pit, because it is not in your nature or your usage wantonly to prolong the miseries of a poor old woman" (1:26).

If the British were not ruling India, and if Sleeman were not a colonial official, he would not have been in this predicament, but his description makes it seem hardly unique to colonialism. He struggles with a problem common to many who hold professional authority over other lives—like the physician faced with a woman's desire for an abortion or a dying patient's plea for euthanasia, to take related and controversial contemporary cases. Formulaic political or moral solutions break down under the stress of Sleeman's detailed picture of the situation: if the old woman died of starvation, not only would he have failed to save her but "the family would be disgraced, her miseries prolonged, and I myself rendered liable to be charged with a wanton abuse of authority." Since Sleeman had independently prohibited suttee in his district in this year just before governmental abolition, he could not fall back on higher "orders." If he relented, however, and permitted this particular suttee, he would not only violate his own humanitarian principles but also publicly weaken his personal authority in the district.

Having reduced the problem from mythic to quotidian proportions, Sleeman shows himself behaving with earnest professional clumsiness. He alternates threats with bribes: if she commits suttee, her family's ancestral shrines may be destroyed, and the government may repossess their rent-free lands; if she chooses to live, however, he will build her a "splendid habitation," which he as well as her children will visit daily (1:28). Unmoved by his administrative ordeal, the woman remains fixed to her rock and to her resolve. In the end, Sleeman consents, rather to the surprise of the community.

The outcome matters less in the narrative than the antecedent drama, just as the scene of the burning remains subordinate to the dialogue. Further reading in *Rambles and Recollections* shows that dialogue distinguishes Sleeman's whole enterprise as a colonial memoirist. He casts many unlikely topics in the form of conversations: for example, the chapter about epidemic disease does not follow the model of a "report" on health conditions but rather presents a sequence of somewhat bizarre interviews about disease with figures ranging from native judicial officers to soldiers and servants. Elsewhere, he transcribes his conversations with peasants, pandits, Maharajahs, the aged mothers of Maharajahs, water carriers, landowners, Muslim scholars, and others. So much dialogue is made possible by Sleeman's unusual grasp of Indian vernaculars and by his habit, increasingly rare among nineteenth-century colonial administrators, of wandering around asking all sorts of people about their lives: "Perhaps few Europeans have mixed and conversed more freely with all classes than I have" (2:54), he uncharacteristically boasts at one point, before going on to regret his lack of even greater linguistic proficiency. Some of the book's most amusing as well as embarrassing episodes expose the confusion caused by his compatriots' ignorance of Indian languages.[48]

It must be acknowledged, however, that no wonderfully moving speeches come out of Sleeman's reported dialogue. He lacks a great novelist's talent for devising persuasive speech forms on the written page. Moreover, he is stuck with the problem that English translations of Indian vernacular tend toward high-flown platitude. Even in native English, the effect of high seriousness in common vernacular speech eludes nineteenth-century poets and novelists.[49] Dickens hardly manages it; neither does Wordsworth or George Eliot. English writers often elevate common speech through biblical phrasing and cadence, the King James Bible serving as a common resource for emotional dignity in speech across regional and class lines. But a Brahmin widow's religious faith does not easily translate into the idiom of the King James Bible, even if a few words like "paradise," "soul," and "ashes" can be flung across the gap.

Sleeman succeeds as well as he does mainly by displaying in this woman's resolve human virtues that seem separable from their specific religious content and linguistic form. While the woman (and the entire ritual of *sati*) refers to a religious mythology that remains fantastical and obscure in English translation, her fortitude and dignity, her firm choice of spiritual over material reward, her resistance to worldly coercion, her bravery in the face of physical pain compose a portrait of heroism recognizable to a Westerner, at least in the nineteenth century. At the same time, Sleeman's attentiveness to the strangeness of her beliefs and behavior preserves her foreignness; he does not merely assimilate the Hindu woman to his own imaginative system, like Wordsworth with his leechgatherer or beggars. In comparison to Wordsworth, Sleeman listens to strange voices with more attention and less awe. He is not a Romantic wanderer, hungry for new myth and symbol, but a working administrator whose encounters with individual Indians complicate rather than simplify his problems.

Ambivalence toward Hindu (and other) mythology colors the whole of Sleeman's memoir. He equates all myth with fiction, and while more engaged by fiction than most of his colleagues, he responds much more passionately to practical issues, such as crop blight, land distribution, and the organization of markets and transport for food. Hinduism causes more trouble than other mythologies, he explains, not because it is falser or more vicious but because it penetrates deeper into practical and social life (1:228). Yet if excessive belief in fiction menaces the practical welfare of the community, rational practicality also fails to provide Sleeman with a totalizing myth. He is a lax Utilitarian, with some traces of the older, conservative colonialist's interest in foreign oddity and some touches of Victorian envy for the power of religious fictions to comfort all true believers, including Hindus: "Happy people! How much do they escape of that pain, which in hot climates wears us all down in our efforts to trace moral and physical phenomena to their real causes and sources. Mind! mind! mind! without any of it, those Europeans who eat and drink moderately might get on very well in this climate. Much of it weighs them down" (2:101).

Sleeman implies that his kind of mild skepticism might suffice in a temperate climate. But he is in India. When he needs the support of a creed, he falls back on a qualified version of the imperial reform credo: "I believe, that in spite of all the defects . . . the life, property, and character of the innocent are now more secure . . . and all their advantages more freely enjoyed, than they ever were under any former government . . . or than they now are under any native government in India" (2:331).[50]

For all Sleeman's skepticism, the British imperial creed survives intact in his book, and potentially subversive observations scatter among the particulars. The old woman of his suttee story remains a rare phenomenon: "one of the most extraordinary old ladies I have ever seen" (1:24). While he does not force particulars into conventional plots, his openness keeps him from carrying through the construction of counterplots. His penchant for anecdote, and for the exceptional, remarkable situation, corresponds to a general reluctance to allegorize his material. The old woman of his anecdote more nearly represents the particularity of India (and of life, more generally) that resists allegorization.

While Sleeman exemplifies the virtue of intelligent openness to particularity, his narrative also exposes the vulnerability of this virtue to more aggressive, totalizing energies. Not only is his practical intelligence weaker than the Hindu faith of the old woman, but he also gives in to the Reformist clichés of British rule. In another chapter, he describes showing the local suttee shrines to the great Reformer, Governor General Bentinck himself, during a visit Bentinck made to the Nerbudda. Bentinck appears to lack Sleeman's talent for the particular. Although Bentinck abolished suttee, he could not recognize the relics of the ceremony when he saw them. Sleeman reports the scene as dialogue, but the technique is pointless here, since Bentinck says virtually nothing, and Sleeman does not tell him his own suttee story. In the presence of his superior, Sleeman declines into a subservient tourist guide: "He asked me what these tombs were; for he had never seen any of the kind before. When I told him what they were, he said not a word; but he must have felt a proud consciousness of the debt of gratitude which India owes to the statesman who had the courage to put a stop to this great evil, in spite of all the fearful obstacles which bigotry and prejudice opposed to the measure" (1:140). Lacking the self-assertive or ironic impulse to make much of Bentinck's silence, Sleeman as a writer only straightens up into the functionary's posture he had maintained in the scene itself. He becomes the anonymous "Indian Official" of his book's title, ventriloquizing a cliché version of suttee myth to fill in Bentinck's speechlessness.

Yet particularities skillfully arranged, or simply allowed to coexist without much visible arranging, can also create ironic dislocation. When Sleeman starts "Suttee on the Nerbudda" by laconically noting that a shrine to the woman now exists, even though he had expressly forbidden it to be built, the detail flatly records the weakness of a power exercised through its own bureaucratic mechanisms, separate from the community will. A more baffling effect comes from the odd dialogues that follow the main story. Just after so impressively normalizing the "extraordinary" old lady of the Nerbudda, Sleeman entirely destabilizes his own sympathetic understanding by shifting to an even more extraordinary local incident. This story, too, emerges through a sequence of reported conversations. A "native gentleman" first tells him about a low-caste cultivator's wife, thirty years before, who heard that the local Brahmin banker had died and "declared, all at once, that she had been a suttee with him six times before; and that she would now go into paradise with him a seventh time. . . . She was between fifty and sixty years of age; and had grandchildren; and all her family tried to persuade her that it must be a mistake, but all in vain. She became a suttee, and was burnt the day after the body of the banker!" (1:34). "And what became of the banker's widow?" Sleeman quotes himself as asking, with his usual practicality. The Hindu gentleman's reply is in another tone, hard to decipher: "She said that she felt no divine call to the flames." Sleeman almost wryly maintains his concrete literalness when he learns that the banker was only about thirty when he died: "Then he will have rather an old wife in paradise?" His Indian friend is unfazed: "No, sir; after they pass through the flames upon earth, both become young in paradise" (1:35).

Narrated directly, this incident might seem merely exotic. It is the Hindu gentleman's unruffled fluency, together with Sleeman's mildness, that makes the interchange novelistic, an Anglo–Indian encounter of the sort that E. M. Forster might do a century later. Sleeman's persistent curiosity, however, leads further than Forster goes. A few days later, Sleeman mentions the incident to another Indian friend, the educated, English-speaking principal of the local college: "He said, 'That in all probability this woman had really been the wife of the Brahman [*sic*] in some former birth—of which transposition a singular case had occurred in his own family'" (1:37). The principal goes on to tell of two snakes who entered the suttee fire of his great-grandfather's three wives and were thus memorialized as two additional wives in the family shrines. A few days later, yet another opportunity for conversation occurs, when the youngest brother of the long-deceased banker happens to visit Sleeman and quite cordially agrees to recount the old family story. Initially, he recalls, they were "astounded . . . and told her that it must be a mistake," since they were Brahmin and this self-proclaimed spouse belonged to a low caste. But the woman had her explanation for how she had descended from the caste of her previous incarnations, and she was not to be dissuaded. Finally, "she prevailed upon her husband and his brother to assist her in her return to her former husband and caste as a Brahman [*sic*]. . . . The husband and brother set fire to the pile, and she was burned" (1:38–39). The equanimity of the conversation seems almost as unnerving as the story itself. "And what did your father think?" Sleeman asks. Eventually, the father accepted the claim; the family paid for the funeral, observed all the appropriate ceremonies, and built her shrine: "Her tomb is still to be seen at Khittolee, and that of my brother at Sehora."

"Suttee on the Nerbudda" concludes with Sleeman's brief account of his visit to these tombs and the neighboring village and town, where he found that "all the people" knew the story and confirmed that the woman had surely been the banker's wife. The chapter ends by simply repeating, almost like a ballad refrain, "Her tomb is at Khittolee, and his at Sehora" (1:40).

The tonal inflection of this narrative is difficult to determine. Is this pathos? irony? mockery of superstition? tender family lore? The dialogues have a disorienting effect, stranding the nonadept Western reader somewhere between Sleeman's experienced poise and a touristic vertigo. In the chapter as a whole, one extraordinary old woman jangles against another, while male Indian voices open glimpses into the vast, intricate fabric of Hindu caste and social community. Far removed from the British suttee romance, Sleeman's conversational narrative recaptures some of the wildness of eighteenth-century legends, while also drawing near to that other mythic discourse laid out by the Indian psychoanalyst Sudhir Kakar, who interprets the overt and hidden dynamic of Indian men and women as narrated through folktale, fiction, fantasy, and clinical interview.[51] In this specifically Indian discourse, Kakar explains, images of powerful women haunt men who convert their sense of helplessness into stories and rituals of worship.

Since Sleeman "in the end" always returns to the more familiar main road of British official policy, how to read his narrative excursions comes down to a matter of judgment. A political impulse to discredit Western individualism as an overrated feature of authors, as well as of administrators, motivates much current emphasis on the collective and anonymous character of cultural texts. The by now predictable use of the cultural text is to show the "hegemonic" discourse, the machinery of the system that, by the end of the radical analysis, can be seen to control all apparent individual accomplishments in art or social reform, except those by members of hitherto unrecognized subaltern groups: women, racial minorities, or colonial subjects. The demotion of the status of some major figure or text is often the goal of the project, which easily handles the instrumental lesser texts along the way.

A different standard of judgment, however, can differentiate quality among minor as well as major cultural texts according to the fullness of their rendering of tensions inherent in the social material. Radical cultural criticism tends to minimize this tension, either by consigning it to unconscious processes of ambivalence or anxiety or by reproaching the colonialist narrative for presumably correctable vices. Said, for example, laments the "common human failing" of preferring "the schematic authority of a text" over "the disorientation of direct encounters with the human."[52] What would constitute a direct human encounter with a Hindu widow in the nineteenth century, or even now? With the extreme situation of *sati*, every position is conspicuously governed by textual and other schemes of authority. Hindu pandits, Brahmin families, British Reformers, and even Marxist, feminist, and Subaltern critics all encounter the human reality of widow burning in structures no less distancing than those of colonialist Reform. Sleeman as an administrator encountered *sati* and other situations through the unarguably restrictive structure of power that authorized his interviews. While this authority can be seen to color his narrative, it is also the case that, in his writing, he succeeds in opening the structure of authority for uncommon perceptions and complications.

A fundamental tension nevertheless inheres in the irreducible discrepancy between a particularity that attends to the exceptional, the mysterious, and the bizarre in human events and the generality that is necessary for any formulation of social policy or theory. Sleeman's memoir is most individualized when he elicits and records Indian challenges to British self-satisfaction, a form of encounter he appears to have preferred to social exchanges with other British, who hardly appear in his book and never vividly. If he does not extend his dialogues with Indians into abstract questions of government, part of the reason is that his intelligence seems most vigorous in relation to the particulars of his practical work. Sleeman's anecdotes remain disorienting as well as provocative because they expose the gap between general principles, theories, or policies and the resistant strangeness of human experiences the closer you get to them.

For readers, freedom from intellectual orthodoxy may depend not only on antihegemonic theories and declarations but also on the concrete choices made by individual writers who can move outside their own (and our) critical systems, if we let them. Such opportunities turn up in surprising places; the cultural archive is the repository not only of prejudice and fantasy but also of urgent, practical dilemmas and bewildering uncertainties, sometimes recorded with impressive acuity and vividness. For all its embeddedness in colonialism, Sleeman's memoir has the power to disorient any simple judgment of *sati* and also of other aspects of governance, not limited to British colonialism in India. If he leaves us baffled by his suttee stories, that is surely partly because we recognize in them problems that still elude satisfactory resolution.

4

Victorian Oblivion and The Moonstone

"If he could only have recovered in a complete state of
oblivion as to the past, he would have been a happier man.
Perhaps we should all be happier," he added, with a sad
smile, "if we could but completely forget!"

—Wilkie Collins, *The Moonstone*

The Moonstone has long been recognized as crucial, if not entirely original, in the development of the detective novel, but its status as a colonial text is and probably will remain unsettled. The disguised Brahmins stalking the Yorkshire countryside in quest of their sacred Indian jewel contribute a shiver of Oriental sensationalism to the novel's domestic crime plot, but Wilkie Collins's readers in the 1860s and for a hundred years after did not worry themselves about the political implications of the crime's Indian origin. The crowds gathered in anticipation of the next installment of the novel were not arguing politics but betting on where the stolen jewel would eventually be found.[1] *The Moonstone* presents the case of an entertainment whose very popularity militates against serious consideration of it as social or political critique.

John Reed in the 1970s was the first commentator to give Collins credit for representing "the unacknowledged crime" of imperial depredation in *The Moonstone*: "It is a national not a personal guilt that is in question in this novel, and national rather than individual values that are tested."[2] More in accord with Victorian response, as well as with the categories of recent postcolonial analysis, Ashish Roy counters that Collins stays safely within conventional colonial discourse; he sees *The Moonstone* as justifying British imperialist rule by exorcising those vicious abuses abhorrent to every good Victorian.[3] Roy follows the structure of postcolonial critical debate by formulating the question in polarized form: is *The Moonstone* an inaugural "anti-imperialist" indictment? Or is it "a prototypical imperialist text," all its intricacy decipherable into rhetorical and political patterns not notably different from, say, those to be found later in the Sherlock Holmes stories of Arthur Conan Doyle?[4]

I want to identify *The Moonstone*'s distinctiveness by moving outside the structure of this debate and noticing instead the novel's depiction of oblivion as the Victorian remedy for colonial as well as other kinds of ethical distress. This detective novel peculiarly concerns itself as much with the swervings and lapses of mind that make responsibility for crime so easy to evade as with the investigation or solution of any crime. The central image of the Shivering Sand—the quicksand in the novel's Yorkshire coastal setting that so rapidly buries (but sometimes gives back) inconvenient knowledge—shapes *The Moonstone* into a surprisingly modern critique of Victorian ethical evasion.[5] The novel's recurrent examples of partial amnesia, inattention, and other varieties of oblivion represent conscience and consciousness as quicksand, a conception that in itself significantly departs from the solid ground of moral confidence sought if never entirely secured in Victorian colonial orthodoxy.

The best-known reference point for the false innocence of British imperialism has been the notorious sentence frequently extracted from the 1883 book *The Expansion of England*, by the Victorian imperialist historian J. R. Seeley: "We seem, as it were, to have conquered and peopled half the world in a fit of absence of mind" (8).[6] Collins's plot device of an opium trance in *The Moonstone* anticipates by twenty years Seeley's notion of a "fit" of unconsciousness as the alibi for illegitimate if not definably criminal aggression. The joke of Collins's novel is that, out of eagerness to solve the mysterious theft of the Moonstone diamond from the cabinet of his beloved cousin, Rachel Verinder, the amiable romantic hero, Franklin Blake, must first discover that he has himself performed the robbery, albeit while in an opium trance (later exploited by another cousin, Godfrey Ablewhite, the novel's only unambiguous knave). Franklin had not coveted the Indian jewel that he was assigned to deliver to his cousin's house as a birthday gift bequeathed in the will of a wicked uncle any more than he sought the passion of the servant, Rosanna Spearman, who (in the novel's interesting subplot) is driven to suicide by his obtuse unawareness of her infatuation with him. The circumstance that Franklin owes his trance to opium, Britain's most infamous colonial trade in oblivion, adds another irony. Franklin is an innocent, unwitting participant in the taking of opium, as in other crimes. Collins's interwoven plots ingeniously play with images of innocence as "absence of mind," a kind of not knowing, a not noticing of harm that nevertheless has the same effect as more overt and aggressive power.

Collins anticipates Seeley also in his ironic if ambivalent knowingness about the Victorian alibi of oblivion. Postcolonial criticism has tended to reserve knowingness for itself, leaving Victorian authors blindly enclosed in their culture's dynamic of denial, repression, and repudiation of responsibility. Thus Roy detects residues of anxiety that "betray" the inadequacy of imperial justification in *The Moonstone* but relies for this insight on poststructuralist techniques of semiotic analysis rather than on any skeptical irony within the novel itself.[7] Through the figure of the half-caste doctor's assistant, Ezra Jennings, however, Collins proposes an alternative experimental method of reading to recover buried meanings in puzzling or seemingly incoherent texts.[8] As Jennings explains in relation to his transcript of Mr. Candy's fevered delirium on the night of the theft:

> "I filled in each blank space on the paper, with what the words or phrases on either side of it suggested to me as the speaker's meaning. ... In plainer words, after putting the broken sentences together I found the superior faculty of thinking going on, more or less connectedly, in my patient's mind, while the inferior faculty of expression was in a state of almost complete incapacity and confusion" (375).[9]

Jennings's method works well, not only for the fragmented narratives within Collins's novel, but also for the baffling sentence of J. R. Seeley, whose comment about colonial "absence of mind" has been too readily isolated as a symptom of his own mental and moral confusion. As I have argued elsewhere, what is sometimes now called "Seeley's absentmindedness" has misleadingly turned Seeley into a synecdoche for Victorian oblivion.[10]

In its context, Seeley in *The Expansion of England* can be understood to be enlivening a lecture on imperial history with a bit of wit. He was neither endorsing nor repeating the notion of an unconsciously acquired British empire but, on the contrary, caricaturing what he regarded as a common Victorian distortion of history. Seeley's own position was that imperial ambition had been "the great fact of modern English history" (12) for the preceding three hundred years and the continuing basis of England's prosperity and power. His Cambridge University course, featuring England's imperial competition with other European powers, especially with France in the eighteenth century, proposed to correct the overemphasis on England's domestic progress and politics popularized by Whig historians such as Macaulay, along with the Victorian press. Seeley's far-fetched conceit of global conquest accomplished in a "fit of absence of mind" deliberately makes this alibi for colonial expansion look absurd: "as if it were merely the unopposed occupation of empty countries by the nation which happened to have the greatest surplus population and the greatest maritime power. I shall show this to be a great mistake" (13).

Seeley complicates his image further by analyzing a complex, semiwillful dissociation of the English popular imagination from the policies and goals of what he calls "the political community": "While we were doing it [conquest] . . . we did not allow it to affect our imaginations or in any degree to change our ways of thinking; nor have we even now ceased to think of ourselves as simply a race inhabiting an island off the northern coast of the Continent of Europe" (8). Although Seeley has the reputation of being an imperial apologist, that ignominious label oversimplifies his openness of speculation about the ethics as well as the practicality of colonial possessions involving peoples of different cultures, races, and religions. More in accord with the spirit of his hero, Burke, than with Burke's more complacent Victorian interpreters, Seeley anxiously considers the precarious future of Britain's empire in the light of the relative meanings of the term "civilization" and the larger vicissitudes of worldly power.

The Moonstone anticipates Seeley's picture of the Victorian domestic imagination. When the cursed jewel arrives at the Verinder house, the elderly housesteward, Betteredge, feels indignant: "here was our quiet English house suddenly invaded by a devilish Indian Diamond—bringing after it a conspiracy of living rogues, set loose on us by the vengeance of a dead man. . . .Who ever heard the like of it—in the nineteenth century, mind; in an age of progress, and in a country which rejoices in the blessings of the British constitution?" (46).

Collins exercises his wit more in the Walpolian role of bystander than as either historian or polemicist within what Seeley calls "the political community." Collins was a popular novelist with a fascination for strange mental states, a sensitivity to the injustices of social class (especially as they affected women), and a sharp eye for the shallow complacencies and semiwillful constrictions of consciousness in the Victorian audience he at the same time was resolved to entertain.

Some of the novel's challenges to Victorian alibis of oblivion are quite forthright. In regard to the suicide of the servant, Rosanna Spearman, for example, the novel's underclass social rebel, Lucy Yolland, goes so far as to call Franklin Blake a "murderer" for his careless ignorance of the servant girl's suffering: "Don't tell me he didn't mean it, and didn't know it," she protests to Betteredge, "He ought to have known it" (191). Lucy, to be sure, is an ineffectual protester. With her lame foot and bad temper, Limping Lucy flares up and then disappears in the novel, like a weird apparition, her revolutionary outcries for warfare against the rich and against men unheeded (and even unheard) by the novel's genteel characters.

Like the earlier texts in this study, *The Moonstone* combines critical boldness with provisions for preserving the comfort of its patrons, the middleclass readership Collins called "King Public."[11] Disturbing apparitions in *The Moonstone* could be laughed off or blamed on Collins's own extremity of physical and mental distress at the time of composition, as emphasized in his ingratiating preface.[12] In later conversation and correspondence, Collins proposed an alibi of oblivion for himself by insisting that the heavy doses of opium he was taking for gout at the time left him "scarcely aware of what he was doing during much of the writing."[13] The exaggeration in this disclaimer has been demonstrated by studies of Collins's careful working notebooks.[14] Nor does it accord with the novel's remarkably coherent patterns of imagery and irony. What does seem beyond dispute is Collins's eagerness to befriend rather than offend his audience, as his mentor Dickens feared he had a tendency to do.[15] In a variant of Puck's epilogue in *A Midsummer Night's Dream*, Collins blames his own absence of mind rather than the audience's for any offense:

> If we shadows have offended,
> Think but this, and all is mended:
> That [I] have but slumb'red here,
> While these visions did appear.[16]

Uncertainty about where, exactly, offense is to be located enters *The Moonstone* in the prologue, "Extracted from a family paper" written in 1799 by an East India Company officer to his relatives in England. The extract is a long letter explaining the unnamed writer's motive for breaking relations with his cousin and fellow officer, John Herncastle, a looter, murderer, and reckless adventurer whose theft of the precious Moonstone after the Battle of Seringapatam threatens to curse the entire family.

It has been usual to take the righteous voice of the prologue at face value, as if it were exempt from the open satire of self-righteousness that later makes the figures of the phony philanthropist, Ablewhite, and his falsely pious admirer, Miss Clack, so contemptible. Straightforward reading of the prologue, however, has the misleading effect of instating the most self-righteous strain of eighteenth-century colonial discourse as Collins's own unquestioned inheritance. Outrage against isolated individual malefactors was a legacy of eighteenth-century colonial historiography and political polemic, one already disputed at its outset by skeptics such as Walpole and Burke (at least before he began his unrelenting prosecution of Hastings). It is curious that for a novel so dependent on skepticism toward a whole sequence of partially obtuse narrators, no question of irony has entered interpretation of the righteous cousin of the prologue. Reed, for example, simply repeats the respectable cousin's moral certainty: "It is clear from the first that Herncastle is nothing more than a felon, and common in his greed, for while the 'camp-followers committed deplorable excesses' upon the storming of Seringapatam, Herncastle, instead of controlling them, joined them."[17]

The apparent clarity of the prologue's narrative does not hold up very well under the Ezra Jennings method of contextual interpretation, especially if the historical clues half-buried by Collins are followed. The splitting of felons from moral commanders among the English in Seringapatam and other situations of colonial conquest crumbles under the evidence Collins would have encountered in his historical research.[18] Collins's reading, and even popular knowledge, recognized not only the enormous significance of Seringapatam for the consolidation of British power in south India at the end of the eighteenth century but also the brutality of the battle. Seringapatam introduces colonial India through imagery of bloody conquest associated not only with the preceding generation but also with recent history, in particular the annexation of the Punjab in 1849, after the Sikh wars, the very years established as the "present" of the novel's events.[19] In contrast to many of his contemporaries, who celebrated the glories of British conquest in paintings and retellings of military feats, Collins tended more to the cynical wit of a Walpole, as can be heard in his 1859 account, in *Household Words*, of an abortive invasion by the French of the Devonshire coast that occurred at the same time as Seringapatam: "The rules established in all cases of conquering" were followed, Collins remarks: "Having started with setting something on fire, it went on, in due course, to accomplish the first objects of all Invasions, thieving and killing."[20]

The destruction at Seringapatam of Mysore's strongest military leader, Tipu Sultan, removed the fiercest Indian resistance to British conquest in the eighteenth century. Although blamed by the British for provoking the conflict and demonized as a savage "tiger" (Tipu's own heraldic device), he was also recognized as a formidable foe. Collins would have found, in Theodore Hook's biography of Seringapatam's General David Baird, disturbing details of how Tipu's corpse was plundered by a common soldier after he was murdered "in cold blood."[21] The prologue glances at the inglorious brutality of the battlefield in the cousin's report of Tipu's dead body discovered ignominiously buried "under a heap of the slain" after the planting of the English flag (13). As for the savagery of the common soldiers, the righteous cousin remarks only that after the battle they "disgraced themselves goodhumouredly" (14).

Plunder in the righteous cousin's account of Seringapatam becomes vulgar lower-class misbehavior, while no mention at all appears of the widely reported vast thievery and payoffs to the officers and even to General Baird. The plunder at Seringapatam was a matter of public record in memoirs and popular histories, even those that celebrated the victory. Memoirs cited by Hook recall that, for example, "One gentleman in particular, when he perceived Colonel Wallace and the aid[e]-de-camp approaching, affected to be highly incensed against the men, and actively employed in preventing the pillage, while at the very moment they saw him filling his own pockets."[22] Another memoir gives a fuller accounting of the division of spoils, including General Baird's disappointment in his share:

The idea at first was that every officer in the army had made at least from £10,000 to £20,000. And even General Baird, whom I dined with, expressed his disappointment at receiving so small a sum as £12,000. He expected at the very least £100,000 ....The wealth captured was enormous, and consisted of all sorts of property from every Court in Europe. There was splendid china from the King of France, clocks, watches, shawls of immense value, trinkets, jewellery from all nations, pearls, rubies, diamonds and emeralds, and every other precious stone made up into ornaments—even solid wedges and bars of pure gold.[23]

The prizes acquired render the command against looting a distinction more of social class than of morality. Collins's Betteredge (more sensitive to hierarchies of justice in England than in India) observes class discriminations in relation to thievery as they have affected the servant, Rosanna, once imprisoned as a common thief: "Rosanna Spearman had been a thief, and not being of the sort that get up Companies in the City, and rob from thousands, instead of only robbing from one, the law laid hold of her, and the prison and the reformatory followed the lead of the law" (34).

Nineteenth-century reform of the East India Company into a more regulated bureaucratic organization relegated the excesses of eighteenth-century profiteering to a distant past—that remote period of "origins" that Burke (a decade before Seringapatam) had recommended covering with a discreet veil.[24] The self-righteous cousin participates in the cleansing of history by limiting his outrage to the individual violence that he sees when he encounters John Herncastle: "a torch in one hand, and a dagger dripping with blood in the other" (14). The cousin's sensational language dissociates this spectacle of imperial frenzy from the regular East India Company business of conquest and plunder at Seringapatam. Herncastle is made to seem diabolical because he is driven neither by recognizable high-class greed nor by vulgar "goodhumoured" rambunctiousness. He actually believes in the curse carried by this jewel and is mysteriously drawn to its danger by his "love of the marvellous" (13).

Herncastle's cousin concludes: "Let our relatives, on either side, form their own opinion on what I have written, and decide for themselves whether the aversion I now feel towards this man is well or ill founded" (16). The Victorian relatives opt for "aversion," a form of turning away that stops short of actually repudiating what has now become lawful property. The family's aversion remains private, in accord with the privacy of the cousin's letter. He makes much of the point that he has made no public, official charge against Herncastle; his narrative is for the family alone (11, 15). The continuing privacy of the investigation conducted after the domestic theft of the jewel from the Verinder house reinforces the sense of property that circulates on an ambiguous border of the legal system. English inheritance law brings imperial loot into the domain of legal private property, so that its subsequent thievery from the Verinder house is a crime. But the investigation of this crime in the novel continues as a family matter, with private detectives and, ultimately, private punishment.

The prologue's demonization of Herncastle brings together the Victorian aversion to the eighteenth-century type of the eccentric Indianized Englishman and repudiation of the wicked past. Later details fill out the portrait of Herncastle as a figure who, Franklin remarks to the elderly Betteredge, "belonged to your time, not to mine" (42). Upon returning to England after Seringapatam, Herncastle was ostracized as a "blackguard" and barred from the respectable houses of his family. He was rumored to indulge in opium, old books, "strange things in chemistry," and "carousing and amusing himself among the lowest people in the lowest slums" (44). Colonial misbehavior joins social-class transgression as related violations of propriety. Although Herncastle appeared indifferent to his outcast state, his eventual resentment and desire for revenge against his sister's closed door against him presumably motivates him to bequeath the cursed jewel to his niece, Rachel.

The young Franklin takes a lighthearted tone of disregard for his bad uncle: "The wicked Colonel's will has left his Diamond as a birthday present to my cousin Rachel. . . . And my father, as the wicked Colonel's executor, has given it in charge to me to bring down here" (42). Although Betteredge, staring at the Shivering Sand, expostulates that he would have bet the elder Blake "wouldn't have touched the Colonel with a pair of tongs!," the novel's plot amusingly endorses the insinuation in Herncastle's will that his respectable relations have only superficial aversion to plundered Indian property. Betteredge's impulsive desire at the outset "to shy the Diamond into the quicksand, and settle the question in *that* way" (52) becomes a joke about Victorian materialism through Franklin's jocular reply: "'If you have got the value of the stone in your pocket,' answered Mr Franklin, 'say so, Betteredge, and in it goes!'" (53). By inserting the purloined jewel into the domestic system of inherited wealth, Herncastle's will challenges the family's (and nation's) dissociation from eighteenth-century colonial crimes: the material inheritance is a temptation they cannot resist.

No clear rules in the Victorian period (or since?) adjudicate the legitimate ownership of property derived from conquest. Here, too, Collins's knowledge from contemporary events as well as from books provides potentially ironic analogy for the novel's situation. In regard to purloined jewels, the most famous contemporary example was the stupendous Koh-I-Noor diamond, which Collins mentions in his preface of 1868 as "one of the sacred gems of India" (3), also under a supposed curse against predators. This gem was taken into British possession as the booty of conquest (from the Punjab in 1849); rather than being hidden away in a private vault like the Moonstone, it was famously presented as a triumphal gift to Queen Victoria, then exhibited with fanfare at the Great Exhibition of 1851. Afterward, presumably because of anxiety about its provenance, the royal family sent it to Amsterdam to be cut into pieces (later deposited in the royal treasury).[25] Collins introduces that Victorian solution to the dangerous possession of once sacred purloined jewels through Ablewhite's desperate plan to have the stone cut up in Rotterdam to facilitate its sale, the proceeds of which will pay off his illicit debts (459). Nothing of Herncastle's "love of the marvellous" restrains Ablewhite; his greed and hypocrisy seem to descend directly from the righteous cousin and his fellow officers, for whom the loot of conquest is merely coinage to pay debts and secure position at home.

The Moonstone's prior misadventures in the remote Indian past further complicate ethical judgment in the prologue. The cousin presents this history as a "fanciful story" (13), but correspondence to documented events collapses the distinction between history and legend. The story begins in the dim, ancient past when the jewel was worshipped as the eye of the four-handed moon god in the ancient temple city of Somnauth. When that temple was seized and looted by marauding "Mahometan"[26] invaders under Mahmud of Ghazni in the eleventh century, three Brahmin guardians successfully removed the Moonstone to Benares, where it survived for six further centuries in a new shrine, protected by a succession of guardians and by the curse of Vishnu on any desecrater. The jewel fell definitively into secular history only at the beginning of the eighteenth century, the prologue explains, when a soldier of Aurengzebe seized it in defiance of the curse. Thence, through a century of violent transfers, it came to adorn the dagger flourished by Tipu Sultan, last of the great Mohammedan resisters. The failure of Tipu's weapon against the British could signify either the fulfillment of the ancient Hindu curse or its nullification in a purely secular contest of military strength. In British historiography of the eighteenth and nineteenth centuries, the saga of Mughal conquest served to exonerate British aggression. Since Mohammedan invaders had already been destroying the ancient Hindu order for centuries, it was argued, and since the despotism and military weakness of the eighteenth-century Mughal empire now demonstrated its decadence, British activity could be justified as not violating any existing political or ethical order in the subcontinent; the only source of order would be that which the British would bring from their own civilization.[27]

The only English character in *The Moonstone* who thinks more than a minute about any of this history is the Indian expert and traveler Murthwaite. In a sense, he is the true inheritor of the eighteenth-century Colonel's "love of the marvellous," now welcomed into the house in the marginally respectable Victorian form of traveler and proto-ethnographer. Murthwaite's knowledge of Indian languages and ritual, his boredom in England, and his incongruous admiration for the likely ruthlessness of the Brahmin stalkers runs through the novel as entertaining diversion for the other characters (and the reader) until the book's epilogue, with Murthwaite as narrator, again moves outside the range of the English family's awareness or interest.

Betteredge voices the family's "abhorrence" for any further involvement in the lost Moonstone in his final narrative: "I hold that unlucky jewel in abhorrence—and I refer you to other authority than mine, for such news of the Moonstone as you may, at the present time, be expected to receive" (462). A closing in of the family around renewed innocence shows in Franklin's playful mimicry of investigation, when the only "news" that "something is going to happen in the house" now refers to his and Rachel's forthcoming baby (463). This entirely predictable follow-up to the marriage parodies detective discourse in Franklin's final conversation with Betteredge: "'May I venture to inquire where you got your information?' [Franklin] asked. 'I only got mine (imparted in the strictest secrecy) five minutes since'" (463). Investigation declines into a commonplace joke about the pseudo-secrets of marriage. It is no secret that the sudden death of the elder Blake has left Franklin "heir to his great fortune" (296); now that the condition Franklin first proposed to Betteredge for letting the diamond go has been fulfilled, no sense of sacrifice attaches to the jewel's loss.

In the epilogue (a letter from Murthwaite to the family lawyer), the eccentric traveler has become a secret spectator of the Moonstone's ritual reinstatement in its original shrine at Somnauth. Through what now becomes a solemn voice of witness to sacred mysteries, the epilogue recasts the sly Indian trio into priests who have completed an arduous mission to reclaim an ancient spiritual legacy. Murthwaite has from the beginning granted their spiritual claim, but always with an ominous insistence on the likely murderous ruthlessness of their methods. At the end, Murthwaite witnesses instead the harsh if not violent punishment of lifelong penitential pilgrimage imposed on the priests for their violation of Hindu taboos against travel abroad. In what seems the book's final irony, Hindu and English culture come together in their penchant for casting out the agents who deliver what the culture desires and keeps. Here is a cynical view of cultural universality, though gravity and pathos dominate the tone of Murthwaite's letter.[28]

Although, at first glance, the very idea of the jewel's return might seem the most fanciful part of Collins's Indian fiction, an actual parliamentary scandal about returning sacred treasure to Somnauth in the early 1840s offers further ironic perspective for Collins's plot. At the end of the ignominious British military failure in the Afghan wars (an embarrassment overcome eventually by the Punjab triumph at the end of the decade), the newly installed Governor-General Ellenborough made time during his retreat to seize the carved gates from the tomb of the same eleventh-century Mohammedan invader mentioned in Collins's prologue, Mahmud of Ghazni.[29]

Ellenborough's plan was to return the gates to the Hindu temple of Somnauth, from where they had reputedly been looted at that same ancient time
that Collins invokes as the beginning of the Moonstone's history. Ellenborough's motives are left ambiguous in the historical record: a gesture to humil-
iate the Afghan Mohammedans who had held out against the British? Or a
display directed more to Hindu India to show British rule as their protection
against ancient foes? The most famous contemporary account allows no rational motive at all, denouncing the plan as "an indiscretion and temerity almost beyond belief," evidence of a man "unfit for high public trust."[30]

This was Macaulay's denunciation in 1842, calling for censure of Ellenborough in the House of Commons. Macaulay's invective sets off by contrast
the lyrical gravity and pathos of Hindu ritual in Collins's epilogue. Hinduism, Macaulay declares, is the most "degrading" and "pernicious" religion ever known: "In no part of the world has a religion ever existed more
unfavorable to the moral and intellectual health of our race."[31] He invokes
suttee, thugee, and the other standard items in the Victorian litany of Hindu
barbarism, then derides with equal vehemence the architecture of its tem-
ples, the ugliness of its ornament, and the absurdity of its mythology. "All is
hideous, and grotesque, and ignoble." For Macaulay, aid to restore any idola-
trous Hindu shrine sets back the progress of civilization, while from the perspective of policy—policy never being far from morality to Macaulay—such
aid gratuitously insults the Mohammedan minority in India whose support
British rule also requires. "Morally, this is a crime. Politically, it is a blun-
der."[32] The most lenient judgment of Ellenborough that Macaulay can
muster is that this "eccentric folly" is a throwback to the tolerance for pagan
idolatry of "some prejudiced Anglo-Indians of the old school."[33] In other
words, the idea of restoring a Hindu shrine is a vestige of eighteenth-century
infatuation with Hinduism, a folly England in 1842 now repudiates.

By the time of *The Moonstone*, in 1868, mutiny atrocities ascribed to Indian barbarism—both Muslim and Hindu—had overridden Macaulay's distinctions between Indian religions, while intensifying his denunciations of
Indian savagery. By the discursive standards of 1868, Collins grants his
Brahmin guardians of the Moonstone extraordinary restraint and self-disci-
pline. They acomplish their mission astutely and with patience; the only casualty is the despicable Ablewhite. Moreover, in the light of Macaulay's invective against Ellenborough, it seems astute as well as brave for these
Hindus to rely for restitution of their lost sacred treasure only on themselves.

Victory in the Punjab, Queen Victoria's Koh-I-Noor diamond, Macaulay
and the Gates of Somnauth—these mid-Victorian points of colonial reference bind the not-so-distant past of Seringapatam to the novel's present time
of 1848–1850. Neither the Verinder family nor Collins's readership in 1868
are eager to pull on the chain of Anglo-Indian history that Collins locates
with half-buried clues. The image of a chain that can pull up a canister of

"evidence" sunk under the Shivering Sand belongs to the story of the domestic servant, Rosanna. Franklin seeks out that canister only because mis-
conceptions about his guilt interfere with his courtship of Rachel. But none
of the novel's English characters suffers personally from not knowing more
Indian history. Collins's historical framework teases this indifference without attacking it head on.

Mockery of the privileged English community's willful self-absorption
does, however, undercut the affirmation of values attributed to the novel by
many critics. Reed, for example, proposes to separate the good-humored individuality he sees embodied by Rachel and Franklin from the exploitative
crimes of the society in which they find themselves: "If imperial depradation
is the true crime of *The Moonstone*, this discovery of the authentic value of
individual humanity is its true subject."[34] This affirmation accords with the
optimism of Betteredge, who contentedly prepares to live out his old age in
service to the new generation of the family started by Rachel and Franklin.

I see more irony and skepticism in the novel toward "respectable" domestic values, and more insinuation of how the conventions of Victorian personal life underlie and replicate the dynamic of the nation's colonial behavior. The pleasingly witty tone of the novel only partially masks Collins's
sharp observation of a community that in its behavior at home as well as
abroad chooses not to know the origins and consequences of its happiness
and prosperity. Collins's intricate design of multiple, interconnected plots
and partial narratives gives the reader this knowledge in pieces to put together—or not.[35]

Betteredge, for example, calls attention to Rachel and Franklin as conventional "gentlefolks," their attractive intelligence and charm notwithstanding: "Gentlefolks in general have a very awkward rock ahead in life—the rock
ahead of their own idleness. . . . Nine times out of ten they take to torturing
something, or to spoiling something—and they firmly believe they are im-
proving their minds, when the plain truth is, they are only making a mess in
the house" (62).

The main (and messiest) activity of Rachel and Franklin's courtship is the
"decorative painting" of Rachel's cabinet door—an innocent pastime that
later proves noxious because it is the smearing of this wet paint on some garment of the thief that becomes the main clue in the criminal investigation.
Collins accomplishes an amusing double spoof through Betteredge's irrever-
ent account of gentlefolks' "work" of painting:

> They began with the inside of the door. Mr Franklin scraped off all
> the nice varnish with pumice-stone, and made what he described as a
> surface to work on. Miss Rachel then covered the surface, under his
> directions and with his help, with patterns and devices—griffins,
> birds, flowers, cupids, and such like—copied from designs made by a

famous Italian painter, whose name escapes me: the one, I mean, who stocked the world with Virgin Maries, and had a sweetheart at the baker's. Viewed as work, this decoration was slow to do, and dirty to deal with. But our young lady and gentleman never seemed to tire of it. When they were not riding, or seeing company, or taking their meals, or piping their songs, there they were with their heads together, as busy as bees, spoiling the door. (63–64)

Collins mimics the philistine steward's impatience with intellectual and aesthetic pursuits. Betteredge's only book is *Robinson Crusoe*, and his primary duty is to keep the house clean. Forgetting the name of Raphael is a little joke at Betteredge's expense. Collins himself, as the son and brother of professional painters in a household that was something of a salon for the art world of early Victorian London, knew and cared more than Betteredge about painting.[36] But the spoof goes in the other direction, too, as the affectionately scolding Betteredge becomes an instrument to mock overprivileged Victorian amateurs. Betteredge's small eruptions of class consciousness do establish a critical distance from Rachel and Franklin. Even Betteredge's philistinism indirectly works to deflate certain elevating pretensions of Art. A self-professed "universal genius," Franklin returns from the Continent with techniques and designs to turn the genteel Victorian maiden's cabinet into an innocent bower of bliss. Betteredge's loose association to the Italian painter's "sweetheart at the baker's" inserts a little jab at the artificial transfigurations practiced by high art and its genteel domestic derivatives. The Virgin Marys in Raphael's paintings may be simply the bakery girl in other clothes. Collins mocks the aestheticized eroticism of the courtship, and its protection of virginity, as signified by the decorated door.[37] The small joke contributes to the novel's larger effect of questioning the vast apparent distance between Rachel, the charming virginal daughter of the Verinder family, and Rosanna, the absurdly infatuated servant with a disreputable past—a distance that is utterly unbridgeable in the social world of the novel.

In the middle sections of *The Moonstone*, the social and sexual domestic drama involving Rosanna, Rachel, and Franklin dominates the plot, all but burying the colonial crime, except as analogy to the social-class discriminations that make Rosanna's neglect so pathetic. It is arguable that the subplot of Rosanna's unhappy passion works better as an idea than as social drama. Collins overloads the house servant with conventional disqualifications for romantic interest: not only a servant but a convicted thief with a prison record; also a deformed shoulder and (at least by the consensus of the other servants) "the plainest woman in the house" (35). Her obsessive, unrequited infatuation with Franklin Blake risks seeming an overdrawn image of irrational passion and its hysterical devotions, on the order of Henry James's comically melodramatic governess Mrs. Wix in her infatuation with the charming Sir Claude in *What Maisie Knew*. The somewhat labored parallel between Rachel and Rosanna involves no dramatic relationship between them of the sort that James devises for Maisie and Mrs. Wix. Whereas James's story depends on the heroine's growing perceptions, Rachel's consciousness seems fixated on her single nighttime vision of Franklin removing her jewel from her cabinet. She displays virtually no development of consciousness, at least none that we come to know, since Collins deprives her of her own narrative. Rachel, as others have also noted, is not a very interesting figure in the novel, even though she is said to have a mind of her own.[38] Collins's art keeps us at a skeptical distance from the limited consciousness of all his characters. The most interesting to scrutinize for the novel's critique of oblivion is that of the increasingly confused and steadily obtuse Franklin Blake. As *The Moonstone* shifts from the mystery of criminal theft to the equally mysterious gradations of innocence and responsibility in personal relationships, it is Franklin's thin consciousness (or, rather, absence of mind) that Collins satirically inspects.

Franklin is a lively, intelligent, good-humored young man: "I hate hurting a woman's feelings" (148), he assures Betteredge, when first confronted with evidence that he has treated Rosanna badly. The other men in the book understand that he bears the servant girl no particular ill will; if he entertains some vague hope that she might prove to be the thief, the reason is that her guilt would conveniently solve the mystery that is interfering with his courtship of Rachel. Otherwise, Rosanna is simply invisible to him as a human being. "He took about as much notice of her as he took of the cat," Betteredge bluntly remarks (69).[39] When Betteredge confides to Cuff his own conviction that "Rosanna had been mad enough to set her heart on Mr Franklin," the shrewd Sergeant, with lip corners curled, identifies the predicament as perfectly conventional: "Hadn't you better say she's mad enough to be an ugly girl and only a servant? . . . You think Mr Franklin Blake hasn't got a suspicion of the girl's fancy for him? Ah! he would have found it out fast enough if she had been nice-looking" (123).

A greater limitation than Franklin's selective vision in regard to women is his incapacity to endure their critical gaze on himself. After Rosanna's death, Limping Lucy treats him to a theatrically staged punishment of scrutiny. Franklin recalls the intolerable experience in his narrative:

"Stand there," she said, "I want to look at you."
There was no mistaking the expression on her face. I inspired her with the strongest emotions of abhorrence and disgust. Let me not be vain enough to say that no woman had ever looked at me in this manner before. I will only venture on the more modest assertion that no woman had ever let me perceive it yet. There is a limit to the length of the inspection which a man can endure, under certain circumstances.

I attempted to direct Limping Lucy's attention to some less revolting object than my face. . . .

"No," said the girl, speaking to herself, but keeping her eyes still mercilessly fixed on me. "I can't find out what she saw in his face. I can't guess what she heard in his voice." (308–9)

Rosanna's suicide letter, pulled up from beneath the Shivering Sand, focuses further distressing scrutiny on Franklin. Rosanna wrote in the bitterness of unrequited love and may have been unfair, as when she insinuates that Rachel derives her attractiveness mainly from her social advantages: "Suppose you put Miss Rachel into a servant's dress, and took her ornaments off——? . . . But who can tell what the men like?" (318). As the letter proceeds to describe Rosanna's discovery of the stained nightgown that attests to Franklin's nighttime presence in Rachel's room, her insinuations arouse in him so much resentment that he stops reading the letter entirely: "'Read the rest for yourself,' I said, handing the letter to Betteredge across the table. 'If there is anything in it that I *must* look at, you can tell me as you go on'" (322). One of the longest suicide letters in the history of fiction never does get read by its addressee until Franklin puts it in place much later in his retrospective narrative. At the time he does not press Betteredge to read it to him, nor does Betteredge encourage him. "It will sorely distress you, whenever you read it," he protectively advises. "Don't read it now" (334).

Franklin embodies the English gentleman's reflexive aversion to distress. Later, in the climactic scene where the corpse of the villainous thief, Ablewhite, is stripped of its Indian disguise, Franklin turns away, even though the lawyer's base messenger boy, Gooseberry, enthusiastically urges him to watch: "Gooseberry danced with excitement on the chair. 'Come up here, along with me, sir! He's washing off his complexion now!'" (447). Franklin finds the boy's "enjoyment" of the horror "hideous" and unsuccessfully attempts to remove him from the room. He himself settles for merely averting his eyes, twice turning away, first to the open window and then to other objects in the room. Set off against Gooseberry's vulgar excitement, his aversion is a kind of gentlemanly delicacy: "My nerves were not strong enough to bear it. I turned away again."

Franklin also turns away from internal distress and his memory of it. There are, for example, the several versions of an interesting scene in the billiard room, where Franklin rebuffs Rosanna's attempt to speak to him about the theft. She brings up the scene in her letter as a crisis in her despair. Another version featuring Franklin's uneasiness appears in one of Betteredge's narratives, which gives Franklin's account at the time:

"It was an awkward position; and I dare say I got out of it awkwardly enough. I said to her, 'I don't quite understand you. Is there anything you want me to do?' Mind, Betteredge, I didn't speak unkindly! The poor girl can't help being ugly—I felt that, at the time. The cue was still in my hand, and I went on knocking the balls about, to take off the awkwardness of the thing. As it turned out, I only made matters worse still. I'm afraid I mortified her without meaning it! She suddenly turned away. 'He looks at the billiard balls,' I heard her say. 'Anything rather than look at me!' Before I could stop her, she had left the hall. I am not quite easy about it, Betteredge. Would you mind telling Rosanna that I meant no unkindness? I have been a little hard on her, perhaps, in my own thoughts—I have almost hoped that the loss of the Diamond might be traced to *her*. Not from any ill-will to the poor girl: but—" He stopped there, and going back to the billiard-table, began to knock the balls about once more. (147–48)

Collins nicely registers the bland self-distancing from emotional distress in English upper-class idiom. Forster, as I observed earlier, directly drama-tizes this inadequacy of speech in the colonial context through the dialogue of his Anglo-Indians, even the well-meaning Fielding in *A Passage to India*.[40] Franklin's physical gestures correspond to his speech. In conversation with Betteredge, Franklin repeats the same awkward turn away to the billiards that he describes having resorted to with Rosanna. He can't really finish a sentence that (barely) admits how convenient it would be if Rosanna were the thief. He leaves it to the house steward to make amends for him. Reacting to Rosanna's pained allusion to the scene in her letter, when he finally brings himself to read it in the security of new prosperity, he allows his restored self-assurance to wipe away all trace of mental and moral uneasiness from his recollection of the scene. Even his nervous staring at the billiard balls (the most painful detail in Rosanna's letter) simplifies itself in memory to become an instance of misunderstood generosity: "For her own sake, I had purposely shown no special interest in what was coming; for her own sake, I had pur-posely looked at the billiard balls, instead of looking at *her*" (334–35). With this cleansing memory, Franklin terminates the presence of Rosanna in the novel, turning to "interests which concern the living people of this narra-tive" (335). The habitual motions of Franklin's consciousness cover his fail-ings in the past with a "discreet veil," in Burke's phrase.

Such close inspection of Franklin's resilient conscience may seem too fas-tidious for the kind of popular entertainment offered by *The Moonstone*. Yet Collins explicitly takes up the issue of remembering and forgetting very early in the book. Memory appears mainly as a form of suffering; only disabled characters seem afflicted: Rosanna, Limping Lucy, Ezra Jennings. Early on, Betteredge tries to comfort a depressed Rosanna by the reassurance that, in regard to her earlier errors and imprisonment, "your past life is all sponged out. Why can't you forget it?" (37). Rosanna responds by pointing to the still visible location of a stain on Betteredge's coat that Rosanna herself had treated "with a new composition, warranted to remove anything": "The grease was gone, but there was a little dull place left on the nap of the cloth where the grease had been. The girl pointed to that place, and shook her head. 'The stain is taken off,' she said. 'But the place shows, Mr Betteredge—the place shows!'" Rosanna's depressive pessimism about the ineradicability of the past sets off by contrast the ultimately happy and prosperous couple, who prove to be experts not only in up-to-date decoration but also in solvents to take off any stain.

Collins's irony is pointed yet in a way indulgent toward English expertise at the self-cleansing moral life. The trait forms a large part of Franklin's "inscrutable appeal" to the less happy people. Rosanna's infatuation and her intense disappointment in Franklin follow from the attractiveness of his charm as it beamed into her weary struggle to lead a reformed life: "You had come across it like a beam of sunshine at first—and then you too failed me" (319). The half-caste doctor, Jennings, uses the same image without the reproach: "You, and such as you, show me the sunny side of human life,"he exclaims with "breathless eagerness" early in their acquaintance (381).

In evaluation of *The Moonstone* as a colonial text, not much critical notice has been taken of Jennings's adoration of Franklin, an infatuation almost equal in its excess to Rosanna's. The impression of bedazzlement becomes important for the colonial theme that Jennings brings back in new terms to the final third of the novel. From one perspective, Jennings's role in reconciling Franklin and Rachel may seem to remove the stain from colonial history, as well as from this one family. With his piebald hair, dark complexion, and ambiguous racial origin, Jennings is the hybrid offspring of colonialism who is socially ostracized by the English but who serves them devotedly and blesses their happiness without resentment. His experiments, strange books, opium habit, and disgrace in the past connect him to Herncastle, but he works to remove curses rather than to spread them. Unlike the Brahmins in search of their purloined jewel, Jennings wants nothing more than to serve English prosperity and innocence—and then die: "Is it possible . . . that I, of all men in the world, am chosen to be the means of bringing these two young people together again? My own happiness has been trampled under foot. . . . Shall I live to see a happiness of others, which is of my making—a love renewed, which is of my bringing back? Oh merciful Death, let me see it before your arms enfold me, before your voice whispers to me, 'Rest at last!'" (399).

How are we to take this voice of pious self-sacrifice? Collins in part makes Jennings into a figure of healing and exorcism, in Roy's term.[41] In this variant of the loyal colonial servant, Jennings's piety testifies to the redemptive force of Christian colonialism for master and subjects alike. Yet, in a more original way, the metaphoric pattern of the novel also lets us take the sick and unhappy half-caste doctor's assistant to represent the dull place under the stain of colonialism that unreliable English "sunshine" cannot purify.

Collins's ambitious conception of the colonial hybrid in England stands out by comparison with the less impressive character probably modeled on Jennings in Dickens's unfinished *The Mystery of Edwin Drood*.[42] Like Jennings, Dickens's Neville Landless evokes Macaulay's ideal of the educated colonial subject: "Indian in blood and colour, but English in taste, in opinions, in morals, and in intellect."[43] But instead of serving as a class of "interpreters" in the colonies, as Macaulay proposed, both Jennings and Landless are immigrant figures, struggling to assimilate to domestic English society. Both not only submit to English civilization but fall positively, if also hopelessly, in love with it.[44] Collins, however, gives Jennings competence and authority withheld from Dickens's dark orphan from Ceylon. Jennings's neurological knowledge crucially advances the detective investigation, after the eminent Cuff has quit to grow roses. His understanding of the hidden underlife of consciousness proves more sophisticated than English common sense. His subordination of his own suffering for the sake of his professional vocation represents a kind of disciplined work unique among the characters of the novel.[45]

Dickens conforms more to conventional Victorian expectation by debasing and infantilizing his colonial figure. Neville Landless submits abjectly to the tutelage of the genial Rev. Septimus Crisparkle, who wastes no opportunity to correct the traces of savagery in his speech and gestures. When Neville calls the stepfather who beat his helpless sister and himself "a cruel brute," Crisparkle's "shock" makes Neville hang his head and apologize (45). Neville's ominous habit of clenching his fists in barely suppressed rage also produces gentle but steady correction from Crisparkle. "'Neville,' hinted the Minor Canon, with a steady countenance, 'you have repeated that former action of your hands, which I so much dislike'" (81). Dickens's Neville sorrowfully confesses to his perpetual struggle with "deadly and bitter hatred," which he ascribes not only to early persecution but also to his upbringing among "an inferior race": "and I may easily have contracted some affinity with them. Sometimes, I don't know but that it may be a drop of what is tigerish in their blood" (46–47). Dickens's own narrative language reinforces the anxiety about bestial blood that he gives to the colonial character. Sympathy for Landless and his sister as victims coexists with stereotyped images of the bestial racial "Other": "something untamed about them both; a certain air upon them of hunter and huntress; yet withal a certain air of being the objects of the chase, rather than the followers. Slender, supple, quick of eye and limb; half shy, half defiant; fierce of look; an indefinable kind of pause coming and going on their whole expression, both of face and form, which might be equally likened to the pause before a crouch, or a bound" (42–43). Collins is relatively free of this racial stereotyping in his conception of Ezra Jennings, who becomes tutor rather than tutee of Franklin and the entire English community.

Collins's intimate, dependent association with Dickens adds further interest to the many signs of difference and even tension between them in matters of race and colonialism in the 1860s and earlier. During the controversy following General Eyre's massacre of Jamaican rebels—the major colonial scandal of the 1860s—Dickens but not Collins joined the Eyre Defense Committee organized by Carlyle and other Victorian intellectuals.[46] Earlier, in response to news of atrocities against the English at the time of the 1857 Rebellion, Dickens in a letter went so far as to fantasize himself "Commander in Chief in India," proclaiming to "the Oriental race" his official duty to "do my utmost to exterminate the Race upon whom the stain of the late cruelties rested,"[47] a locution especially shocking to the modern reader by its foreshadowing of Kurtz's expostulation at the end of his "eloquent" report for the "International Society for the Suppression of Savage Customs" in *Heart of Darkness*: "Exterminate all the brutes!"[48]

Collins's resistance to Victorian racial hysteria appears during the decade before *The Moonstone* in his sole piece of journalism specifically devoted to the Rebellion, an article titled "A Sermon for Sepoys," written on assignment from Dickens for *Household Words*. Although the article begins in the form of a tutorial in civilization for "the human tigers" in India, it quickly turns into a parable taken, he says, from the reign of the seventeenth-century Mughal Emperor Shah Jehan. A sequence of reflective conversations among the Emperor, a pious Vizier, and a sage weigh the obligations of the political as compared to the contemplative religious life. The concluding moral affirms that benevolent public action is as pious a service to the divine as religious retreat.[49] A very odd lesson to send to the "tigers" of the 1857 Indian Rebellion, who, from the perspective of the English, were showing only too little propensity for contemplative withdrawal!

Collins's parable in "A Sermon for Sepoys" has so little pertinence to the issues of the 1857 Rebellion that it seems a merely space-filling way of at once fulfilling and avoiding Dickens's assignment. Yet to turn a sermon for rebels into a tribute to the Indian cultural tradition is also a provocative gesture of dissent, as is the article's seemingly bland opening sentence about the British colonial enterprise: "While we are still fighting for the possession of India, benevolent men of various religious denomination are making arrangements for taming the human tigers in that country by Christian means."[50] In Collins's phrasing, the British struggle, put bluntly, is "for the possession of India," not for any civilizing mission nor for revenge on atrocities against English women and children (the main British line in 1858). Christian benevolence, moreover, is presented only as an adjunct to conquest.

But if Collins intended to be dissenting from post-Mutiny colonial discourse in "A Sermon for Sepoys," he also succeeded in being so quiet about it as to go unnoticed. By the time of *The Moonstone*, his established reputation and financial success might have supported more boldness. Still, Dickens's *All the Year Round* was publishing *The Moonstone* in serial form, and Dickens's expressed impatience with the story as it progressed contributed to the painful schism between the two men during these years.[51]

Reluctance to cause offense, however, does not entirely account for something excessively mystifying about Jennings in *The Moonstone*, as in Collins's journalism. Because Jennings orders all his journals and papers destroyed at his death, except those pages that refer to Franklin, the secrets of his life are truly and forever consigned to oblivion for the reader also. We never know his colony of origin, or the nature of his physical disease, or the disgrace that has ruined his life. He only briefly mentions to Franklin in conversation "the cloud of a horrible accusation" (379) that required him to leave a woman he loved. He protests his innocence but keeps silent about the charge. To call him repressed, in the psychoanalytic sense of the term, is misleading, however, since he is not presented as unconscious of his pain.[52] He is withholding and secretive, rather than repressed. Was there a disgrace of illicit union or children (such as existed in Collins's own secret life)? Was it something about opium (also known firsthand to Collins)? Or is there some homosexual issue, as seems vaguely intimated by the excessive rapture of his attachment to Franklin and his cryptic reference to being one of those men born with "female constitutions" (373)?

Or did Collins as author keep Jennings's disgrace a secret because he did not himself see it clearly? The clues for Jennings don't fit together very well, even applying Jennings's technique for filling in blank spaces. He tells Franklin that his "one last interest in life" is to earn enough money "to provide for a person—very dear to me—whom I shall never see again" (380). But no further mention of this financial concern appears, even in the preserved journal extracts. His financial records and wishes disappear along with the rest of his papers at his death. Rather than a realized figure of repression or some other psychological dynamic, Jennings seems more simply an only rough sketch for a character whose fuller history and psychology exceeded the reach of Collins's imagination in the 1860s. A plain servant's infatuation with a gentleman lay within that reach. A hybrid offspring of colonialism who has internalized the values of a society willing to use his services but without accepting him socially is a type that fully enters British and postcolonial literature only in the following century.

What Collins can precociously register is the intense doubleness of such a figure. Perhaps by extrapolation from his own feelings of social isolation, illness, and addiction at a time when he was also laboring to please the public through composition of the novel, Collins punctuates Jennings's effusions in his journal about the joy of serving Franklin with references to his "complete prostration" (401) and despair. He doesn't want to "alarm or distress"

Franklin with his own suffering. Yet he also records a number of details that suggest his notice of the charming young couple's total self-absorption. At the time of the experimental reenactment of the crime, Franklin is again "amusing himself at the billiard table" (411) (justified, to be sure, by the necessity of reenacting his activities of the preceding year). More baffling is Rachel's expectation that Jennings's most thrilling experience would be to be Rachel herself. In one journal entry, Jennings juxtaposes his own opium nightmares of "the one beloved face . . . hideously phosphorescent in the black darkness" (397) with Rachel's plea for permission to sit and watch the lovely Franklin sleep: "Oh, Mr Jennings, if you were me, only think how you would long to sit and look at him" (429). Again, after kissing Franklin's forehead: "She looked back at me with a bright smile, and a charming colour in her face. 'You would have done it,' she whispered, 'in my place'" (430). If Rachel didn't seem so close to the mark in imagining how Jennings would like to be in her place, loving and being loved by Franklin, her rapt self-absorption would be less unnerving.

Other details reinforce the analogy between Jennings and Rosanna as parallel unrequited lovers of Franklin as a kind of English country house sun god. Both confess their love only posthumously, in the form of written documents—in Jennings's case saved pages of the journal intended for the friend as if they were a kind of letter: "In years to come, he may feel an interest in looking back at what is written there" (460), he says on his deathbed. Although Franklin attends to the flattering journal more eagerly than to Rosanna's reproachful letter, there is no sign in the book that he retains much interest in Jennings once the doctor has served the purpose of solving his problem. "Mr Blake is to write, and tell me what happens in London" (430), Jennings fervidly writes in his journal, when the lovers are about to depart for London. Three months go by in the book's calendar with no mention of a letter until Mr. Candy writes to announce Jennings's death. The sadness of Rachel and Franklin as they leave Jennings behind for London lasts only for a single, rather formulaic paragraph in Franklin's narrative (432). Then they are in London; pursuit of the real thief takes over; then marriage, then the baby. Franklin never mentions Jennings again.

Disturbing and ironic details are spread throughout *The Moonstone* like kindling for a fiery critique of this society's fundamental oblivion to any concerns other than its own domestic happiness. But no explosion happens. If this absence of detonation be taken as a weakness in Collins's social critique, it is a limitation that the novel seems deliberately to defend within its own design. At the time of his experiment, Jennings records in his journal the anxiety of one elderly Mrs. Merridew in the party, who anxiously remembers that at school, experiments "invariably ended in an explosion." She asks Jennings if he could warn her of the explosion this time. "With a view to getting it over, if possible, before I go to bed" (416). Jennings comforts her with his usual overdone courtesy: "I attempted to assure Mrs Merridew that an explosion was not included in the programme on this occasion" (416).

Collins is similarly solicitous of the Mrs. Merridews in his readership. It is not just that he needs to please them. He actually likes them all, not with the rapture of Jennings for Franklin but even with ironic perception of their limitations and conventionality. Jennings expresses something of this affection when he thinks of the whole audience gathered for his experiment: "I thought of Mrs Merridew and her embroidery, and of Betteredge and his conscience. There is a wonderful sameness in the solid side of the English character—just as there is a wonderful sameness in the solid expression of the English face" (417). In this caricature of English moral serenity, the blank surface of the English seems more soothing than repugnant. As a neurologist, however, Jennings specializes in piecing together the fragments when the superficially solid surface breaks down. The distinctiveness of *The Moonstone* comes from Collins's own attentiveness to the less solid side of the English character—the Shivering Sand of conscience and of consciousness. *The Moonstone* gives us more than enough pieces to constitute a strong exposé of his society's devotion to preserving moral comfort through habits and skills of oblivion and aversion. Like Jennings, however, Collins in *The Moonstone* wants to befriend these English characters rather than explode their oblivion in their faces. We may think that the Mrs. Merridews and Betteredges and, particularly, the Rachels and Franklins should be made to lose more sleep. But although Collins is capable of imagining a defiant Limping Lucy, the pleasures as well as the limitations of *The Moonstone* are inseparable from his reluctance to be one.

II

AFTER INDEPENDENCE

Prologue to Part II

It took British consciousness another century to reach Franklin Blake's accommodation in *The Moonstone* to permanent return of Britain's inherited "jewel" of India. In the 1920s and 1930s, with Indian nationalist agitation in full force, Orwell still classified dissent from imperial self-justification among the "forbidden things" shared in whispered late-night train talk among disillusioned colonial officials after many bottles of beer.[1] Orwell lasted five years in the 1920s in his unhappy police service in Burma; his outspoken anti-imperial declarations in the autobiographical segment of *The Road to Wigan Pier* belong to the book's Depression-era investigation of domestic injustices buried under middle-class British consciousness, such as the dehumanizing and invisible labor of English coal miners, providing warmth, as if by miracle, to houses oblivious of its source in human toil. For Orwell as for Collins in the 1860s, empire abroad and social class structures at home came to form a single network of entrenched injustice that his writing in the 1930s explored in compelling terms. A literary survey of anti-imperial dissent during the interwar decades would feature Orwell along with fuller examination of Edward Thompson, E. M. Forster, and a handful of other skeptical liberals whose loss of confidence in England's own social structure after World War I extended to questions about the empire that underlay it.

I choose, however, to shift attention away from England for the remainder of this book in order to attend to selected writings by a number of Indian writers in the twentieth century about their own and India's relationship to English language and culture once the end of British rule had removed the most palpable rationale for English as an Indian language. Should the English language itself be made to "quit India," sent packing along with the foreign rulers, administrators, and educators who had initially instituted it as an instrument of cultural as well as political domination?

Already in the nineteenth century, proto-nationalist Indian writers, especially among the elite intelligentsia in Bengal, had advocated development of an indigenous modern literature in the Indian vernaculars.[2] Fluency in English, even attachment to works of English literature, did not necessarily lead educated Indians in the late nineteenth century to accept that English could effectively carry the rhythms, textures, and intimate associations of Indian life, especially in prose fiction, where dialogue and everyday personal detail count for so much. Tagore's poetry could be transposed from Bengali into a universalist spiritual English rhetoric that excited Yeats and T. S. Eliot (although not many readers of English poetry since), but discerning Bengali readers then and subsequently have regularly deplored these translations as misrepresentations of Tagore's poetry; even worse, novels and short stories by Tagore and other Bengali writers depend on the nuances and connotations of a language that resisted (and still resists) effective English translation. The closest relationship for a non-Bengali audience to Tagore (and other Bengali fiction writers) is still through the film versions by Satyijat Ray, where simple subtitles work as narrative signposts, while ironies and subtleties come through the Bengali filmmaker's visual art accompanied by music and the sounds of the Bengali language.

Ambivalence toward the English language increased during the Indian nationalist movement, making distinctions between orthodoxy and dissent difficult to stabilize. If English as the language of "civilization" was the imperial orthodoxy instituted by Macaulay, all Indian nationalists were dissenters.[3] Yet contradictions and qualifications within this generalization immediately require notice.

A brief early sample of Gandhi's complexity appears at the start of his address to students at the dedication ceremonies of Hindu Central University College at Benares in 1916. Attended by the British Viceroy, Lord Hardinge, and other notables both British and Indian, the celebration was already in its third day by the time of Gandhi's speech, which no doubt adds spice to his wry comment on the nation's (and his own) fatigue with speechmaking as an activity in general, and specifically in English: "I wanted to say," he remarks in advance of his own contribution, "it is a matter of deep humiliation and shame for us that I am compelled this evening, under the shadow of this great college in this sacred city, to address my countrymen in a language that is foreign to me" (129).[4] At the sessions of the Congress earlier that year in Bombay, he observes, only the speeches delivered in Hindi "touched" the audience, even though Hindi is not the spoken vernacular of that region: between "the vernaculars of the Bombay Presidency on the one hand, and Hindi on the other, no such great dividing line exists as there does between English and the sister languages of India" (130). The compulsion for English on this ceremonial academic occasion seems due in part to the high British presence in his audience and at least as much to the status of English as the official language of Indian higher education. Gandhi uses the occasion to declare himself opposed to this institutional coercion on several grounds: it wastes youthful Indian energies in the learning of a foreign language instead of more important subjects; it impedes the growth of national sentiment and alienates the educated from the mass of the population, including even their wives; and, most important, it drains verbal expression of power to speak to the heart.

Among the paradoxes of the speech is the fact that in the midst of these repudiations Gandhi presents himself as speaking from and to the heart, albeit in English. He defends what he calls his "transgressions" in the speech as the liberty of a man who is venturing to "speak feelingly" and "think audibly": "I have turned the searchlight all over, and as you have given me the privilege of speaking to you, I am laying my heart bare" (132). The English language did not keep Gandhi on this occasion from speaking intimately to this audience in English and "touching" them so deeply that their uproar of emotion actually prevented him from finishing his speech. Nor was Gandhi merely tapping jingoistic passions, since the import of his message was that Indian self-government required Indians to improve themselves first, in ceasing behaviors such as spitting in public, lording it over the poor on trains and elsewhere, and ostentatiously displaying ornaments that would astonish a Parisian jeweler, such as he had noticed at this very ceremony. The cause of disruptive uproar is hard to infer from the written transcript of the speech; it offers something to offend and arouse every one of his listeners. What is beyond doubt is that Gandhi's English could touch Indian emotions; it would be hard to imagine him achieving more colloquial directness and force if he were speaking Hindi (especially since Gujarati, not Hindi, was his own vernacular).

More paradoxes: although Gandhi's Benares speech showed his ability to speak feelingly in English, his opening argument also invites an uproar to interrupt and silence speech. This is a speech against speeches: "we have now reached almost the end of our resources in speech-making, and it is not enough that our ears are feasted . . . , but it is necessary that our hearts have got to be touched and that our hands and feet have got to be moved." By 1916, Gandhi had already devised ways to transcend Indian language divisions through nonverbal manifestations of solidarity, resolve, and action, such as *satyagraha* (the nonviolent protest campaigns) and publicized fasts and imprisonments on behalf of Indians in South Africa; the dramatic call for a nationwide *hartal* (strike) against the repressive Rowlatt bills was only three years in the future. At the same time, Gandhi continued his masterful strategic management of India's linguistic complexity. In 1919 he assumed editorship of both the English weekly *Young India* and the Gujarati weekly *Navajivan*. His famous autobiography, *The Story of My Experiments with Truth*, began as weekly columns in the Gujarati journal in 1922, while he was in prison, but soon became available to the rest of India (and the English-speaking world) through translation into English by his secretary, Mahadev Desai.[5]

Gandhi's autobiography shows his adroitness with contraries of concepts, as well as of languages. His introduction acknowledges complaints he has received from others about this project because autobiography is regarded as a Western practice, without Eastern models except by those under Western influence. Gandhi sidesteps the differentiation among influences on him by simply asserting that this writing of his is not a "real autobiography" but something sui generis: "the story of my experiments with truth." He does not belabor the critical question of models and influence. *My Experiments with Truth* is in actuality an idiosyncratic text, with its often odd choice of anecdote and its didactic and spiritual excursuses. It is nevertheless also a real autobiography that narrates the fascinating development from childhood of a figure who became modern India's foremost dissenter and maverick, no matter what orthodoxies would later be instituted in his name.

The ambiguous status of English in India continued, with somewhat different coloration, in the post-Gandhian period. While the new Constitution legally established Gandhi's dictum that Hindi should be India's national language, the Constitution itself was written in English. Threats to the very survival of the federated nation from group and regional conflicts that took the form of language wars turned English from a compulsion to a refuge of neutrality in the 1950s.[6] Nehru himself, moreover, owed not a little of his domestic and international prestige to his impeccable (if sometimes rather stiff) English style, honed at Harrow and Cambridge University. Like Gandhi, he wrote an autobiography that became famous throughout the world. *Toward Freedom: The Autobiography of Jawaharlal Nehru*, written while he was imprisoned by the British government in India during 1934–35, defines its intended audience in its preface as "my own countrymen and countrywomen," but when published and circulated in England and America in 1941, it commanded important international respect for the cause of Indian nationalism. Education abroad in English also distinguished other of the founding leaders: Muhammed Ali Jinnah, for example, commonly labeled the father of Pakistan, went at age eighteen to study law in London, where he was initiated into nationalistic politics as well as the bar.

The English language continued to be as crucial for the institutional life of secular literature as for government. The formal study of modern literature was conducted mainly in English, with work in other European literatures often read in English translation. Modern Indian secular literature in any language was an extracurricular activity until very recently. Cultivated Bengalis might cherish their noble vernacular literary tradition and even many non-Muslims might be able to recite (if not read) Urdu love poetry, but translations from one Indian vernacular into another (or into English) was and still remains a labor too costly and too arduous to realize the often-repeated vision of a multilingual national vernacular literature accessible to all Indian readers. Nor has Hindi as yet become a national literary language.[7] The vulgar form of Hindi spread through the popularity of "Bollywood" film may have done more than any law to create a national language in India, but it has not erased loyalty to the various vernaculars or to English for those who care about serious written literature. Predictions that English will eventually be displaced by projects of inter-Indian translation and the eventual rise of a national literature in Hindi continue even while Indian writing in English during the past twenty years has achieved unprecedented prosperity, thanks, to be sure, to its phenomenal commercial and critical success abroad.

This overcompressed summary of India's multilingual complications seems a necessary prologue to any consideration of postcolonial Indian writing in English. Exclusive emphasis on English as merely a vestige of a "colonized" mentality more grossly simplifies an intricate history than does even my brevity. Unmitigated resentment against the status of English, while always a strand of Indian nationalist sentiment, gained doctrinaire authority only belatedly, if at all. At the level of formal intellectual and academic debate, important influences in this direction in the 1960s came from outside India: from French African and West Indian intellectuals, such as Frantz Fanon, Albert Memmi, and, later, Ngugi wa Thiong'o, from Kenya.[8] In the 1980s, Indian critique of colonialism's continuing contamination of the Indian mind generated a flurry of books with melodramatic titles: *Crippled Minds, The Intimate Enemy, The Imprisoned Mind, Masks of Conquest, Nationalist Thought and the Colonial World: A Derivative Discourse?*[9] These diagnoses of mental victimization and of dependence more insidious than mere foreign rule go beyond Gandhi's call for a national language and culture, since his anti-English stance was joined to an equally forceful critique of Indians' own responsibility for class privilege, civic neglect, and personal selfishness, a critique that Gandhi constructed by drawing freely on progressive social thought from a great variety of both Western and Indian sources. Hindu revivalism, sometimes sheltered under Gandhi's name, fostered a more simplistic nativism in the 1980s, as did retrospective denigration of the Anglicized character of the earlier nationalist generation. A paradoxical reinforcement of nativism has also come from the Western centers of opinion that nativists presumably want to repudiate. Some of the most militant denunciations of English language and literature as "masks of conquest" emanated in the 1980s from graduate students and faculty pursuing careers in English and comparative literature in the West.[10]

Simple opposition to English language and literature has obvious limitations as a professional position for Indians (and anyone else) making a career out of English literary study, since the triumph of the oppositional argument would logically entail dismantling the enterprise. But professional survival is only one contributor to the recent turn to hybridity and cultural mobility as bywords in academic postcolonial studies in the 1990s. The *fatwah* against Rushdie in 1989 opened fissures in the commitment to "purity" as a cultural ideal. In addition, new institutional as well as ideological advocacy of multiculturalism in response to changing academic demography, especially in

America, has fostered the integration of postcolonial studies into the larger drive toward cultural diversity in all areas of education. Finally, there is the sheer proliferation—and success—of new Indian writers, both in India and from what is now termed the Indian Diaspora. An Indian writer can no longer be simply categorized as either renouncing or embracing some essence of Indianness by virtue of residential address or language choice. The growth of the Indian Diaspora has increased the number of writers (and readers) who claim Indian cultural identity while residing or even having been born elsewhere. Restrictive definitions of "authenticity" continue, but without the power that they had even a decade ago. Indian writing in English is a fascinating field at the beginning of this new century precisely because it is so much in flux, so much less containable in any simple formulation than ever before.

My own critical attention in the midst of this creative flux has been attracted, first, by a number of writers and texts from the 1950s that anticipate recent developments but within the more easily mapped cultural scene of an earlier period. Nonfictional prose genres of autobiography, travel reportage, and cultural commentary came to dominate my selections because the authorial self-presentation in these genres so quickly and sharply displays tensions, anxieties, and dilemmas often concealed by a poised storytelling persona in works of fiction. Nirad C. Chaudhuri, V. S. Naipaul, the writers of *Quest* magazine, and, in my epilogue, the young contemporary writer Pankaj Mishra all seem themselves attracted to nonfictional prose for opportunities to challenge received opinions and pieties. Their realism is more critical than magical, so that their conflicts with others (and, at times, with themselves) are manifest, even if complicated by irony or self-contradiction. At the same time, they are literary writers; their authority comes not through accumulations of data or applications of specialized methodology but from the imaginative and verbal designs of their prose. Their style becomes part of the argument of their writing and makes for its complexity. Chaudhuri's iconoclastic irony, for example, affirms the superiority of his Bengali cultural inheritance at the same time that he exposes and analyzes the failure of the Bengali ideal in his own experience. The comic pathos of V. S. Naipaul's upset while traveling to India challenges sanguine judgments not only of India, but also of Naipaul's own ambitions and character. The lesser known and less masterful writers in the 1950s Indian journal *Quest* struggle to articulate an independent cultural position in the face of a variety of threats from nativist authorities within India and also from the journal's American sponsors. The frustrations expressed in *Quest* foreshadow harsher and more menacing dilemmas in our current era of violently clashing loyalties. The tension between *Quest*'s version of cultural freedom for India in the 1950s and concurrent liberal Anglo-American ideas displays schisms that still undermine so-called liberal cultural exchange between East and West.

I single out Pankaj Mishra from the many talented young Indian writers for my concluding commentary in part because he most clearly extends into the contemporary moment the quest for intellectual independence that has occupied my attention in both parts of this book. Like Chaudhuri and Naipaul, Mishra excels in the kind of prose in which analytic acuity, descriptive particularity, and a strong personal voice are the components of an effective style. In language notably free of academic or other kinds of jargon, Mishra demonstrates the difference between multicultural hybridity (American style) and the possible meanings of a new cosmopolitanism oriented specifically to Indian conditions. Mishra's continuing location in India gives further salience to his provocative social and political writing about contemporary South Asia. Although the diverse talents that make Indian fiction in English such an enlivening part of contemporary world literature are to be celebrated, no matter where the authors reside, there is special interest for this book in the endeavors of a gadfly who brings precocious literary knowledge and skill to bear on an India more hostile than receptive to his offering. I call my commentary on Mishra an epilogue, because it gathers up many of the themes earlier discussed, but it might equally well serve as a prologue to reflections on the new period of creativity in Indian writing that, like Mishra himself, has such a promising future ahead.

5

The Beast in Nirad Chaudhuri's Garden

If your first order of business is to "decolonize" the mind, there seems little to be said on behalf of Nirad C. Chaudhuri's *Autobiography of an Unknown Indian*,[1] with its fond childhood memories of Palgrave's *Golden Treasury* and the *Encyclopedia Britannica* in turn-of-the-century Bengal. Many anticolonial critics simply fix Chaudhuri as one of Macaulay's freakish progeny: the Anglicized mind in brown skin created to serve imperial power in British India. But now that the idea of hybridity has joined if not replaced authenticity and resistance as legitimate offspring of the colonial encounter, Chaudhuri's complex meditation on his multiple cultural affiliations may receive more appreciative regard.[2] Rushdie, at the time of the *fatwah* against him, bravely challenged what he called the "bogey of Authenticity" by arguing that the "hybridity" and "eclecticism" of actual postcolonial conditions impose modernism on postcolonial consciousness.[3] He writes specifically on behalf of emigrant writers like himself, but he also argues that cultural displacement in some form is a more general modern reality: "the past is a country from which we have all emigrated. . . . its loss is part of our common humanity. . . . And those of us who have been forced by cultural displacement to accept the provisional nature of all truths, all certainties, have perhaps had modernism forced upon us."[4]

Yet Chaudhuri's style of cultural displacement has little in common with the fluid, mobile, populist modernity associated with Rushdie. Although the *Autobiography* is routinely named an Indo-English classic, its Bengali hauteur, its irony, and its densely allusive style assert a superiority of culture and intelligence that comes across as aggressively exclusive, especially to Indian readers.[5] Like many autodidacts, Chaudhuri displays his learning with a pride that looks like ostentation, while his overplentiful citations from French and Latin, as well as from English literature, give a learned weight to his pessimism that runs counter to contemporary taste. Instead of the dynamic, transgressive crossing of borders that now makes the idea of cultural hybridity appealing to many postcolonial writers and critics, Chaudhuri seems to be the vestigial voice of a doomed liberal hope for synthesis and integration, specifically associated with a Bengali culture already outmoded early in the Indian nationalist movement.

I argue here that Chaudhuri's *Autobiography* invites new interest not only as a relic but for the subtle and original drama of the style Chaudhuri creates to analyze and withstand the experience of violence and loss. The elaborate, idiosyncratic English that Chaudhuri devises to recount the troubled story of his early life also gives compelling form to the more general breaking apart of public as well as personal structures in the closing decades of British rule in India. The writing of the book itself seems a feat of self-creation that wards off the powerful disintegrative forces that the book also vividly displays and analyzes. For Chaudhuri, disintegration is not fun, in a postmodern sense, but an intimate menace that his writing actively struggles to overcome.

Chaudhuri's literary achievement defies both Macaulay (who wanted only to train a class of English-speaking Indian clerks) and those nativists who denounce Macaulay to bolster the worth of the Indian traditions Macaulay despised. Chaudhuri is equally sensitive to the false exaltation of xenophobia and to the insult of foreign rule. Not that skepticism and independence are offered here as recipes for worldly success. Colonialist anglophilia (the fault for which he is most often indicted) bears the onus of careerist opportunism under imperial rule. Yet Chaudhuri ends his volume with an account of cataclysmic failure and breakdown in his twenty-first year. Nor does his authorial persona represent any ordinary recovery. The figure that emerges from the autobiography is an anomaly: a Victorian Indo-English *sadhu*, fanatically driven to renounce or undermine every opportunity of worldly success, yet believing in no gods but reason and strength.

Chaudhuri traces the aspiration toward cultural synthesis that dominated his adolescence more to his Bengali heritage than to Western teaching. The chapter in the *Autobiography* called "Torch Race of the Indian Renaissance" traces the development in nineteenth-century Bengal of an ideal "synthesis of the East and West" (179), in which the best of Western civilization would help to shape a proud Indian program of social, religious, and political reform for the modern era. In retrospect, Chaudhuri sees the beginning breakup of that ideal coinciding with his own coming of age in the years just after World War I. By the time of his writing the *Autobiography*, in 1951, Chaudhuri's youthful longing for synthesis and integration had been further shattered by Partition. As a Hindu, he was easily able to continue living and working in New Delhi (where he had been a military broadcaster during World War II), but Partition barred him from any return to East Bengal, which had become part of Pakistan. In its lovingly detailed description of East Bengal before Partition, the *Autobiography* is in part an elegy to Chaudhuri's lost childhood place, just as *Midnight's Children* mourns the Bombay Rushdie lost when his Muslim family moved to Pakistan. As for Rushdie, Chaudhuri's skepticism about nationalist zeal is rooted in painful direct experience of the subcontinent's continuing violent divisions. For Chaudhuri, personal losses were reinforced by the lessons of his omniverous reading, in which conflict, failure, decay, and violence emerge as the rule in human history generally, not only in India. From this broader perspective, Chaudhuri's English-language *Autobiography* belatedly joins his Indian story to those early modernist narratives where autobiographical stories of cultural disintegration are shaped into idiosyncratic concoctions made out of salvaged cultural fragments.

Chaudhuri was anomalous among cosmopolitan Indians of his generation in coming to his skeptical insights while staying put in India for the first half-century of his long life. At the time of writing the *Autobiography*, he had never even visited the West; his first trip to England occurred after the *Autobiography* had been published. He did not emigrate until 1970, when, at the age of seventy-three, he moved to Oxford (where the apparently invigorating effect of his version of iconoclasm kept him going until his death at age 101 in 1999). The stubbornness of his staying throughout the most troubled years of India's independence struggle, together with his unyielding insistence on measuring the new nation, as well as himself, by cosmopolitan cultural standards, gives a kind of heroism to the narrative voice of this book, written apart from any intellectual community and sent off in quixotic hope of publication to an England he had never seen.

Chaudhuri's sense of himself as an anomaly rather than a model for others comes through his pronouncement, in 1954, that the English language could have no regenerative cultural power in modern India, where English belongs to an "unreal shadowy culture," given artificial strength by government patronage.[6] This dark prognosis appeared only three years after the stylistic tour de force of Chaudhuri's own ambitious book in English. In his 1954 essay, Chaudhuri diagnoses the terminal weakness of English writing in India quite as harshly as would the most adamant nativist, arguing that as a merely foreign, secondary, and elite language of public bureaucracy in India, English has no chance of creative vitality. Its "lack of concreteness, . . . remoteness from workaday affairs and ideas; over-readiness to pick up foreign fashions and jargon; indifference to Indian conditions and traditions; dilettantism equivalent to preciosity" only reinforce the worst vices of a new breed of "culture-wallah."

Why, then, did Chaudhuri discard his own beloved Bengali language to write his *Autobiography* in English? He had the example of his revered boyhood poet-hero, Michael Madhusan Dutt, who outgrew his infatuation with English by the age of thirty and went on to initiate the nineteenth-century Bengali Renaissance by adapting motifs from Homer, Dante, Virgil, and Milton for his Bengali blank verse epic on a Ramayanic theme (188). Chaudhuri praises Dutt along with other nineteenth-century exemplars of cultural synthesis in Bengali such as Bankim Chandra Chatterji, who also settled into

Bengali fame after a "youthful misfire" in English. As a child Chaudhuri had thoroughly accepted Dutt's "password" of 1865: "Let those who feel that they have springs of fresh thought in them fly to their mother tongue . . . gents who fancy that they are swarthy Macaulays and Carlyles and Thackerays . . . are nothing of the sort" (189). Chaudhuri's cryptic reference to his own literary career in this context—"Why from this early conviction my thoughts finally turned to English has its own history"—identifies another of the large, implicit themes of the *Autobiography*, with its tragic and elegiac consciousness of a lost "mother tongue," given up with the motherland of Bengal and the entire Bengali Renaissance dream.[7]

Chaudhuri, however, presents himself as culturally dislocated before Partition, and even before he left East Bengal for Calcutta as an adolescent student in 1911. Western influences had been complicating the cultural identity of his entire Bengali community of colonial civil servants and professionals throughout the whole nineteenth century. In the particular case of his family, the eclectic and hybrid Bengali atmosphere was intensified by his father's personal enthusiasm for all kinds of reform, beginning with a Westernized definition of the "true family" as consisting of parents and children only, apart from the claims of the "joint family" and the ancestral village (137). Chaudhuri admires the modernity of his "true family," but the intimations of violence and madness he discloses within it undermine any simple faith in progress.

In his self-consciousness about psychic as well as geographic fissures, Chaudhuri accepts what he calls "estrangement" (257) as the condition not only of his pain but also of his knowledge and creative power. Perhaps the deepest sign of Western influence in Chaudhuri's *Autobiography* is the very patterning of self-development in terms of a Wordsworthian estrangement into consciousness, from "fair seedtime" in a small rural town to uprooted urban wandering in a society itself torn apart by revolutionary political hopes and fears.

Chaudhuri begins from Romantic and Victorian models, especially Wordsworth.[8] He too recalls a childhood fortunately ordered by the rituals and pastimes of the seasonal round, although Wordsworth's "faces of the moving year" in East Bengal shift only from wet to dry, and, instead of "huge and mighty forms" of mountains, it was the "mountainous carcass of the buffalo" (65) bloodily sacrificed in the annual Durga festival that lifted Chaudhuri's childhood fear to awe.

An English literary atmosphere seems more than a precious overlay in Chaudhuri's style partly because the details of that literature actually belong to the story of his early development. With a precocity surely beyond Macaulay's imagining for Indians, Chaudhuri had as a child absorbed English literature into the fabric of his imagination—not only ideas and principles but images, metaphors, sentence structures, narrative patterns, and a whole mental habit of thinking concretely through verbal details in complex and dramatic relation to each other. His 1954 essay specifically faults Indian writing for its "lack of concreteness"; the superabundant detail in Chaudhuri's narrative testifies not only to his remarkable memory but to his taste for a prose style that organizes concrete detail into rich figurative and thematic patterns.

At Chaudhuri's rural school, Bengali teachers presented Palgrave's *Children's Treasury* alongside the *Ramayana* and the *Mahabharata*, so that, in addition to the Hindu sacred stories, the anthology of English poetry from Shakespeare to Tennyson became for him what he calls a "chiaroscuro" of knowledge that was "extremely sensational"—exotic but also immediate, with "intense highlights in certain places and deep unrelieved shadows in others" (97).[9] "Sensational" here carries the Wordsworthian meaning of sense experience—personal, concrete, immediate, and connected to the round of daily life.

Chaudhuri's move to go to preparatory college in Calcutta at the age of fourteen is presented in the *Autobiography* as an irrevocable uprooting from the nourishing "sensational" life of his childhood. Calcutta, he insists, never became a "natural habitat" for him even after thirty-two years of living there. Calcutta denaturalized him from plant-like rootedness in the sensory world to something more like an airplane that "has to drag its heavier-than-air body with infinite strain . . . perpetually remembering that as soon as that colossal horse-power and those thousands of revolutions per minute have ceased to shake and tear one's being, one would plunge headlong and crash" (258). Chaudhuri likes to elaborate his strain through shifting metaphors; a single page shows not only plants and airplanes but snails, hermit crabs, and the windjammer sailboats of an earlier era: "There is a world of difference between being buoyed up by one's environment, so as to be able to glide naturally on it, and having to beat it until it unwillingly generates the force to keep one afloat" (258).

The frequently noted artifice of Chaudhuri's English style, with its extended conceits and elaborate syntactic poise, displays English literary composition as in itself a form of the strain he associates with survival in Calcutta. Chaudhuri's metaphors call attention to his style as a way of "beating" the subject: controlling and even punishing it through force in order to counter some downward pull. The book's narrative design as well as its style sustains the anxiety about survival that the book recalls from the past, for although he is obviously afloat enough to write the book by 1951, he chooses to break off his story with his catastrophic "crash" after his failure to achieve his M.A. in history in Calcutta in 1920. The narrative movement is toward failure and collapse. During the long, dark sixteen years that followed, he summarizes at the end, the only alternative to intolerable strain was a kind of narcissistic paralysis whose perverse appeal he now mythologizes in an imagery of decadent self-love: "It was as if the spirit of a man lying dead on the wayside had taken a perch on a withered branch nearby and were crying bitterly as it contemplated the inert body for which it still felt a passionate and agonizing love. Yet it was neither absinthe, nor lust, nor disease, nor remorse for some hideous suppressed crime, nor unrequited love which had brought me to this pass. My low spirits were absolute. There seemed to be no cure for them" (455).

How Chaudhuri was eventually able to harness the "colossal horse-power" of his mind and will to pull out of this *accidie* forms the subtext of the *Autobiography* and the thematic significance of its style. Sickened almost to death by academic failure, he is eventually revived by the nineteenth-century British cure of autobiographical composition. What paralyzed Chaudhuri in 1920 was his "insane ambition" to become not just a professor of history but the "epitome of universal knowledge" (330). Without explicitly invoking Wordsworth's dangerous bout with the demons of "speculative abstraction" or John Stuart Mill's depression or Casaubon's fatal intellectual ailment in *Middlemarch*, Chaudhuri presents himself as infected with a recognizable nineteenth-century Western disease of the intellect. He failed his M.A. in Calcutta because he could not study, and he could not study because he planned to read every book, even those in languages he did not know. So, when he was not seeking distraction in the making of cardboard boxes and designs for an Indian national army, he was idly lost in fantasies of his Key to all Histories: "The idea of a gigantic corpus piling itself up in annual volumes throughout a life-time, a single-handed *Monumenta* of Indian history rivalling the corporate *Monumenta Germaniae Historica*, and the idea of a stupendous synthesis written on a grand scale over decades and revised on an equally grand scale over succeeding decades obsessed me at the same time. . . . No wonder I crashed" (352).

Read within the Western tradition of intellectual confessions from Rousseau to Wordsworth, Mill, and Henry Adams, rather than as the "objective" work of Indian history some of his detractors stubbornly persist in demanding of him in spite of his confessed failure, the *Autobiography* explains why Chaudhuri's grandiose ambitions as a historian were doomed.[10] Chaudhuri's preface offers the *Autobiography* as a "contribution to contemporary history," but history on the grand scale is just what he avoids. There is no documentation, for example, in the chapters of "background" and "context"; the movement among remembered experience, general observation, and theoretical speculation is fluid and unapologetically subjective, its air of certitude notwithstanding. A version of Indian history is present, to be sure, but only implicitly and often as the unstated referent of the allegorizing style. At times, Chaudhuri concentrates the whole of India's situation into the synecdoche of his own experience, as if autobiography could after all become a *Monumenta* of Indian history. But Chaudhuri also intermittently acknowledges that he is too idiosyncratic to be a fit allegorical figure; Bengal also is too special and too mixed in itself for the synedoche to carry more than intermittent weight. The autobiographer has to bury and mourn the inert body of his earlier aspiration to synthesis and objectivity.

Part of Chaudhuri's strain, however, is that he cannot entirely relinquish his earlier aspiration, even while narrating its failure. At certain points, he is driven to dig up the remains of his dead self and display its ornaments, such as his long-lost essay "The Objective Method in History" (337–46). After thirty-four years of half-burial—first "under the debris" of an earthquake at home, then as salvaged scrap paper for younger brothers, then twice lost again—it appears for the first time in print here to memorialize the monumental history he could not accomplish.

Although Chaudhuri is imperfectly cured of love for his former self, the *Autobiography* itself overcomes the inert narcissism of his youth by enduring the strain needed to combat paralysis. Like Joyce, Eliot, and Pound, who were representing comparable personal and cultural predicaments at the same time that Chaudhuri was first collapsing, his recovery eventually involved separating himself further from a culture whose paralysis came to seem the very image and cause of his own. Unlike some of the great Western modernists, however, Chaudhuri engaged in this combat while staying at home. Nor has he overlooked the irony that the charges of inauthenticity launched against him were so often developed by Indians educated or living abroad.[11]

Chaudhuri's early resistance to the idea of emigration, or to vulgar ideas of the "eclectic," makes sense in terms of his Bengali faith in high ideals of synthesis and reform. Chaudhuri explicitly mocks the grotesquely "eclectic" solutions to cultural displacement adopted by some Indians of his era. There is, for example, his neighbor in Calcutta in 1911, with two wives in two separate households. Next door was installed the Bengali girl to whom his parents had married him in accord with a common Bengali trust in a "marital insurance policy" before young men went to England to study, and a few streets away was the English wife he had nevertheless brought home; "our neighbour showed himself to be eclectic" (290), he remarks with irony. Double marriage for Chaudhuri exposes a vulgar "eclecticism" that is only a euphemism for lack of scruple on the part of parents and children alike.

The same neighboring household displayed even more shocking forms of domestic hybridity, in which fundamental human categories of identity broke down. Chaudhuri recounts that although the "eclectic" neighbor remained loyal enough to Indian domestic virtue to take his needy older brother and family into his household, he could not control the brother's bestial behavior, as when he would "howl like a jackal" at his wife's locking the door against his return from drunken escapades. Chaudhuri also recalls this crude man's fondness for "boasting" about how a vicious bulldog he had once owned had turned on his little daughter and held her throat in his teeth: "at first he thought of going to her help but while he was hesitating how to do it his wife dragged him into a room and bolted the door, saying 'Don't throw good money after bad'; at last the sweeper heard the child's cries and came running to rescue her" (290). Chaudhuri reports this bestial violence laconically, adding only that he later saw the scars around the girl's throat, as if the plain details themselves speak the moral point. Chaudhuri's self-assurance of moral judgment links him to his father—a progressive humanist and, by profession, a criminal lawyer. Chaudhuri remembers his father marveling that these neighbors were not ashamed to tell such stories of themselves.

Yet Chaudhuri's own stories get most interesting when he swerves from his father's ethical certainties to expose curious secrets about his own hybridity. For example, he secretly envied the wife-beating, child-abusing, drunken cur of a neighbor because he was such a masterful gardener. In Chaudhuri's adolescent eyes, the man was a master of form in the garden, "even in the restricted space given to him, and the worst of soils." Chaudhuri goes so far as to say that the brutal man was "redeemed" by his artistry with flowers. As often in the *Autobiography*, Chaudhuri's degree of irony is hard to assess. How can flowers "redeem" such viciousness? According to what values can gardening weigh in the scales against bestial violence?

Chaudhuri's high-flown word "redeemed" is more than a bit of preciosity. The topic of gardening is what actually launches his entire account of the neighbors in the chapter "Experiences of Adolescence." Gardening was one of the hobbies adopted by Chaudhuri with his characteristic fanaticism when the family moved to the Calcutta suburb of Ballygunje in 1911. The redemptive value of gardening for Chaudhuri becomes intelligible through its connection to his other adolescent obsessions, such as military history and the technical aspect of warfare, which were initiating him into a more aesthetic conception of morality than his father's Bengali Puritanism taught. With an intensity reminiscent of Stephen Dedalus, the adolescent Chaudhuri is shown cultivating a precocious taste for "clear and well-disposed forms" (309): the military form of "breechblocks" as well as the cultivated nature of flowering borders. His fascination with war diverted him from the new chauvinist terrorism that was beginning to attract other young Bengalis at this time, for Chaudhuri loved only orderly armies, arrayed like flowers, as in history books. The sordid alternative was the mob violence and criminal terror that he reports as already common in the rural Bengal of his childhood. As a local criminal lawyer, his father was used to handling disorder, but to Chaudhuri as a boy, domestic as well as official violence often seemed very nearly out of control: family guests, for example, sleeping with wool scarves around their necks to impede the knives of possible assailants; unlucky combatants with bleeding wounds in the courtyard of home: "with the blood clotted and the gashes staring, because to interfere with the wounds before the Government assistant surgeon had certified them would have had the likelihood of prejudicing their case" (44).

In Calcutta, a different, equally disturbing relationship of violence to order seems epitomized by the drunken neighbor who is simultaneously beast and gardener, the source of moral chaos and the maker of beauty. However the adolescent handled this incongruity, the autobiographer chooses irony to preserve ambiguity and a sense of disjuncture between his contradictory moral and aesthetic impulses. No logical or spiritual synthesis allows flowers to redeem child abuse, any more than a principle of "eclecticism" validates bigamy. Chaudhuri's verbal irony registers and disclaims the failures of orderly synthesis in his neighborhood.

Irony allows a similar double expressiveness when it involves the more intimate confession that he was himself responsible for the most bizarre violence in the garden at Ballygunje. Like a crazed Marvellian mower inflamed by jealous rage, Chaudhuri "stealthily" went to the neighbor's garden one night and tore up the most gorgeous of his flowers: "In the afternoon when I was in my garden I saw the old man discovering the mischief. He went pale, and such a look came on his face as made me feel an unspeakable skunk. I suppressed the whole mean episode even from my brothers, and if any of my parents had come to know of it, I should, of course, have received the severest whipping of my life" (291). Although the whole episode is dropped in as just a passing anecdote, its bad odor carries over into the next paragraph when he goes on to describe the two literary magazines, one "orthodox" and one "liberal," that his father brought into the house to promote the balanced cultural synthesis he wanted for his sons. The skunk in the garden hovers just beyond sight of this noble parental teaching.

Chaudhuri's only explanation for his secret viciousness is that "one day the ancient malice to which I was heir got the better of me" (291). But to what ancient inheritance does Chaudhuri mean to trace his malice? It is this kind of hauteur that has made for his anti-Indian reputation; he has a disconcerting penchant for condescending to himself as deeply Indian whenever he comes to deplore his own worst deeds. And malice, especially of a greedy or violent character, heads Chaudhuri's catalogue of ancient (and modern) Indian sins. Even in paradisal East Bengal, he explains earlier in the book, a low cloud of malicious violence polluted the community, bringing "murder, assault, robbery, arson, rape, abduction . . . misappropriation of money, betrayal of widows and minors, forged wills, and purloined title-deeds" (46–47).

Chaudhuri does not locate malice, however, at the core of his Indian inheritance. The structure of his childhood universe was more complicated. In the middle was the "thin layer" of violence, whose bloody effects were especially visible to him because of his father's law practice, but below that was "a rock-like foundation of quite different composition never permeated or corrupted by it. We called this lower stratum religion and morality, things in which everybody believed and things to which in the last resort everybody returned" (47). Both the father and the mother stood firmly on this foundation of traditional Hindu ritual that bound the human life to nature and divinities. Above, in a space that seemed to coincide with the sky, was a higher layer, surprisingly not populated by gods, though it had the Western attributes of God: "an immutable sphere of justice and order, brooding sleeplessly over what was happening below. . . . The common people still called it the Company, others Queen Victoria, and the educated the Government." In Chaudhuri's childhood cosmology, the British Empire was above, in place of divinity; the Hindu religion was below, as a foundation for everyday life in rich sensory and spiritual connection to nature. Only in between was the chaotic, mobile, treacherous layer of human malice.

The disintegration of this structure, from both above and below, is the historical collapse that engulfs Chaudhuri's personal life and is in turn allegorically represented by it. And it is this large, slow collapse, already beginning to be palpable in 1909 and culminating in the nightmarish chaos of Partition still vivid as Chaudhuri writes in 1951, that he sees to have spread violent malice from top to bottom of the Indian universe: "Today everything is giving way. The thing overhead, once believed to be immutable, has blown up, and the primordial foundation of rock below, on which we thought we had our feet firmly planted, is rotting into dust" (47).

In addition to the Indian ancestry of Chaudhuri's "ancient malice," however, there is a further and simultaneous Western inheritance implicit in his language and imagery. Considering that Milton was the most influential English poet in the Bengali Renaissance, Satan is surely one of Chaudhuri's ancestors in the garden, and, staying with the English poetry that figures explicitly in the *Autobiography*, there is also Webster's famous wolf in the dirge, who digs up corpses buried by nature's friendly creatures:

> There were two other poems which made an even greater impression on us and they were placed one above the other in Palgrave's *Children's Treasury*. . . . The first of them was Shakespeare's "Full fathom five . . ." and the second Webster's "Call for the robin-redbreast and the wren." . . . What a magic country it was where the drowned were transformed into pearl and coral and where the robin and the wren covered the friendless bodies of unburied men with leaves and flowers, and the ant, the fieldmouse and the mole reared hillocks over them. . . . But when we read the last two lines: "But keep the wolf far thence, that's foe to men, For with his nails he'll dig them up again," our boyish animalism got the better of us. Going on all fours on our earthen floor and stretching and spreading out our fingers as a cat stretches out and spreads its claws, we fell to scratching the ground. (112)

Webster and Shakespeare, along with Wordsworth and Milton, are not the sources that postcolonial studies prefer to find in non-Western texts. Did T. S. Eliot draw from the same anthology for his eclectic fragments in *The Waste Land*? Chaudhuri never mentions Eliot. Palgrave, that most effective instrument of British cultural expansionism, seems to have led Chaudhuri independently to the most famous lyrical fragments also retrieved by English modernists, and to the impulse to dramatize personal experience through ambiguous and ironic relation to them.

Chaudhuri introduces the dirges of Shakespeare and Webster directly after recalling the vision of "purity and peace" that he came to associate with Wordsworth's "Composed upon Westminster Bridge," also in Palgrave. The magic of these poems induced in the children an inversion of Rupert Brooke's faith: "We had a feeling that if we died in England what would become for ever England would be a little foreign flesh, and with that faith there was happiness in perishing in an English glade, with the robin and the wren twittering overhead" (112). Abject colonial self-obliteration, of the sort represented in *The Moonstone*'s Ezra Jennings and *Edwin Drood*'s Neville Landless,[12] is here exaggerated to the point of parody. In this context, the animalism that disrupts Indian longing for annihilation in an English glade seems not so much malicious as vital—a protest of vitality against the fatal attractiveness of English images of purity and peace. There is a certain welcome mischief to Chaudhuri's prosaic understatement about how here, as later in the garden of Ballygunje, the beast within "got the better" of attraction to aesthetic loveliness. Compared to T. S. Eliot, Chaudhuri may even allow more normal vitality to scavenging creatures: "boyish animalism," though a stiff Victorian phrase, names an instinctive, inspiriting protest against the seductive redemptions in English lyric poetry. In Bengal, Chaudhuri elsewhere remarks, Satan was the hero of *Paradise Lost*, and even his orderly father had as his favorite line "Better to reign in hell than serve in heaven" (101).

Chaudhuri, however, is not a Christian, and the bestial malice recurrent in his narrative takes on a more specifically Hindu aura in the light of the cosmology he formulates as his "credo" in the epilogue to *Thy Hand, Great Anarch!* There he credits his early Hindu training for keeping him skeptical of any theology that dualistically separates good from evil: "it was easy for me as a Hindu to realize from my study of zoology that all the failures in behaviour which the Christian theologians and moralists have called evil, are the outcome of man's loss of that part of his animal status which contained the innate controls on his biological urges, which in animals are as operative as are the urges themselves . . . if man had remained a full animal in his animal functions with only *sapienta* added, there would have been no evil at all anywhere in the universe, because it does not exist except among men."[13] That is the eighty-five-year old Chaudhuri, trying to generalize a "faith" from his long life of imagination and experience. The *Autobiography* settles for less doctrine and allows the beast of malice to prowl through the garden of his imagination and memory with more disturbing freedom.

Objections to what is seen as Chaudhuri's infatuation with literary allusion ignore the ironic and dramatic play of his imagination. Joyce's artistic stature (along with his assiduous training of his early readers) has established multiple layering of allusion as the privilege if also the arrogance of the modernist artist. But in a Bengali of Chaudhuri's generation, the sheer use of allusion to Western literature in itself evokes the mockable stereotype of the hybrid Babu, ready to give his life for the solace of English poetry and English countryside. Like Joyce and T. S. Eliot, however, Chaudhuri is drawn to a lyric like Webster's dirge at least in part for the tensions that complicate its expression of solace within the English poetic tradition. Webster, after all, envisions not only the comfort of English earth to the corpses of outcasts but also the vulnerability of the outcast state to wolfish aggression. An Indian imagination for which Shakespeare, Webster, and Wordsworth have become "sensational knowledge" has not necessarily repudiated its own identity but may instead have acquired additional resources for investigating its own predicament and secrets. There is a great difference, moreover, between the grand synthesis of history dreamt of by Chaudhuri the colonial graduate student and a modern autobiography haunted by "But keep the wolf far thence that's foe to men." It is like the difference between T. S. Eliot's thesis on Bradley and *The Waste Land*, or between Stephen Dedalus trying to synthesize an aesthetic theory from Aristotle, Aquinas, and Shakespeare and the Joyce of *Ulysses* displaying Stephen turning an Irish riddle into a Websterian nightmare of a fox who digs up his grandmother's corpse in the night.[14]

Why Chaudhuri, with all his remarkable range and specificity of verbal imagination, never reaches the intensity of Eliot or Joyce is perhaps no more explicable than any mystery of genius. Some inhibiting forces are nevertheless conspicuous. Although Chaudhuri shows us his own and other cultures reduced to fragments, his own sentences are at the same time self-protectively held above the destructive element. Perhaps he should have thrown away his five-hundred-page manuscript of compulsively well-composed sentences the way Joyce threw away "Stephen Hero" to be free to write *A Portrait of the Artist as a Young Man*—or maybe he needed an editor as aggressive as Pound was with Eliot, instead of publishers overimpressed by the Victorian eloquence of an unknown Indian. Although Chaudhuri submitted his book as late as 1951, the Victorian spell over Indian writing in English remained well into the 1960s, when the question was boldly posed to the "avant-garde" Writers Workshop of Calcutta by David McCutchion (a young Cambridge graduate who went from teaching English in India to the role of supporter and gadfly to English-language writers in Calcutta): "Is Indian literature in English going to set itself standards or not, and are those standards to be Victorian or modern? . . . Is it to come to grips with mature experience or sentimentalize? . . . here on earth or in the Seventh Heaven?"[15] McCutchion echoes Chaudhuri's gloomy 1954 prognosis for Indian writing in English that keeps itself apart from "concrete reality" and the "feel" of things, and he defends Chaudhuri's own power of particularized detail against Indian complaints of "morbidity." But Chaudhuri was less in touch than McCutchion with modernist alternatives to outmoded Victorian syntactic structures and with the Empsonian and Leavisite English criticism that promoted modernist principles. For the three decades between the 1920s and 1950s, Chaudhuri had been too passive, too familial, even intermittently too involved in political and patriotic hopes to pick himself up and leave the structures he had seen collapsing as early as 1921. Indian prose narrative in English decisively broke free from Victorian linguistic authority only with the appearance of *Midnight's Children* in 1981.[16]

Further recognition of what I am proposing as Chaudhuri's latent modernism is likely now to come from Chaudhuri's readers and interpreters, both Indian and Western, if only because his books are most approachable in pieces, in a version of the hole-in-the-sheet viewing devised by Rushdie as a deliberate narrative technique in *Midnight's Children*. There is a dreamlike surplus and redundancy to the best episodes in the *Autobiography* that make them vibrate with each other through echoes and recurrent patterns of detail across the intermediate stretches of sometimes verbose and pompous exposition. Chaudhuri's dramatic imagination comes to life when fragments are seen in relation to each other, as for example the imagery of violence already discussed here, which reverberates strangely with the figure of the mother elsewhere in the *Autobiography*. Chaudhuri resembles Joyce in *Ulysses* in his power to interweave the adolescent's uneasy attachment to his mother into the drama of a whole colonial culture in crisis.

Chaudhuri's mother is an even more haunting figure than Stephen Dedalus's dying and dead mother because she suffered from protracted mental illness, a mysterious version of hysteria manifested in "fits": uncontrollable states of wild moaning and silent prostration for days at a time. Since between these fits she was as firm, strict, and devoted to integrity as his father, Chaudhuri's feelings for her from childhood fluctuated through many shades of love, horror, admiration, guilt, and shame. Here was another and intimately terrifying specter, stalking the peace imagined by the parents in their Westernized oasis of the "true family." Chaudhuri describes his father's patient attendance on this illness, which mysteriously occurred only when he was around and could then be soothed only by his direct care. The true etiology of the mother's illness could never be ascertained from her own multiple explanations: that her mother-in-law had laid a curse on her; that she had been poisoned in the house of her in-laws during the labor of her first (still-born) child; that a secret tragedy was buried in letters she would some day disclose; that a demonic female assailant had tried to murder her with a scimitar. Here was another inheritance of "ancient malice" without knowable origin.

This family drama becomes intertwined with the outbreak of violent public nationalism in the chapter "Citizen-Student," which ends in the earthquake that destroyed the family's house in East Bengal in 1918 (the disaster that incidentally buried his college essay on "objective method"). The earthquake occurs during Chaudhuri's vacation just after he has completed his B.A. examinations. As an actual event, the earthquake is not such a severe calamity. Although the house is destroyed, the family suffers only some months of discomfort. Chaudhuri's academic "crash" is still two years in the future. Nothing really catastrophic happens in 1918, only portents and symbols, and nightmare memories: his mother and sister rushing and shrieking while he stands trance-like not helping them; the slow-moving descent of "fallen masonry" around him; his own body stretched out unconscious on the ground. There is also, afterward, the corrugated-iron roof of the veranda embedded in the garden like a containing wall; his father rushing back from court with only one shoe on; and, most strange of all, his futile search for Wilkie Collins's *The Woman in White*, the book he had been reading when the tremors began.[17]

Chaudhuri prepares for the large symbolic reverberations of the earthquake episode through the political details in the first part of the chapter. This was one of those times in India (Joyce represents the same moment in Ireland) when no hyphenated compound, such as "Citizen-Student," could integrate the political and academic aspirations of young Bengalis. The Defense of India Act, devised to control subversion during World War I, was "seizing the revolutionary movement by the throat" (312), but its violence only generated more nationalist violence in response to police persecution. And the fear of violence produced further, more intimate forms of it, even among those who did not want it. One fellow boarder of Chaudhuri's in Calcutta committed suicide to spare his family police persecution (313). Chaudhuri's own younger brother was brutally beaten by his elder brother while being held down by Chaudhuri and his mother because the family was worried about the risks posed by his suspicious political activities. As Chaudhuri describes the event, the imagery of violent beasts returns to the narrative: "At first the boy resisted, but he was held down too firmly to be able to move. It was like whipping a chained dog, and as weal after weal appeared on his back, he began first to moan, then to slobber and twist, and at last sank on the floor exhausted. My mother, who had seen the whole business through without flinching, had him cleansed and washed, put him to bed, and walked away with the same firmness she had shown during the whipping. The boy lay as if in a swoon for something like four hours. . . . My mother never again referred to the incident, and I had not the stomach to ask her" (316).

Chaudhuri had no stomach for revolutionary activity or for its suppression. He was still trying to transcend conflict through his academic dream of objective intellectual synthesis. His essay on the objective method in history had been written specifically in response to a "tremendous patriotic harangue" by one of his favorite young history professors. The paradoxes of the student's conflicting passions emerges ironically in the narrative's colloquial images. In a "boiling rage" of protest, Chaudhuri composed his praise for history that is "cool in tone, impartial in statement, reserved in judgement" (338). But this would-be Thucydides was also afraid, both of his own rage for coolness and of the violent response it was likely to evoke in the hectic political atmosphere of the university. The burial of the essay in the earthquake, he explains, was not pure loss, for it provided a valid excuse for not going into print with these unpatriotic ideas at that time. The figure of Chaudhuri before the earthquake on his bed in East Bengal reading *The Woman in White* is, among other things, a figure trying to withdraw from the violence of nationalism and the equal violence involved in opposing it.

Collins's popular sensational novel is both a natural and an extremely peculiar choice for escapist reading during a political earthquake. Although devoid of explicit political reference, it resembles other of Chaudhuri's literary references in being a text that phantasmagorically reproduces rather than resolves the conflicts and ambiguities within Chaudhuri's actual Indian world. Collins's mystery novel reflects Chaudhuri's own helpless terror in the coloration of Victorian sensationalist fiction.

Collins's narrative constructions are famous for displaying the impossibility of objectivity; like *The Moonstone* later, *The Woman in White* is split among a series of partial narrators, none of whom can securely get to the center of the criminal plot or to a just resolution of it. The title alone points in confusing directions. Instead of the conventional (Western) associations with a virgin or bride, the white garment of Collins's title has more than one entirely private meaning: the novel begins with the hero's spectral encounter with the escaped lunatic woman in white on a road in Hampstead; later, the costume marks the mysterious bond between a seemingly unrelated dead woman and her foster daughter in the country. In the course of the story, mysterious exchanges and connections of identity contribute to the novel's bizarre power and terror. The heroine is said to have been buried as a corpse, while she has really been falsely incarcerated as a lunatic; the "real" lunatic is the one who is dead. But this confusion occurs only after the heroine has been made virtually insane (and corpse-like) by a sinister conspiracy of villainous intimates who are after her inheritance. The virtuous hero, Hartright, meanwhile, is helplessly off the scene for most of the women's ordeal. In short, *The Woman in White* is another story of tainted inheritance, confused identity, and impotent anxiety in the face of ancient malice. The reading of such fiction is thus an imperfect escape from Indian terrors in 1918. In the *Autobiography*, the novel (including its mysterious disappearance in the earthquake) mirrors Chaudhuri's Indian predicament rather than simply distracting from it.

Whereas Wordsworth and other English poets stand for the "sensational," in that they present experience through the concreteness of the senses, Chaudhuri's account of the earthquake introduces the melodramatic horror of "sensational" Victorian fiction as the atmosphere of Indian reality in 1918. The episode begins with the "low hum" of women's conversation reaching Chaudhuri from the veranda while he is reading *The Woman in White* on the bed. He first feels the tremors through the bed and as they mount, he resists the impulse to go under the bed and jumps instead to the quavering floor. Fixed as in a trance, he is unable to help his mother and sister, whom he sees through the doorway shrieking and rushing through the house. Eventually running out the door himself, he tries to balance himself with outstretched arms and spread-out legs, but no balance is possible as a "low all-pervading rumble" rises out of "a vast preternatural and unconquerable silence." Chaudhuri watches, still trance-like, as the house collapses. He then falls down unconscious on the ground. Miraculously, the falling masonry does not land on him or on his mother and sister; later he finds them crouching near where the roof of the veranda had acted as a containing wall against the debris.

Emotional response to the scene in Chaudhuri's dreamlike account is limited to the father, who rushes from court, one foot shoeless, crying, "It has come down," and almost weeping with relief at the family's survival. Like Hartright in Collins's novel, Chaudhuri is conspicuously useless during the women's ordeal. His lack of even appropriate emotion seems yet another invidious contrast with his revered father. The main activity Chaudhuri ascribes to himself after he recovers consciousness is his obsessive pursuit of his lost volume of *The Woman in White*. The book, he immediately decides, is the casualty not just of natural disaster but of human malice: "somebody had had the presence of mind to steal it. I had to pursue the loss of the book, because it was not mine but belonged to the public library. One of my brothers retrieved it from a house in the neighbourhood a year later" (322).

Chaudhuri's weirdly detailed justification for his obsession with his lost book makes sense only in terms of some dream logic of displaced blame and self-blame. "Malice was having its day with us" (311), he remarks in the earlier, political part of the chapter, but whose malice? Who is the criminal and who the victim? Which is worse: stealing the book, looking for it instead of tending to the family amid the "fallen masonry," or losing it for the library that acts as a kind of protective "containing wall" in his life? *The Woman in White* was not entirely a protection, in any case, for it poses the same interrogations in veiled but equally anxiety-laden terms. Who is the lunatic? Who is the corpse? What differentiates lunatic from corpse? How can malice be resisted when it invades and shakes every corner of a house from roof to foundation? In Indian politics, similar splittings and blurrings of distinctions appear, as the mother organizes a brutal whipping that precisely duplicates the persecution of the police that it is intended to prevent. And the university presents yet another version of the same reversals and paradoxes, as Chaudhuri proposes "the objective method" while "boiling in rage" against his favorite professor. As in the *Autobiography* as a whole, neither the origin of calamities nor the effective recourse against them can be decisively established. The dreamlike memory of paralysis in the midst of chaos may also seem a screen memory for helplessness in the midst of the greater earthquake of Partition, still thirty years away.

"History to be above evasion or dispute must stand on documents" (339), Chaudhuri had written in his student essay on the objective method. If Chaudhuri ever got to finish *The Woman in White*, he would have noticed that the well-meaning Hartright undertakes to resolve the criminal plot by tracking down documentary evidence: a forged marriage entry in a church register. At the end of the novel, however, Hartright's documentary evidence works only indirectly, by forcing one of the villains into starting a fire that destroys both himself and the incriminating document in the same conflagration. Collins's novel both represents and spoofs Victorian obsession with documentary evidence. As an aspiring historian, Chaudhuri had invested documents with similar transcendent value, and his documents also tend to get lost or stolen or destroyed in catastrophe. In another sense, however, all Chaudhuri's personal documents are recovered: the historical essay and *The Woman in White* and poems by Webster and Shakespeare and Wordsworth, as well as many other texts in whole or in parts, such as his beloved articles on artillery from the 1911 *Britannica*. But none of these documentary fragments, separately or together, constitute an impartial resolution of private or public history, nor can they be synthesized and integrated. The fragments Chaudhuri incorporates into his *Autobiography* gain their significance dramatically, in the way they so intimately communicate the strain of fashioning an identity as a dislocated East Bengali intellectual in the first half of the twentieth century. The memorable images do not exactly add up to a political position of either collusion or resistance in the era of Indian nationalism; what is memorable is the figure of a young man whose troubles are "sensational" in all meanings of the English word:—at once an inert body laid out on the road or in the garden and also a hybrid wolf/dog/skunk, instinctively driven to dig everything up.

6

The Politics of Cultural Freedom: India in the 1950s

Dissent in British writing about India during the colonial period is comparatively easy to recognize and define, even while it changes tone and shape in response to shifting historical contingencies over the long period of British rule. In India, after independence and the trauma of Partition, the nationalist consensus against imperial domination that had held the freedom movement together broke apart into complex and aggressive internal conflicts: regional, political, religious, and social. As Vikram Seth displays in detail in *A Suitable Boy*, a mixture of large and petty concerns tore Indian politics and society into myriad hostile factions in the 1950s, so that competitive division rather than orthodoxy became the rule. In *A Suitable Boy*, a disgruntled Party member imagines instructing the Prime Minister to give up his high rhetorical calls for unity: "Dear Chacha Nehru, I felt like saying, this is India, Bharat, the country where faction was invented before the zero. If even the heart is divided into four parts, can you expect us Indians to divide ourselves into less than four hundred."[1]

Less evident in Seth's novel or in other recent literary accounts of India in the 1950s is the additional external pressure on Indian writers in English as British dominance yielded place to the competitive courtship of Asia by America and the Soviet Union. Then, as now, America sought to strengthen educated, politically liberal and democratic intellectuals in Asia. But writers drawn to the West by distrust of the Soviet model and by ideals of liberal humanism, learned in part through their British education, encountered as much frustration as support from their new foreign sponsors, who often had little regard for their specific concerns. The activity of dissent for these Indian writers involved struggle on two not always coordinated or even compatible fronts: within India, there was the effort to oppose the rising forces of Hindu fervor, and even what was perceived as authoritarian tendencies in the Nehru regime; in relation to the Western international community, there was the no less difficult determination to resist new forms of foreign coercion and cooptation that seemed to repeat colonial patterns rather than support freedom from them.

To demonstrate the constrained predicament of aspiring liberal intellectuals in India during the 1950s, I take as my principal text the collective writing venture in the journal *Quest*, a "bi-monthly of Art and Ideas," which tried to create in India an intellectual forum not bound by party or specific policy commitments, a journal of a sort familiar in postwar America, where prestigious journals such as *Partisan Review*, *The Nation*, *Commentary*, and others pursued what could be called a "liberal" or "left-liberal" political line but also went beyond the specifically political for far-ranging literary and cultural commentary, and for even the publication of new literary work. The frustration of *Quest*'s goal makes a poignant, fascinating historical story and also an all too pertinent analogue to the continuing predicament of contemporary "liberal" intellectuals in the non-West who are still objects of urgent American courtship fifty years later. Beyond the cautionary value of *Quest*'s failure as a collective enterprise, however, there are some individual writings remarkable for their own force and expressiveness; they stand out not by transcending the journal's historical predicament but by conveying exceptionally distinct and moving images of it.

Not everyone remembers how much of an anti-Soviet banner "cultural freedom" became in the West after World War II. The organization called the Congress for Cultural Freedom was founded in Berlin soon after the bombs stopped; it was to be an international federation of "free" intellectuals, which could bring together artists, academics, and opinion makers whose very diversity could testify to the value of democratic freedom.[2] In addition to large international conferences of notable intellectuals, intended to compete with the Soviet international circuit of "Congresses," a number of attractive national journals were launched by the organization; *Quest* was the Indian publication, as *Encounter* was Anglo-American, *Preuves* was French, and *Der Monat* was German. The best goal of the Congress for Cultural Freedom's publishing enterprise was its support for enlightened, liberal, cultural commentary in far-flung locations where lack of resources and a possibly hostile political atmosphere presented all but insuperable obstacles to such activity.

A less exalted interpretation of purpose came to the fore in 1967, when the Central Intelligence Agency's (CIA) covert sponsorship of the Congress for Cultural Freedom became public in a scandal seized upon by the American Left as evidence of the liberal complicity in American imperialism that they were already denouncing in relation to the war in Vietnam.[3] All those glamorous international conferences of the 1950s in Berlin, Bombay, Milan, and Rangoon, all the literary symposia and seminars and journals of art and opinion in English, German, French, and Spanish, all the wooing of world-class intellectuals to the democratic ideal of individual freedom—all the rhetoric and travel and high-class intellectual hobnobbing on one continent and another through the 1950s and early 1960s turned out to have been secretly paid for by the CIA.

For the diverse assortment of mainly liberal and socialist participants from Europe and Asia, the "secret" of American government subsidy was hardly a mystery at all.[4] Even if many were queasy about the details of sponsorship, only the Americans fetishized the concept of "independent" intellectuals. For non-Communist intellectuals in postwar Europe and Asia, it was the job of America in some form or other to pay, since paying the bill was regarded as the principal contribution America could make to world culture. Disdain for the vulgarity and materialism of American culture comfortably coexisted with anti-Communist politics for Europeans and Asians, and even among many of the Americans in the Congress for Cultural Freedom.[5] What was commonly termed the "non-Communist Left" shared or at least recognized worldwide low esteem for American culture in the postwar period. That is why the journal *Encounter* (the only Congress publication with an American coeditor) was established in 1953 as a journal from London and allowed to sustain a degree of the anti-American snobbery that united postwar intellectuals of the world despite all their other disagreements.

While the complicated ambiguities and scandals of the secret American government role in the Congress for Cultural Freedom has been variously analyzed—in tones ranging from regret to righteous glee[6]—the crucial Asian component of the story has disappeared from view. But the urgent need to woo the intellectuals of "free" Asia (China having already been "lost") was an explicit raison d'être of the entire Congress for Cultural Freedom enterprise. This Western anxiety explains both the choice of India for the second international meeting in 1951 and Nehru's refusal of New Delhi as site for an event by the Congress, which he regarded as just an "American front."[7] The meeting found an alternate Indian location in Bombay.

Irving Kristol, the first American coeditor of *Encounter*, euphemistically recalls "gentle interventions" from Congress headquarters in Paris urging attention to Asia, and particularly to India, the last hope in Asia for "the free world."[8] *Encounter* fulfilled its assignment by giving more space to Indian topics, and even to Indian writers, than any comparable English-language journal in the 1950s on either side of the Atlantic. *Encounter* was marketed as India's "fastest growing monthly" and did succeed in winning the journal the largest Asian readership of any cultural periodical in English.[9]

The impressiveness of this distinction shrinks in the light of the indifference to India among *Encounter*'s rivals.[10] The English had finally quit India, and had sufficient problems to cope with at home. American postwar intellectuals were preoccupied with Europe's turmoil. Many of them indeed came from Europe; India still barely existed for them beyond the name of Gandhi. Virtually the only article about India during this period in the *Parti-*

san Review, for example, aside from Orwell's ambivalent memorial tribute to Gandhi, is James Burnham's account of his trip to the Congress for Cultural Freedom conference in Bombay.[11]

The launching of *Quest* belonged to this courtship, but tension and cross-purposes existed in the endeavor from the start. Changes in editorial policy and personnel as early as 1958 reflect basic and never-resolved problems of identity and allegiance.[12] For while American money began flowing to *Quest* only because of the Cold War, its Indian contributors were preoccupied less by anxieties about Communism than by internal cultural aspirations of little interest to their foreign sponsors. *Quest*, for example, celebrated the film accomplishment of Satyajit Ray in no fewer than four articles in the mid-1950s. His prize-winning "Pather Panchali" exemplified its ideal of a genuinely modern and independent Indian creative accomplishment—an Indian subject in an Indian spirit, yet worthy of respect by the highest standards of international cinema. *Encounter*'s many articles about India never mention Ray at all (though the magazine had ample space to argue about James Dean and the films of Britain's new Angry Young Men).

For *Quest*'s reviewers, the obstacle to "free" cultural development in India was not Communism so much as inadequate standards and technical knowledge; what India needed, from their perspective, was a kind of independent criticism fostered by neither Nehru's state control of resources nor the growing power of Hindu revivalism. Yet, to anticipate one of my main contentions, the Western sponsors of international cultural freedom were more obsessed with Nehru's suspect "neutralism" in international politics than with his monopolistic control of culture within India, and they were flirting with Hindu revivalism as a possible bulwark against the Red Menace.

By the end of the 1950s, the directorate of the Congress for Cultural Freedom had written off *Quest* and the entire American courtship of India as nothing but a source of frustration. While *Quest* limped on until its shutdown in the Emergency declared by Indira Gandhi in 1976, disappointment was expressed from the Indian perspective too. Despite its lively and optimistic beginning, *Quest* could not foster any creative regeneration of Indian culture, however often it kept repeating that goal. Its increasingly dispirited tone in the late 1950s acknowledged that cultural freedom in India would have to occur in different terms, if it was to happen at all.

The Indian editors and writers of *Quest* initially accepted foreign sponsorship in order to gain opportunities they could not otherwise afford. The irony of postcolonial "independence" is reflected in the limited choice of funding for an Indian journal of art and ideas in the 1950s: there was American money, packaged under a variety of government, foundation, and university labels, and then there was Soviet money, also ingeniously and variously labeled, and finally there was (not very much) Indian money, mainly from the cultural funds of the Nehru government.

The origin of American money was less shrouded in secrecy in India than in America, where the mystery of who-knew-what-when about the CIA sponsorship is still being disputed. In 1952, a remarkable little book, *American Shadow over India*, by a journalist, L. Natarajan (with the help of an unnamed American correspondent), laid out full details of the interlocking personnel and funding that joined America's wartime intelligence office (OSS), the CIA, and not only the Congress for Cultural Freedom but also the Ford and Rockefeller foundations, the Social Science Research Council, and the newly established "area studies" programs at leading American universities.[13] At the same time, the competing Soviet "shadow over India" becomes rather visible in the book's foreword, where "American financial imperialism" is castigated by the standard of Soviet "social justice."[14] Natarajan's book was published by a company in Bombay called the People's Publishing House.

The Indian Committee for Cultural Freedom featured an executive committee led by the distinguished Indian socialists Minoo Masani and Jayaprakash Narayan. To understand how an "American front" could attract these heroes of Indian nationalist and socialist fame, one has to attend to the factional struggles within Indian politics in the early years of independence. The longtime leader of the left-socialist wing of the Congress Party, Jayaprakash Narayan, had broken away after independence to challenge Nehru from his separate Praja Socialist Party. Disappointed in this effort by the early 1950s, he withdrew entirely from electoral politics in favor of spiritual and cultural opposition from outside the circle of power. If Narayan had not withdrawn, it was said, he would have continued as Nehru's formidable natural rival.[15] But his commitment to nonviolence and to "a living and immediate revolution in the minds of men and their mutual relationships" (*Encounter* 3 [December 1954]: 11)[16] brought him into odd congruence with the internationalist movement of cultural freedom, where he could be as outspoken as he pleased in protesting the violence and brutality of the involuntary revolutions in the Soviet Union and in China. Narayan's preaching tried to combine Indian spirituality and economic realism into an ethic of social cooperation that he saw as the sole alternative to coercive state Communism, with its dictatorships of army and secret police.

Other critics of Nehru who also preferred Western to Soviet affiliation included the first editor of *Quest*, Nissim Ezekial, a young Indo-Jewish writer who would later become an important Indian poet and literary critic in English, and (as one of three advisory editors) Nirad C. Chaudhuri, newly prominent as the author of the controversial *Autobiography of an Unknown Indian* and as a gadfly to the "culture-wallahs" of Nehru's New Delhi.[17]

It was not love for America that attracted any of these figures to *Quest* so much as a hope that they could use rather than be used by their new sponsors. Ezekial acknowledged the Cold War coding of high words in his 1955 inaugural editorial when he remarked that cultural criticism at the current time is not for political "innocents": abstractions like "cultural freedom," along with "peace" and "social justice," he explained, all belonged to the rhetoric of a global conflict not designed to promote India's independent interests (1 [August 1955]: 2–3).[18] In nevertheless accepting Western sponsorship, Ezekial argued, *Quest* was choosing the alliance that most supported a version of cultural freedom crucial to and within India, namely the freedom to criticize established authority within the state. Ezekial wanted to use *Quest* for a specifically Indian project of internal "opposition to authority," in accord with the position argued more recently by African critics such as Abiola Irele, that *after* the struggle for anticolonial freedom, there needs to come a "second phase" of internal debate within postcolonial nations themselves.[19]

The Cold War framework of *Quest*, however, demonstrates how foreign sponsorship constrains, if not fatally contaminates, such a project of internal criticism. The Indian experience in the 1950s speaks to the continuing difficulties of postcolonial cultural freedom in the context of multinational power struggles in no way eliminated by the ending of the Cold War.

One low point in the Indian politics of cultural freedom, 1950s style, was reached in a dreary Calcutta seminar sponsored by *Quest* in 1959 under the characteristically dispiriting title "The Relevance or Irrelevance of Philosophical, Moral, and Political Considerations in the Evaluation of Creative Literature." The account in *Quest* (no. 21, April–June 1959: 47–52) by David McCutchion, the young Cambridge graduate I mentioned earlier as a critic of the lingering Victorianism of Indian writing in English,[20] largely ignores the content of the speeches and goes for the cross-cultural drama of the event. Not that there was much drama to report. Arthur Koestler was the inaugural speaker. He held forth repetitiously on the difference between creative literature and other writing: "The tragic life is cosmic (he was frequently to insist), and when we are on that plane our day to day pleasures and disappointments seem of no importance" (47). Ignoring Koestler's lead, the Indian academic speakers drifted off vaguely on their own. A professor from Aligarh "began the discussion with an elegantly phrased speech in which however he did not seem to make any striking points . . . those who spoke after him hardly made any reference to what he had said" (48).

The only break came when Koestler interrupted with a "petulant" demand for more concreteness from the Indian speakers. Briskly enumerating a list of arguable "greats," including Baudelaire, de Sade, Nietzche, Céline, Evelyn Waugh, Ezra Pound, Françoise Sagan, and a Japanese epic of which "he did not recall the name—based on a blood-feud code of honour" (49). Koestler demanded that the Indians be "democratic" and cast votes on the morality of each, yea or nay. But nobody would play Koestler's game of democracy except a Jesuit, Father Fallon, who ventured a yea vote for Baudelaire. Koestler left the meeting disgruntled: "'There is no bringing these people down to earth,' he was heard to comment on the way out." The next morning of the seminar was enlivened only when a Polish delegate by the name of Szimansky opposed virtually everything Koestler had said about tragedy, morality, and other subjects. He agreed only with Koestler's point about the deplorable haze of abstraction in Calcutta: "He had attended more than two hundred writers' conferences in Poland, he began, but never one like this. For in his country, they always discussed the relevance of a particular work to a particular subject, and never lost themselves in such abstractions" (52).

McCutchion's deadpan narrative probably answers the seminar's topic question about the relevance of politics to literature better than any points made in the speeches themselves. What else but politics could have brought a Hungarian ex-Communist from America to Calcutta to force a democratic vote about literary morality on a Jesuit priest, a dissident Pole, and Indian professors from Aligarh and elsewhere?

Other vignettes from the pages of *Quest* and *Encounter* from the 1950s give further evidence of the political as well as rhetorical struggle that *Encounter* rather euphemistically preferred to call "troubled dialogue" (6 [February 1956]: 73). In the early summer of 1956, for example, Ezekial informed *Quest* readers of the visit to Bombay of the American writer James T. Farrell, author of the classic *Studs Lonigan* trilogy and president of the American Committee for Cultural Freedom. Although Ezekial pays tribute to Farrell as noted champion of freedom and human rights, he stays on the cool side of adulation, with remarks about Farrell's lack of development since *Studs Lonigan*, for example, and unflattering comparisons between his "deliberately flat and pedestrian style" and James Joyce's rich "emotional and intellectual texture" in *A Portrait of the Artist as a Young Man* (1 [June–July 1956]: 33–34). The literary slight is noteworthy mainly as a foretaste of the open conflict that erupted by summer's end.[21]

It is Farrell who, after his departure, publicized this conflict in the pages of *Quest* by rebuking Indian intellectuals for British-style "aristocratic disdain of material things and of work" (2 [August–September 1956]: 65–66) and for reckless anti-Americanism, the kind of thing that hardworking America was getting mightily sick of appeasing with dollars. Like Koestler, Farrell talks tough to bring Indians down to earth: "The American worker, rising at five and six a.m. daily to earn his bread and giving a few weeks of his labour in taxes is not going to react well and in good temper when he learns that some of his foreign friends refer to America as Uncle Shylock and Uncle Sucker."

An elegantly phrased letter from the principal of Fergusson College, Poona, in the next issue of *Quest*, calls attention to a few general points neglected by Farrell, namely "the phenomenon of the U.S. standing on the side of Totalitarian, Imperialistic and Racist powers," such as Portugal and Guatemala (2 [October–November 1956]: 63). With assurances of regard for the "friendly ways and unassuming manners" of the Americans he had recently met, the writer concludes that it might be useful to his new friends to take less for granted "their scale of priorities about the evils in this world that have to be destroyed": "For the Asians and Africans, at least, racial equality is a long way ahead of anti-communism."

Farrell kept the dispute going from New York the following winter, insisting in a further letter that he was not the type to "go about trying by checkbook and slogan to win quick liking for myself and my country" (2 [December–January 1956–57]: 57–59). He again invoked the overtaxed American worker, slaving away to support elitist foreign intellectuals. Ignoring the question of principle in American foreign policy, Farrell brought the slur of racism down to a matter of personal honor: "I happen to be one of the many Americans who has fought in many ways for complete equality in America." In regard to racism as a global evil, Farrell simply refused to accept Indian challenges to American moral authority: "I distinguish between equality and a reversal of roles. . . . A cult of superiority appears at least threatening to break out among the opponents of colonialism."

By the time of this last salvo, Farrell had already resigned from the presidency of the American Committee for Cultural Freedom, following his return from what Alan Wald in *The New York Intellectuals* evokes as an ordeal in more places than Bombay. In August, the *Chicago Daily Tribune* received a ranting letter by Farrell sent from Turkey: "we must stop taking as much as one insult from anybody in the world."[22]

In actuality, Americans in the 1950s were required to take a lot of insults from people all over the world. Indeed, sensitivity to the anti-Americanism prevalent among British, European, Asian, and (some) American intellectuals after World War II was what generated among the founders the policy of masking American sponsorship of the Congress for Cultural Freedom, even to the point of locating the organization's headquarters in Paris.

A fair number of insults were nevertheless directed specifically at Americans during the extravagant international conference "The Future of Freedom," sponsored by the Congress in 1955 in Milan, where insult and grievance all but poisoned the festivities, while also providing their main vitality. According to Dwight Macdonald's dryly witty report in *Encounter*, "No Miracle in Milan," the most striking lesson of the five days with 150 intellectual superstars of the "free world" was the hitherto unsuspected richness of "the genus cliché" (5 [December 1955]: 68–74). Macdonald awards the prize for clichéd abstraction in Milan to the Americans who "came to Milan to discuss freedom as an abstract philosophical principle, or as a problem in sociology, political theory, [and] other academic disciplines." Intellectuals from America such as Hannah Arendt, Arthur Schlesinger, Jr., Edward Shils, Daniel Bell, John Galbraith, Sidney Hook, and their like took for granted the benign character of whomever they thought was subsidizing their travel to Milan and did not welcome having their discussion of principles disrupted by low-minded charges that Western "freedom" concretely meant submitting to American power in return for dollars. But, Macdonald reports, "the Asian delegates came to find out what 'freedom' really means to people with white skins—and to present to these cultural representatives of their present or former masters a list of complaints and grievances."

Asian concreteness, in this context, took the form of deconstructing liberal abstractions into the political and economic interests they served. By regarding Western scholars as "representatives" of their states, moreover, the Asian delegates became figurative exactly at the point where literalness mattered to the Americans, who were unprepared to have their individuality discounted. In their view, they "represented" not America but their own thought. The separation between individual thought and government policy was at the liberal heart of the cultural freedom the Americans were in Milan to affirm, without overscrupulous anxiety about latent tensions in their own positions.

As a diplomatist with more official government involvement than most of the other American delegates in Milan, George F. Kennan openly accepted the position of national representative in Milan and, like Farrell in that role, what he represented was the down-to-earth American voice of aggrieved liberalism. As reported in *Encounter* by Stephen Spender (its British coeditor), Kennan's postmortem on the event in Milan was that

> there was little point in Americans attending conferences with
> Asians. . . .whatever Americans did they were always thought to be
> acting from power-lusting, money-grabbing or war-mongering mo-
> tives. . . . He did not mean—he said—that material aid should be
> abandoned, but that Americans should assert bluntly that they only
> helped people because they wanted their 12 per cent profit . . . just as
> there were situations in which it was no use two people going on
> being married, so this relation of America to some of the so-called
> 'undeveloped areas' should lead to divorce. In these parts of the
> world, the British could probably explain things better than the
> Americans. (5 [December 1955]: 54–55)

Like Farrell, Kennan shows the quick movement of the American liberal voice into sarcasm once Asians start to drag the American commitment to "freedom" into the mud with talk about motives. Yet Kennan's marriage trope, like his self-caricature of the ugly American materialist, shows the American voice flailing about among shaky metaphors. Kennan casually assumes mastery in this new American marriage with Asia, though America seems even less capable of managing the role than the British husband of before. He threatens divorce, yet hastily draws back from the implication of abandonment. There is no wish to drive Asia into other arms.

Confusion about what to embrace in India is as conspicuous in *Encounter* as the awkward outbreaks of reproach. Ultimately, of course, the West stood for free development, but more immediately, the Cold War, together with the alien needs and traditions of "undeveloped" areas, led to the bracketing of certain standards of judgment. *Encounter*'s favorite Indian phenomenon in the 1950s—the topic of no fewer than seven articles—was the Ghandian mass movement of Bhoodan: the project of voluntary land redistribution led by Gandhi's spiritual heir, Vinoba Bhave.

For the secular urban intellectuals of *Encounter*, the Bhoodan movement was an incongruous enthusiasm. Photographs of dhoti-clad leaders on barefoot pilgrimages to bring word of "land through love" to India's rural villages, one at a time, accompanied excited statistics about the millions of acres already pledged to Bhoodan. A curiously Victorian lineage was given to this admiration for exotic Indian spirituality by a 1954 tribute in *Encounter* to India's "Dynasty of Saints" by Tennyson's grandson, Hallam Tennyson: "Vinoba reminds one what real religion means," he rhapsodizes: "No discord at the heart of things" (3 [December 1954]: 5).

Other articles about Bhoodan in *Encounter* spell out the political advantages to the West of Indian religion, a familiar colonialist argument updated for the Cold War. The Bhoodan program of voluntary material renunciation proposed a "revolution of the spirit" to overcome the problem of mass poverty—without military or political or even economic coercion. In the colonial period, Indian spirituality was thought by many to protect colonial rule by fostering passive indifference to the identity of secular authority, as long as interference in religious practice was avoided. In this postcolonial period, residues of that earlier sentiment combined with the Gandhian legacy of looking to Indian spirituality as the most potent engine for social improvement in India. What a miracle that would be, not only for Indians but equally for Americans still trembling from the Chinese Revolution! Western commentators who would never have dreamed of giving away a square foot of land themselves did not apply the same cultural standards to India when they embraced Bhoodan's principles of self-sacrifice and spiritual community. In the name of what we might now praise as cultural pluralism, they were satisfied to identify Bhoodan with a separate, authentically Indian spiritual tradition. They were not dismayed by the programmatic repudiation by the Bhoodan movement of art and science and "rootless" urban intellectuals (like themselves); the perception that this Gandhian tradition served anti-Communist politics went a long way to mute contradictions between the spirit of Bhoodan and their own cosmopolitan social and intellectual values.

A politically motivated will to believe in Bhoodan emerges even in the most skeptical article in *Encounter* on the subject, a travel sketch in 1955, "Journey among the Saints," by Herbert Passin, an American anthropologist and a Congress for Cultural Freedom activist. Passin's destination was the *ashram* of Jayaprakash Narayan, who himself personified the incongruous synthesis of Gandhian spirituality and cosmopolitan liberalism. After leaving electoral politics, Narayan not only joined the Indian Committee for Cultural Freedom but also became second-in-command of Bhoodan, behind Vinoba Bhave. Narayan's public, ceremonial dedication of his life to Bhoodan in 1954 gave enormous prestige to the movement, as did his well-publicized pilgrimages on foot across rural India, preaching "living and immediate revolution in the minds of men." Narayan's conversion to a Gandhian ethic of social cooperation was attractive to many of the other ex-Marxists in the Congress for Cultural Freedom, who were also impressed by his unique résumé: ten years in and out of prison for guerrilla activity before independence; twenty years as socialist political leader, now a Hindu *guru*—and all grounded in an American M.A. in economics from the University of Wisconsin, where he had first read Marx in the 1920s.[23]

Passin initially approaches Narayan's *ashram* in a skeptical spirit of attention to incongruities left out of Hallam Tennyson's paen to the harmonies of "real" Indian religion. He tells, for example, how, after twenty-two hours of train agony, he discovered that his sleeping roll had been stolen in the station of Bodh Gaya, where the Buddha had attained enlightenment 2,500 years before. But Passin's irony stops just short of critical skepticism about the revolutionary promise of Bhoodan. Even for himself, the trip to the *ashram* becomes almost a religious initiation: after seventeen hours by broken-down jeep and foot through rivers, streams, and paddy fields full of animal and human dung, he arrives with "spirit triumphant." "Hallelujah, here I go," he exclaims, when recalling how he was too tired to turn his foot one inch to avoid a mess of human dung (4 [February 1955]: 73–74). Passin is good at conveying the exciting release from the "niggling calculations" of discomfort and danger that Indian travel can inspire in Westerners, but he is also candid in limiting the spiritual claims of his touristic adventures, at least by comparison to his Indian guides: "My companions, being saints or apprentice saints, ended with the same imperturbable good humour. . . . I cannot say that my own tortured and set grin was their equal in spiritual grace."

The ambiguous value of Indian "spiritual grace" to Passin becomes especially clear at the end of the sketch, after his departure from the *ashram*: "My fastidiousness, however, had been left behind a long time ago. I drank, without hesitation or thought of typhoid, cholera, or typhus, whatever water was offered me. . . . Wherever we went, peasants greeted us with the cry: *Sub Bhoomi Gopalki?*—'All Land Belongs to God'?—the slogan of the Bhoodan movement. One could sense how deep were the roots which it had struck. . . ." Passin's preoccupation with his medical danger combines uneasily with his tribute to Indian spirituality; by the end of his account the entire Bhoodan movement comes to seem marvelous for the very reason that it is so deeply rooted in a land drenched in disease-carrying dung.[24]

Passin locates the Bhoodan movement in an India legendary not only for plagues and infections but also for turning Western wisdom about health upside down. This inversion becomes literal when he singles out as a notable human encounter in Narayan's *ashram* his early morning sight of "a pair of legs staring me in the face": "My roommate was standing on his head, a morning exercise which he assured me is exceedingly good for the circulation of the blood." Since the voluntary land-gift movement also inverted the property relationships accepted as natural in the West, bemused insinuations of pathology spread from the infested soil and the upside-down figure of his roommate to the entire movement of Bhoodan. For the anti-Communist intellectuals of *Encounter*, however, skepticism about the health of the tradition in which Bhoodan was rooted had to be balanced against even the remote chance that Bhoodan was a dispensation from the (Indian) divine sent to protect India (and the West) from the lethal plague of Communism. Hope for a traditional Indian spiritual cure for Asian poverty controls Passin's irony about Indian saintliness, so that his comico-catastrophic travel sketch participates in the same endorsement of Bhoodan that is spelled out elsewhere in *Encounter* with even less acknowledgement of doubt.

Suspicion of an updated, postcolonial Orientalism in *Encounter*'s overenthusiastic embrace of Indian spirituality sharpens upon observation that the Indian writers in *Quest* at this time in the mid-1950s were sharply debating the cultural implications of Bhoodan and the entire Western as well as native discourse of enthusiasm for Indian spirituality. It is not that *Quest* went any further than *Encounter* into the huge economic and administrative problems of the Bhoodan movement.[25] As journals of "art and ideas," both *Quest* and *Encounter* engaged with the idea more than the feasibility of Bhoodan, but the idea itself was treated differently in *Quest*. Undeterred by Narayan's authority in the Indian Committee for Cultural Freedom, the very first issue of *Quest* featured a protest against the entire "mystique" of Bhoodan for its "romantic return to the past." Longing for release from "the saint and the sage" staples of Indian tradition, the journalist M. G. Bailur disdains the "high-minded piety" of Bhoodan as reversion to archaic Hindu "idealisation of indigence," a reduction, he protests, to "universal pauperization" (1 [August 1955]: 5–10).

In another article, A. B. Shah, a mathematician from Poona warns against yielding to foreign interest in keeping India under "the shackles of the superhuman" and exhorts "democratic intellectuals in India" to resist the contradictory pursuit of democratic freedom through "authoritarian doctrines of indigenous make" (1 [December–January 1955–56]: 25–30). Rather than embrace a separate cultural standard for endorsing the exotic spirituality of Bhoodan, like Tennyson or Passin, this Indian intellectual presumes to apply the Westerners' anti-authoritarian cultural standard to India; he wants to rally Indians to a humanistic "rational ethics with the freedom and dignity of the individual as its central values."

The status of an Indian declaration in favor of rational ethics and individualism became paradoxical in the politics of cultural freedom in the 1950s, and it is still paradoxical today. According to our current terms of postcolonial discourse analysis, formulae like "rational ethics" and "freedom and dignity of the individual" smack of Western cultural imperialism and, when used by an Indian, supposedly indicate a colonized mentality—just what you would expect from a writer paid, as it turns out, by the CIA.[26] But in the specific context of the Congress for Cultural Freedom, the endorsement of rational ethics by Indian writers in *Quest* was turning a language derived from Western liberalism partly against those Western liberals who overeagerly endorsed indigenous Indian traditions when they served their anti-Communist politics.[27]

American cultural emissaries to India in the 1950s, like Farrell and Koestler and Passin, showed remarkably little awareness of how sharply Indian liberal intellectuals resented the political alliance between intellectual cold warriors and Indian saints. Those who aspired to a modern, secular, yet distinctly Indian postcolonial identity found themselves peculiarly without either foreign or indigenous ground to stand on in the 1950s. They faced the all but impossible challenge of devising an independent language for their values. Thus a New Delhi journalist, J. Vijayatunga, writing from the *ashram* operated by the Hindu revivalist poet Sri Aurobindo, laments: "The best we can do is to turn up some old tome and say that in 5000 B.C. we did such and such, that today we are the possessors of great spiritual truths, and that we disdain to emulate the West! . . . We do not even have a living language in which we could confess that we are cowards, that we are hopelessly decadent" (1 [October–November 1955]: 19).

My readings in *Quest* through the 1950s turn up only a scant handful of writings that transcend the constraints regularly lamented in the pages of the journal itself: astute book reviews by Laeeq Futehally and Foy Nisson, some of Nissim Ezekial's editorials and poems, the occasional film review. Nirad C. Chaudhuri looked past *Quest* and chose the international readership of *Encounter* with his two provocative literary essays of the mid-1950s: a critique of E. M. Forster in "Passage to and from India" (2 [June 1954]: 19–24) and a complex appreciation of Kipling's *Kim*, "The Finest Story about India" (8 [April 1957]: 47–53), which begins with one of his characteristic double thrusts: first he lands a blow against nativists by awarding the Indian fiction prize to Kipling, the all but official chronicler of the Raj; then he turns in the opposite direction by remarking that he had read *Kim* for the first time only three years before, because he wouldn't read Kipling while India was under British rule. Whatever Chaudhuri's reasons for choosing to publish these essays in *Encounter*, his relish for contradiction is at once characteristic of *Quest* and more sophisticated in its assured ironic style than the norm of the Indian journal.

One particularly impressive short narrative in a style quite different from Chaudhuri's stands out for the force and suggestiveness of its spare rendering of cultural loss and impoverishment, without grandiose or abject rhetorical gesturing. It is called "A Day in Bithur" (3 [August–September 1957]: 38–41). The author, R. B. Joshi, is identified as a "humanist" versed in Urdu, Sanskrit, and English who is noted for his travelogues and short stories in both Marathi and English.

Through the details of a day trip in 1957 to a centenary shrine of the 1857 Rebellion, Joshi suggests the bleak absence of supports for the national cultural identity that the official centenary wants to celebrate. Joshi sets out by bus through Kanpur to visit the newly installed memorial bust and palace site of the Marathi ruler Nanasaheb, notorious in British annals for ordering the infamous massacre at (what the British spelled) Cawnpore. Nanasaheb was now an official Indian hero in what was coming to be established by nationalists as the first war of Indian independence. Joshi's narrative remains detached, however, from patriotic or other strong emotions. He goes a day after the official ceremony and, when a fellow passenger on the bus complains that the statue is all wrong—"Tell Pandit Nehru . . . Nanasaheb looks like a parcel, Babu; you must do something"—he is at pains to disclaim any authority or influence. Joshi is traveling to the monument as a single passenger, in itself a striking anomaly in this land of mass political as well as religious pilgrimage.

The language of Joshi's narrative confirms his low-key independence. Though his journey includes the heat and delays and mechanical troubles that are *de rigueur* for travel writing about India, he entirely avoids any form of Passin's jovial "Hallelujah." "I am squeezed in," he says laconically, "but do not complain." It is not that he is too saintly to notice the hardship, like Passin's Indian guides. He is just matter-of-fact; he is used to it. At the point when a second unexplained half-hour halt of the bus produces yet more additional passengers in the form of two prisoners tied and led by rope in the hands of three police constables, this impossibly overcrowded bus begins to figure as an emblem of all that must be accepted as matters of fact in India: "I do not know where room can be found for them in the bus. But it *is* found for them—on the roof of this bus, and they climb up, constables and culprits. The sun is beating fiercely from above; there is heavy luggage around, trunks and tins and bundles and bags, all in the sun. They all find place among these" (38).

The microcosm of Joshi's bus needs still to accommodate one more figure, and eventually the lordly local police official is also announced as the cause of a long further delay. Joshi gives ironic humor as well as figurative weight to the social details:

The Darogha Saheb is yet to come. "He is having his meals," says someone. "He has just had his bath and is saying his prayers. It will be at least an hour before he finishes his meals and other things and comes," says another. Everyone has something to say about the Darogha Saheb. But finally he comes. He is a Darogha Saheb to his finger-tips, which are very thick, in keeping with his full paunch and puffy body. There is not an inch of room anywhere on the bus, and the Darogha Saheb will need several inches of it, and he must be found the inches he needs. At least some of them. So he goes and sits to the right of the driver. In that part of the bus where the driver sits, there are now five people, not counting a child thrust into the lap of a none-too-hospitable passenger. (38–39)

Joshi sustains his wry patience for the length of his crowded, uncomfortable, but finally not unbearable trip. A century after the 1857 Rebellion, the Indian community of the bus is not heroic, not saintly, not even hospitable, but room is made for everyone who needs to be on the bus, which against mechanical probability does not break down but manages to lurch forward to its destination.

If Joshi had succeeded only in maintaining this humorous realism, his travelogue would already stand out impressively against *Quest*'s clichéd norm. But Joshi shows Indian reality pushing him beyond realism because his official destination offers so much less material for realism than the bus ride to it. Arrival at the palace site immediately discloses emptiness to be its main feature: a taciturn guide leads him through a scene of nothingness: "We do not meet a soul on the way. The houses on both sides are vacant apartments of mere crumbling walls"; "not a brick of the palace is left standing"; "My guide shows me a well. There is nothing very special about it . . . I ask my guide about this but he knows nothing"; "No one lives there, unless it be hyenas and owls" (40).

While the travelogue of what is not there to be seen provides Forster's ironic starting-point in *A Passage to India*, Joshi moves negation in a newly suggestive direction by probing the historical associations that distinguish Bithur from Forster's Chandrapore or Marabar caves. There is, for example, a mosque built by the Mughal ruler Aureng-Zebe on the spot where, according to the *Ramayana*, Lakshman had brought and left Sita at the behest of Rama. As at Ayodhya and elsewhere in central and northern India, the Hindu past exists as a story underneath the Mughal monument.

Everything in Bithur participates in the same pattern of loss. Joshi wanders in a dreamlike bewilderment, intensified by the sense that memory here has been so peculiarly unhoused, unblessed: "There is no place left here even for the ghosts of these memories to dwell. The British saw to it that none was left. All I see now is a vast plain strewn over with debris and rubble."

The absence of the concrete in this setting comes to signify the colonial condition itself, which has been driven to abstraction through conquest and plunder. Postcolonial India's urge to install new monuments, like the bust of Nanasaheb, becomes more poignant in this context, but also more farcical and insulting in its falsity. Through indifference or ineptitude, the new nation dishonors its own past at Bithur, as in the careless sign pointing to Nanasaheb's memorial: it reads "Nanasaheb Dhu Dhu Pant," a gross error, Joshi remarks; the proper transcription of Marathi ought to read "Dhondo Pant": "No Maharastrian would accept 'Dhu Dhu Pant' for a name or for an alias. It means nothing to him. But perhaps to the monument-makers neither means anything, so it does not matter in the least to them" (40). Joshi implies that the monument-makers of the new united nation know and care little about the regional names and meanings that constitute living history here as in other parts of India.

The local tales offered by the guide implicate the Maharastrians themselves in their own impoverishment. According to one legend, Nanasaheb's predecessor, the Peshwa Baji Rao, once threw away the luxurious pension he had accepted in the settlements famous for securing British imperial domination of the Marathi kingdom in the nineteenth century. Refusing to be disturbed in his daily religious rites on the *ghat* of the Ganga, he once ordered the whole treasure thrown into the river, so that the British had to replace it. The splendid extravagance of earlier conquerors and collaborators alike has left ordinary people like the guide and the local residents as poor as ever. In the bed of the river, a sweeper reportedly once found a golden Ganesh (Indian god of prosperity) but was cheated out of it by a brassware dealer, who sold it to a banker in Kanpur. Passing from the Peshwa to the banker, the blessing of Ganesh still eludes the sweeper, who seems to represent the collective ill luck of the community: "The whole town looks deserted and desolate."

When finally encountered, the memorial bust of Nanasaheb entirely fits this scene of loss, for as predicted, it bears no resemblance to the figure Joshi knows from paintings. Rather than cover loss with substitute images in the manner of the official memorial, Joshi chooses the dignity of simply naming the nothing that is not there and the nothing that is.[28] At the same time, his details of local legend and gossip do people the empty scene with the great names of Indian history and myth—Rama, Ganesh, Aureng-Zebe, Baji Rao, Nanasaheb—so that the ghostly past does circulate here in all its unsanctified sorrow. At the very end, Joshi prefers these ghostly presences to the reality of the bus. He has no eagerness to rejoin that crowded community for the ride back but lingers with the memories he has done so much to deglorify: "Bithur is charged with a crowd of memories. I leave the place behind, but the memories insist on coming with me. I allow them to" (41). A softened tone of reverie at the end almost repudiates the earlier starkness, as if the pain of historical loss acquires its own sweet companionability once the actual scene of desecration is left behind.

Tougher commentary on the monument to Nanasaheb in the next issue of *Quest* adds further irony. According to M. K. Haldar, professor of philosophy at Delhi College, that disappointing bust at Bithur does not even represent Nanasaheb, only a man named Ayodhya Prasad, who was a supplier of the English army in 1857! Worse than the crude error of the sign to the monument, the memorial bust is an imposture. Haldar assertively relishes the irony of the fake monument because it corresponds to his perception of imposture in the whole nationalist centenary. No version of Nanasaheb is a hero to him because he believes princely rulers like Nanasaheb to have been motivated in 1857 mainly by desire to protect their feudal privileges. He distrusts heroes, in any case, for fanning authoritarian tendencies and for distracting people from their real social frustrations. What India needs, he insists, is not heroism, but strengthened belief in "the importance of the independent and free individual" (3 [October–November 1957]: 8–14). Thus Haldar seeks liberation from the losses and betrayals of the past in the credo of liberal humanism. In India in the 1950s, however, the disembodied figure of the "independent and free individual" may seem as uncertain an object for Indian reverence as the false bust of Nanasaheb.

In the absence of more solid figures, India's legendary heroes and historic betrayers continue to hover as the ghostly presences that postcolonial humanism in India must absorb and exorcise. Cultural freedom to explore the complex betrayals of history requires, however, more acceptance of ambiguity and contradiction in the story of nations than easily fits the polarities of either the Cold War or decolonization. Not until a generation later does Rushdie invent a new literary form for this complexity in *Midnight's Children*, in which India in the 1950s is peopled with a fantastical throng of betrayers, ghosts, and imposters. Rushdie also boldly revitalizes the English language as a force for cultural freedom in India, partly by playing so freely with liberal (along with other) clichés. The Goan *ayah's* English nursery lesson: "Anything you want to be, you can be: / You can be just what-all you want" (148) haunts the despair of the ending by the replacement of "can" with "kin": "Anything you want to be, you kin be" (457), suggesting how complex constraining bonds mock the free development of both individuals and nations. In *Midnight's Children*, only Rushdie's own vitality and inventiveness of language stand against "sperectomy" (521), Rushdie's play on the Emergency's sterilization campaign to name the excision of hope, the latest cure for what the novel calls "optimism disease."

Rushdie's role in the continuing politics of cultural freedom seems epitomized by two opposing reviews of his work by Indian critics: one, perhaps coincidentally published in the post-Congress for Cultural Freedom *Encounter*.[29] Maria Couto (identified as a Goan-born professor from the

University of Delhi living in London) praises *Midnight's Children* for its accomplishment of a fresh language for Indian writing in English: "The rhythmic flow and the high figurative content of Indian languages, myth, fable, belief and superstition are integrated into English prose in joyful profusion to suggest India's many-tongued diversity" (58 [February 1982]: 62–63). Feroza Jussawalla, by contrast, writing in the midst of the *Satanic Verses* debacle, harshly criticizes Rushdie as no more than "a successful mainstream westernized immigrant," whose artificial Indianized English is a "mimicry of modernism" that insults and mocks not only Muslims but all Indians, in London as well as on the subcontinent.[30] Jussawalla is a professor in the United States, but she notes that an earlier version of her essay was written for a collection to be published in India, where, however, the publisher was afraid to include quotations from a "banned book," and eventually substituted page numbers for actual quoted text. The disturbing detail, coming at the end of Jussawalla's harsh criticism of *Satanic Verses*, indicates the degree to which the meaning and value of cultural freedom not only has a long, complex history but remains unresolved, a matter for further and more subtle analysis both inside and outside the West.

7

Individuality as a Problem in Naipaul's Indian Narratives

V. S. Naipaul's celebrations of individuality have contributed to his importance as a public intellectual in some (mainly conservative) circles but have for that very reason targeted him in postcolonial critique as the "witness for the Western prosecution," in Said's phrase.[1] Individuality, in conservative usage, defines the accomplishment of the modern West that the rest of the world ought to emulate. More specifically, Naipaul's repeated championing of individuality as the key value for readers and writers of literature brought him into direct conflict with postcolonial radical critique in the 1970s and 1980s, when that field was organizing itself precisely to expose the place of ideas such as individuality in imperialist ideology. But now that interest in multiple and hybrid identities has to some extent displaced the focus on group origins and affiliations within postcolonial studies itself, Naipaul's troubled self-consciousness about the meaning of postcolonial individuality seems newly in touch with current concerns.[2]

Rather than make his preoccupation with individuality a basis for affiliation with other postcolonial writers, Naipaul has held himself aloof, aggressively so, as in a cantankerous 1979 interview in *Salmagundi*, where he specifically invokes the concept of individuality to differentiate himself from other "Asiatics" writing at the time:[3]

> I am an oddity, and have always felt that I was an oddity. . . . In the west, when you write you feel that you write for a certain kind of individual. And you assume that readers can feel themselves to be individuals. This is not an eternal in the world, not a constant. To write a kind of literature that I can find interesting you need to acquire an anxiety about man as an individual, and even in Europe this is a relatively new thing. There are some "Asiatics" writing, it is true. But they are recording for this outside audience their little tribal rites and they're seen really not as new writers enlarging the sensibilities of readers accustomed to works of real literary value.[4]

Aggressiveness in this debate has gone both ways. Fredric Jameson's famous celebration in 1986 of "Third-World Literature" derides individuality as a fetish of "First-World" capitalism and looks to Asia, Africa, and the Caribbean for redemptive alternatives to the "isolated monads" and "dying subjectivities" of Western modernism.[5] In the newly liberated nations of the formerly colonized world, Jameson argues, the collective is always the allegorical if not the literal subject of narrative: "the story of the private individual destiny is always an allegory of the embattled situation of the public third-world culture and society."[6]

The sweeping generalizations and overstated judgments on both sides of this controversy seem rather dated already, because they leave out the ever more flourishing growth of new writing that in a sense branches off from Naipaul's own early work as a displaced Hindu from Trinidad in London, aspiring in the 1950s and 1960s to make a literary career in a wider world than the one he left behind. This new literature, written by hard-pressed émigrés and hopeful immigrants, apostates, and dissenters (including those who never literally leave home) often makes the unsettled relationship of individuals to any single public culture or society precisely the issue at stake. This body of work offers less a represention of any collective than a sense of a variegated *collection* of struggling subjectivities, each with distinct and uneasy relationships to cultures and nations often split within themselves as well as from each other.

Jameson was nevertheless right to italicize the term *individuality*, which Western humanist criticism has so long taken for granted. Even those postcolonial writers most intent on asserting their right to dissent from repressive collectives or to affirm a cultural hybridity that brings gains as well as losses chafe at the imperialist legacy of *individualism* and struggle to liberate their own claim to subjective freedom from oppressive ideological associations.

V. S. Naipaul, meanwhile, has continued to seem an oddity. It is paradoxical, that at the very moment when the spread of ferocious communalist and nationalist passions in India and elsewhere began to alarm earlier advocates of ethnic and nationalist collectives, Naipaul chose to subdue his earlier harsh and pessimistic judgments. The explicit goal of his 1990 Indian narrative, *India: A Million Mutinies Now*, is to expiate the notoriously hostile bias of his first Indian travel account of India, *An Area of Darkness* (1964), by acknowledging that he wrote it in the grip of "neurosis" (7, 8).[7] He explains that he had been flooded in the 1960s by personal fantasies and fears that sprang from his family roots in the Indian migration of indentured labor to Trinidad in the nineteenth century; his first direct encounter with an India he knew only through mysterious family lore had overwhelmed and repelled him. Twenty-eight years later, Naipaul presents himself as more mature and sane, able now to approach India less subjectively, with a different poise and openness to *its* realities.

Naipaul in this book does not discard individuality as a value, but he now transfers it to the myriad Indian voices that he retrospectively sees to have been muffled by the clamor of his panic in *An Area of Darkness*. The title of the long book, *India: A Million Mutinies Now*, refers first to what he regards as the spread of the liberating impulse associated with the 1857 Rebellion. Now, he concludes at the end of the book, "the idea of freedom has gone everywhere in India" (517). In deference to this proliferation of liberated voices, Naipaul chooses to withdraw. The interview format of the book is designed to allow the multiple currents of liberation to flow through Naipaul as a neutral medium, the partisan only of the general goal of freedom.

This seemingly generous role marks a self-conscious turn away from what Naipaul now repudiates as his literary as well as his personal ego in the narrative of 1964. In *An Area of Darkness*, he explains, he was caught not only in a familial neurosis of colonial origin but also in the Western mystique of the writer "as a man with an internal life, a man drawing it all out of his own entrails, magically reading the externals of things" (511). In *India: A Million Mutinies Now*, Naipaul repeatedly denigrates that model of romantic authorial egotism—for example, in relation to the nineteenth-century correspondent William Howard Russell, whose eight-hundred-page diary of the 1857 Rebellion exhibits the writer as "an imperial figure . . . almost as much concerned with himself and his dignity and his character as a special correspondent as with the country he had travelled to see, and the people he found himself among" (393). The architect Le Corbusier stands as an even more egregious example of artistic egotism for Naipaul. His "monument to himself," the city of Chandrigarh, in the Punjab, belongs to the same era as Naipaul's first trip. Chandrigarh was artificial when it was new in 1962, Naipaul recalls, but now the factitiousness of its "megalomaniac architecture" shows more blatantly, in the "stained and diseased" look of its alien materials and design and in its "applied flashiness," which reserves individuality "only to the architect, imposing his ideas of colour in an inflated Miróesque mural . . . and imposing an iconography of his own with a giant hand" (426–27).

The narrative structure of interview has been called a populist form because it appears to validate the people's voice (preferably scores of voices, to represent the hundreds and millions more excluded only for reasons of practicality). Although famous earlier examples exist, from Mayhew to Orwell (Sleeman being a less well-known practitioner),[8] the fashion of interview narrative acquired moral and political cachet in the late 1960s, along with other populist rejections of inherited and elitist authority in art and scholarship as well as in politics. The new "dialogic" emphasis in ethnography recommended by James Clifford[9] derives from this impulse, as do the internationally acclaimed interview books of the Chicago radio-show host Studs Terkel.[10] Two young Chinese journalists, Xinxin Zhang and Sang Ye, give special thanks to Terkel's model at the opening of their impressive collection of interviews, *Chinese Lives* (in another translation, *Chinese Profiles*), published first in a New York Chinese-language newspaper to give overseas Chinese a picture of what seemed like the new "liberation of spirit" in the China of the early 1980s.[11] For so notorious an "elitist" as Naipaul to adopt this populist structure represents a conspicuous choice, an even ostentatious self-criticism of earlier presumptions.

Naipaul's conversion appears less decisive, however, when we consider how long he has been struggling with the imperial ego. Tension between self-assertion and self-effacement has been an ongoing drama in his writing from the start. The problem for me (and the main question that motivates my argument) is why literary and political judgments of Naipaul seem to diverge: politically, Naipaul's new control over subjective bias presumably represents improvement, but Naipaul's writing, at least about India, remains most compelling when tension is most conspicuous and when the gesture of self-effacement breaks down. When Naipaul most effectively withdraws his authorial ego from *India: A Million Mutinies Now*, the unintended effect is the fading also of his Indian subjects. *An Area of Darkness*, for all its obnoxious and neurotic hostility to India, gives more vivid presence to the place and the people because of the very pressure and personal strain that the writing displays. *India: A Million Mutinies Now* is best, I think, when Naipaul's new poise of all-accepting equanimity is most openly shaken up.[12]

Naipaul himself provides analytic terms for understanding his longstanding struggle with his own subjectivity in his autobiographical novel, *The Enigma of Arrival*, published a year before the big India interview trip. Without either the panic of *An Area of Darkness* or the artificial detachment of *India: A Million Mutinies Now*, Naipaul in this book achieves, in his meditative style, perhaps his best balance between enacting his postcolonial predicament and reflectively analyzing it. He recounts that it was in London in the 1950s that he first became disillusioned with the image of "the writer" as "a person possessed of sensibility . . . someone who recorded or displayed an inward development" (EA, 146).[13] Tracing these ideas to the "aesthetic movement at the end of the nineteeenth century and the ideas of Bloomsbury," Naipaul rejected them as "bred essentially out of empire, wealth and imperial security" (146). When, in *India: A Million Mutinies Now*, he disclaims *An Area of Darkness* as itself tainted by the corrupting idea of the writer as "a man drawing it all out of his own entrails," he is not then so much proposing a penitent idea of his late middle age but shifting the chronology of when he began to worry about what identity he could invent for himself as a writer.

In *The Enigma of Arrival*, the crisis of his early years in London centers on the uncertainty of his literary rather than his ethnic identity; put another way, his sense of racial and cultural difference as a Trinidadian Hindu made him seek a literary identity distinct from the confident introspection of the British ruling culture. It was as a writer that he was to establish his identity. To become a writer—to live as a writer—was the adolescent fantasy that initially impelled him to England; it is a fantasy of self-construction rather than self-discovery. With a few glimmers of success (mainly two unpublished manuscripts), Naipaul found that, for him, all the familiar goals of many-faceted human effort everywhere—security, freedom, wealth—more than ordinarily attached themselves to "the writing career." "Security," for him, meant "the security of a man who had at last made himself what he had wanted to be" (EA, 151), namely a writer; "freedom," upon returning to England from a first trip back to Trinidad, referred to "the fact that I had made myself a writer and could now live as a writer" (EA, 152).

The first of Naipaul's youthful alternatives to sensibility, as presented in *The Enigma of Arrival,* was a new cosmopolitanism. Distinctiveness for a postcolonial hybrid writer like himself might come not from his private, internal development but from his special access to multiple external worlds: "the worlds I contained within myself, the worlds I lived in" (EA, 147). Thus, the early fictions located in Hindu Trinidad—*The Mystic Masseur* (1957), *Miguel Street* (1959), *A House for Mr. Biswas* (1961). The project of the first trip to India, resulting in *An Area of Darkness,* extends this same literary conception; India would extend his "writer's capital" (EA, 166); his visit there would add another external world to correspond to the Indianness that was already one of his internal worlds.

Without exactly specifying this aspiration, the design of *An Area of Darkness* right away displays the shakiness of cultural hybridity as a ground for literary or any other kind of identity. Hardly past its account, in the prologue, of the humiliation of Bombay Customs, the narrative flashes back to London and to a grim seven-page memorial to Ramon, another Hindu from Trinidad, who was an obscure, half-criminal London acquaintance of Naipaul's. This secret sharer opens *An Area of Darkness* with an image of the postcolonial émigré as mere "nonentity" (43). Ramon casts the shadow of failure in advance on postcolonial hybridity as a productive escape from sensibility—at least in London. As his name suggests, Ramon was connected to even more "worlds" than was Naipaul, since his Trinidadian mother was half-Venezuelan. Yet the pathetic figure of Ramon marks the possibility of difference that amounts to nothing.

Naipaul gives Ramon virtually no distinctive characteristics. He was invisible in London, "of a piece" with his shabby setting in a dingy Chelsea boardinghouse (39). When he was summoned to court for trial in the abortive burning of a motor scooter, he had no testimonial to his so-called character except his employer's demeaning label of "good boy" (42).[14] Ramon's only distinctive attribute, what Naipaul calls his "ruling passion," his "genius," was his love of driving (40). He had left Trinidad because he had lost his driving license. In London, what he did—all he wanted to do—was drive: "He wished to drive; he drove. He liked a car; he applied his skill to it and drove it away" (40). Even Ramon's crimes were peculiar negations of identity. In London, he compulsively stole parts from cars to fix other cars, also not his own. In the end, he was killed somewhere in some kind of car crash. His funeral (which Naipaul missed) was conducted by another Hindu student from Trinidad in a suburban London graveyard, and Naipaul imagines its hodgepodge as the squalid inversion of postcolonial cosmopolitanism. Ramon merely fades into the colorless grey of London: "I had to imagine the scene: a man in a white dhoti speaking gibberish over the corpse of Ramon, making up rites among the tombstones and crosses of a more recent religion, the mean buildings of a London suburb low in the distance, against an industrial sky" (44).

The first chapter of *An Area of Darkness* presents Naipaul in London as hardly less a nonentity than Ramon. Naipaul wants to be a writer; he went to London to write. Ramon wanted to be a driver; he went to London to drive. What is the difference between a "ruling passion" for driving and one for writing? Doesn't writing—especially postcolonial writing in English—also rely on stolen parts from machines already in circulation? The policeman at Ramon's court appearance assumed that Naipaul too was there to answer a summons for thievery (41). But the pathos of both Ramon and Naipaul is that neither of them is really being summoned to anything. They have no function; their crimes as well as their skills are in a sense superfluous, aimless, undirected to any end beyond the activity itself.

The memorial to Ramon generalizes Naipaul's terror of nonentity in *An Area of Darkness* beyond the specific threat to him of India. Although the book at some points identifies loss of differentiation as the specific shock to Naipaul of discovering himself "faceless" in India, where he "might sink without a trace into that Indian crowd" (46), Ramon's equivalent fate in London identifies a more pervasive postcolonial anxiety that the trip to India, the narrative itself, and indeed, the whole of Naipaul's literary ambition are supposed to solve but instead only exacerbate: "recognition of my difference was necessary to me," he says of his distress upon arrival in Bombay. "I felt the need to impose myself, and didn't know how."

This is a boldly unself-flattering version of postcolonial identity crisis. For Naipaul, the problem of individuality is not so much *who* he is as *how* to impose his self, how to elicit recognition from others of his specialness. Naipaul refers to this "need" for self-assertion with a matter-of-fact melancholy, as if it were an elemental personal drive. But if recognition cannot be won by exotic ethnic multiplicity—either in India or London—and if even "genius," like Ramon's, sinks without a trace, what basis for imposing the self is more secure?

One hint in *An Area of Darkness* emerges still within Naipaul's account of Ramon's failure. What condemned Ramon to nonentity was his incapacity for judgment: "He was incapable of assessing the morality of actions; he was a person to whom things merely happened. . . . That section of the mind, if such a section exists, which judges and feels was in him a blank, on which others could write" (40). The metaphor of being written upon implies the opposite possibility that writing, as distinct from other ruling passions (such as driving), might develop the faculty of *assessment* as a defense against helplessness, against blankness. The need to impose the self might be satisfied through the writer's capacity to assess.

The opening digression about Ramon signals that *An Area of Darkness* is not going to be a "report" about India itself so much as the account of an urgent personal search for alternatives to the blank helplessness of a Hindu Trinidadian in London. Readers with a primary interest in India, however, might (and did) object to an ambitious writer's making "capital" for his literary identity at the expense of their nation's image in the world. There is enough pretension to authority about India in *An Area of Darkness* to suggest that Naipaul was confused himself about the hybrid genre of his narrative, an ambiguity that seemed settled in the wrong direction of greater pretense to authority by Naipaul's later, weaker companion volume of 1977, *India: A Wounded Civilization*. *An Area of Darkness* ends in Conradian fashion with the narrator locating within himself the negation he has identified as India; the title of the sequel less ambiguously externalizes the wound.

Naipaul's notorious judgmental obsessions in both *An Area of Darkness* and *India: A Wounded Civilization* feed on a version of the colonialist parallel between traditional India and medieval Europe, where harmonious but primitive social and religious orders perpetuated superstition and unquestioned ritual.[15] Naipaul darkens the tone of this commonplace analogy to emphasize the tragic necessity of loss for the development of judgment: "It [the medieval mind] had not developed a sense of history, which is a sense of loss; it had developed no true sense of beauty, which is a gift of assessment" (152).

To assess, to judge—this is the ethical and aesthetic capacity that affiliates Naipaul with post-Renaissance Western humanism while also promising him individual distinction in the midst of the Indian crowd that cannot recognize or appreciate his difference. In *An Area of Darkness*, Naipaul ceaselessly exercises his gift of assessment, as if it had become his own essential claim to individuality, a substitute for sensibility and a compensation for ethnic facelessness. In India, where the entire culture, according to Naipaul, still fails to develop the part of the brain that enables assessment, not only he but everyone is in danger of sinking without a trace, written on, virtually obliterated.[16]

Naipaul's term "assessment" narrows the loose, relativistic possibilities of judgment. What different cultures mean by judgment is open to comparative analysis. The English word "assessment" fixes a specifically quantitative and commercial dimension of judgment, implying also a value determined by direct, empirical examination. Naipaul's assessments of India in *An Area of Darkness* bring forward these connotations by their insistence on the authority of individual sight. Set against what he calls "collective Indian blindness," the traveler is in a favorable position to assess, because he directly *sees* what has become invisible to those who take it for granted.[17]

Assessment, of course, also involves evaluative comparison, generalization, measurement according to a standard. Objects in the marketplace have to be sized up in relation to other objects, sometimes to a whole stock that a single item represents. Naipaul's judgments in *An Area of Darkness* regularly affirm the superiority of this empirical, comparative, what may in rhetorical terms be called metonymic form of interpretation over the symbolic and ritual judgments that he sees as dominating medieval European and traditional Indian society.

While many critics have been legitimately outraged by Naipaul's brutal will to assess India on the evidence of his subjective and limited vision, less attention has been given to the impasses and collapses of judgment that make up the book's ironic, novelistic drama of failure. Two incompatible impulses coexist in the book and create its vital tension: there is Naipaul's drive to impose his self through his power of judgment, and there is at the same time the comic pathos of how the "gift of assessment" fails him during his trip. What Naipaul in retrospect calls "neurosis" in the book takes the form of a lurching between self-imposition through judgment and humiliation through ignominious error and defeat.

Naipaul's most grotesque misjudgments occur in the upsetting final episode, "The Village of the Dubes," which recounts how he brutally repudiated the ancestral village that ought to have been the culmination of his trip. The larger pattern of misapplied assessment is there in each of his separate acts of revulsion and devaluation, first in the village itself and later when he scorns the village elder who comes to his hotel with ritual offering of rice from the land his grandfather had redeemed after making some success in Trinidad. Naipaul by this point had already retreated from the village to a hotel in town, where he took further protection behind three official government interpreters, more like bodyguards, and also behind stubbornly literal assessments of what was being offered to him and what was being claimed. His recreation of the scene vividly exposes the revulsion he feels toward the village elder and toward the whole village as a hysterical breakdown of judgment. Deaf to the efforts of his interpreters to soothe him, he is driven to insist on the *worthlessness* of what is being offered:

"What do I do?" I asked the cadets. "I don't want thirty pounds of rice."

"He doesn't want you to take it all. You just take a few grains. Take the *parsad*, though."

I took a few grains of the poor rice, and took the *parsad*, grubby little grey beads of hard sugar, and placed them on the table. (273)

Empirical assessment has hardened into a symptom of helplessness and a defense against the terror of symbolic claims. This is the ignominy that ends the book in baffled rudeness and flight and in a spirit of what Naipaul himself terms "futility and impatience" (277).

At a more quotidian level, there are the semicomic crises pertaining to money that keep the commercial undertones of assessment going all through the book. Naipaul shows himself obsessed with the small sums of rupees he was constantly forced to overpay in India. No overcharge was too small to drive him into a frenzy that survives in the narrative at the edge of farce, paradoxically destroying the authority that the gift of assessment is supposed to secure. Money reduces him to the stereotype of the hapless and helpless tourist or the anonymous "Paying Guest," to borrow the title of a popular Indian film he mentions with horror. Naipaul presents a comic horror story of himself as the stock paying guest. The torture is the impossibility of right assessment. How, for example, could Naipaul assess whether he was being cheated or not on the morning boat in Srinigar? What was it worth? One rupee? Two? Twenty-five? Does the haggling over price possess other than symbolic meaning?

The dispute over the price of the Srinigar boat to the bus station when Naipaul was leaving Kashmir is a nice example of the symbolism concealed within ostensibly empirical assessment. All that is at stake is one or perhaps one and three-quarters rupees: "In four months I had established among the lakeside tongas that I never paid more than one and a quarter rupees for the ride into town. But the circumstances were extraordinary. I offered two. The tonga-wallah refused to touch the notes. I offered no more. He threatened me with his whip; and I found, to my surprise—it must have been the earliness of the hour—that I had seized him by the throat" (191). Murderous violence for one rupee! The excess is a caricature of touristic madness. The same is true of his humiliation and bafflement once he gets on the bus: his ostensibly devoted servant/guide Aziz, with tears of farewell in his eyes, assures him that he himself will "settle" with the tonga-wallah for the "correct" fare—three rupees, after all, because of the morning hour. "Don't worry, sahib. Goodbye" (192). Naipaul, now an anonymous *sahib*, is shamed into thrusting some uncounted extra rupee notes out to Aziz through the bus window. His farewell to Kashmir, scene of the most positive episodes of the book, thus deteriorates into the farcical anguish of the overpaying tourist. Is Aziz to be trusted in his claim on these rupees? "He took them. Tears were running down his cheeks. Even at that moment I could not be sure that he had ever been mine."

Naipaul's uncertainty about how much money he ought to have paid Aziz in Kashmir exemplifies his more general failure to possess the man and, even worse, his consequent inability to retain any self-possession. Futile and impatient assessments of petty sums—demanded, claimed, refused, until finally relinquished in bafflement and shame—almost entirely lose their empirical value in this postcolonial variant of servant-master farce.

What distinguishes Naipaul within this genre is his success in individualizing Aziz beyond the stock figure of Oriental servant. Here is a key example of how the pressure on Naipaul's authorial persona in *An Area of Darkness* gives vivid shape to a competing figure. As Naipaul's character descends into touristic stereotype, Aziz emerges more distinctly, in accord with what the book represents as an essentially competitive distribution of individuality. Naipaul's skill and candor in exposing the competitive dimension of individuality has come to seem to me increasingly significant in his writing. Whenever Naipaul puts two people together, one always seems to impose on the other. In the Kashmir chapters of *An Area of Darkness*, Aziz imposes.

As a character in a narrative, Aziz competes not only with Naipaul himself but also with his precursor, Aziz, in *A Passage to India*. The text evokes the connection especially in the episode where Aziz acts as guide for Naipaul's pilgrimage to the sacred Himalayan cave of Amarnath, recalling Forster's Aziz in his unhappy role as guide for his English guests to the Marabar caves. Naipaul's pilgrimage narrative is most vividly and amusingly a story of Aziz in action: all confidence and busyness, he handles with equal aplomb the ponies, the subordinate guides, and Naipaul (who of course is counting rupees). When one pony driver absconds, Aziz manages to triumph over disaster by performing the work of two men himself. Then, even though he is Muslim, he thoroughly enjoys his own first visit to the Hindu shrine, unfazed even by the unaccountable absence of the ice *lingam* that was the goal of the expedition.

Forster's Aziz, though also an eager, energetic guide, is incompetent in comparison with Naipaul's Kashmiri. Control of the action in the "Cave" section of *A Passage to India* shifts to the foreign visitors at the Marabar caves, despite their varieties of breakdown. Naipaul's confusion on the pilgrimage becomes insignificant in comparison with the distress of Forster's English ladies. When Naipaul backs out of the crowd entering the cave, no meditation as important as Mrs. Moore's on the meaninglessness of love dignifies his withdrawal. Naipaul just places himself in a squalid little corner near the shoe-guard, "in a litter of paper and wrappings and cigarette packets," where he registers only the stereotypical unbeliever's flatness that is a version of his entire experience in India: "at this moment of climax there came the flatness I had all along feared. And it was like the flatness, equally expected, equally feared, of my first day in Bombay. Pilgrimages were only for the devout. I concentrated on the Kashmiri's shoes, the coins on his scrap of newspaper" (179). Direct vision and money—the two foundations of Naipaul's authority in the book—here yield nothing except a meager distraction from inner emptiness. Even the generalization that "pilgrimages are for the devout" seems a false commonplace. After all, the Muslim Aziz has flowed easily into the cave with the Hindu crowd and then out, "tarnished but awed." Aziz does not suffer Naipaul's dizziness at the "spiralling, deliquescing logic" (180) with which the Hindus accept the absence of the ice *lingam* they have journeyed to see. "'You don't come for the *lingam*,' one man said. 'It's the spirit of the thing'" (179). Aziz, though Muslim, has for the moment entered into the Indian "spirit of the thing," while Naipaul shows himself fretting outside that the symbol he doesn't believe in has unaccountably melted away. Naipaul is good at rendering Aziz's attractive capacity to move in and out of collective experiences with admirable lack of apparent strain.

Aziz's adaptability becomes more menacing on the way down the mountain, when the faithless pony driver from the trip up reappears to be paid and Aziz mysteriously shifts allegiance, making Naipaul pay him (with a visible cut for Aziz himself). The trivial if brash transaction becomes a veritable crisis of identity for Naipaul: "Had it been planned days before? Had Aziz intended all his groans and complaints to lead to this, an extra five rupees? It seemed unlikely—that labour up Pissu Ghati had been real—but with Aziz I could no longer be sure. He seemed surer of me: he had taken a gift—in the long run my money—in my presence. . . . I was harmless. Faced with this assessment, I felt my will weaken. No, I wouldn't, simply for the sake of my pride, make a scene; when all was said and done, Aziz was my servant. It would be less troublesome to preserve my character, as he had read it, until we got back to Srinigar" (183).

This language recalls the portrait of Ramon in London at the beginning of the book, helpless because of his inability to assess things. On the way down from the pilgrimage, Aziz, by contrast, accurately assesses Naipaul's harmlessness and thus succeeds in profiting from a reading of his character that Naipaul feels helpless to resist. Aziz defeats Naipaul on his own terms, shrewdly assessing not only his purse but the limits of his will and pride. Naipaul as writer of *An Area of Darkness* in part reasserts his power to impose his self by the fierceness of his judgments of India. But he also dramatizes the weakness of this mental resource when exposed to the pressure of any particular experience during the trip. In the case of Aziz, Naipaul also recoups his own stature as a writer through a literary gift different from "assessment." I mean the novelist's power to write a character different from himself onto the page, thereby both ambiguously controlling the other yet yielding place to him at the same time.

The paradox of *India: A Million Mutinies Now* is that, for all its scores of interviews and all its elaborate deference to the particularities of the new India, no individual Indian is allowed to impose on Naipaul to the same extent that Aziz did in the earlier book; as a result few "characters" emerge vividly at all. If there were contests of power between Naipaul and the subjects of his interviews, most of them have been left out of *India: A Million Mutinies Now*. A pervasive flatness in the outcome of this worthy project calls into question its ostensible advance over the earlier book in both spirit and technique. In *An Area of Darkness*, Naipaul uses his own vulnerable character as a dramatic foil to set off the distinctiveness of Aziz; Naipaul in self-effacing equanimity drains life out of his subjects, too. Narrative poise in *India: A Million Mutinies Now* is preserved through a palpable distance from the Indian characters who now seem incapable of unsettling him no matter what they say or do. Some initial reviewers complained about this impression of constraint, almost of self-censorship. Firdaus Kanga, in the *Times Literary Supplement*, for example, misses the spontaneity of distress that enlivens *An Area of Darkness* and paradoxically inverts the idea of Naipaul's improvement through the image of his giving way now to a "dark temptation" of willful detachment.[18] Worse than neurotic panic to Kanga is the new book's "soporific monotone," what Karl Miller also complains of as "homogenized speech."[19]

Translation of all the Indian vernaculars of the interviews into flat standard English contributes to this inert effect in *India: A Million Mutinies Now*. As the most diverse Indian individuals follow one another through hundreds of pages, they are linguistically hardly distinguishable from each other or from Naipaul, and eventually they begin to fade and blur together. If this flatness is seen as deliberate strategy rather than mere lapse of skill, the apparent goal is to avoid the colonial reproduction of fractured Indianized English that some critics find so objectionably perpetuated in postcolonial Indo-English writing. As a practical problem, too, how would you solve the problem of this variety, where only some voices were speaking any form of English and the majority became a linguistic event for Naipaul only through whatever version of English was offered by his interpreters?

The standardized English, however, also carries thematic importance in *India: A Million Mutinies Now*. These voices, raised above linguistic deviation, embody Naipaul's commitment to abstract from all the diverse Indian figures, and even from their separate manifestations of rage, nostalgia, and revolt, a new "liberation of spirit." Naipaul's own language in the linking commentaries displays his effort to contain diversity within a single vocabulary of Western humanism, with repeated phrases, such as "the wholeness and humanism of the values to which all Indians now felt they could appeal"

(518) or "the concepts—of law and freedom and wide human association—which give men self-awareness and strength" (398). In principle, Naipaul now substitutes a more generous humanist embrace for his earlier rejections. Yet in practice, the humanist affirmation sounds formulaic, standardized, and as alien to the voices he records as the standard English of their speech. The caste and communalist passions that constitute the content of so many of the interviews, for example, manifestly contradict phrases about "wide human association." Some of the interviews, even in their mediated and standardized language, defy Naipaul's values to the point that he cannot restrain his disapproval. Assessment creeps back into the text; Naipaul's careful poise becomes frayed, and when he is willing to let this vulnerability to specific challenge show, much-needed drama enters the book .

Two examples suffice. The first is an interview with a rival model of postcolonial authorship, a poet called Namdeo, well known around Bombay also as the founder of the movement of former Untouchables called the Dalit Panthers. Even though you could hardly guess from the voice translated from Marathi into standard English that this is a poet famous for his pungent street idiom, Namdeo still comes across as a man of unusual complexity, charm, and personal power—also clearly a difficult, elusive, and probably very manipulative character. At the time of the interview, he is ill with venereal disease, and his political movement has all but collapsed. Our first knowledge of him and of the kind of pressure he will exert is that he stands Naipaul up at their first appointment, leaving his wife to represent him. A striking figure in her own right, Mallika, the wife, has published a best-selling book (in Marathi) about her tormented marriage, whose title is translated as *I Want to Destroy Myself.* Naipaul gets to hear all about her book and about the marriage itself in Mallika's three-hour recitation of the splendor and misery of her life with Namdeo.

The Dalit political leader and literary figure thus enters the narrative through the wife's glossy story. Naipaul both allows Mallika to introduce Namdeo through her best-selling tale of passion and marital torment, and at the same time holds her melodrama of romantic suffering at a distance from his own measured and cool prose. It is through Mallika's account that we glimpse Namdeo's charisma as poet of the brothel, as political leader of the downtrodden, and not least as sexual suitor. She tells how he won her away from her respectable family but then imprisoned her in a life degraded by drink, violence, brothel women, and the despair of his failed political movement. She is very willing to tell all, in the style that won her so much success with the Marathi reading public. At the same time that Naipaul is attracted by her (he keeps mentioning her delicate arms and gestures), he also scorns her romantic version of a passion that he deflatingly labels a "schoolgirl romance" (105). Nothing could be further from Naipaul's unimpassioned reticence in this book than Mallika's self-display. Naipaul deglamorizes

Mallika's struggle between love and freedom in the marriage by reducing it to mere "obsession" (109). After reporting that Mallika pursued him the following day with a six-page letter explaining her whole story again, Naipaul drily remarks, "But she had, in fact, said it all when we had met" (111).

A curious competition enters Naipaul's narrative with Mallika and then, more directly, with Namdeo. They are postcolonial Indian "stars," albeit past their heyday. Their terms of stardom repel Naipaul but also resist his control as effectively as Aziz in the earlier book resisted his assessment of costs. With Namdeo, the tension belongs not to master-servant comedy but to the equally recognizable competition between celebrities: these are rival stars. Namdeo is harder to handle than Mallika, so it starts to become quite unclear in the chapter who is going to control the occasion and exactly who is using whom. A few days after the no-show appointment, Naipaul and his interpreter/guide solicitously attend a prostitutes' meeting organized by Namdeo, still in hopes of obliging him enough to get their interview. Namdeo has moved quite ahead of them in planning, however, with notices in the Bombay press that V. S. Naipaul will be the "chief guest" at the event. The embarrassed Naipaul becomes a character in Namdeo's drama as news photographers capture him being garlanded by the women of the brothels. Only then does Namdeo grant the interview, in a room where the newspapers featuring Naipaul's photograph are all laid out.

Naipaul's flat style mutes the comic drama of this contest, while still displaying it. When the interview finally takes place, Namdeo speaks (in Marathi) at great length about his poetry, his politics, his painful "Untouchable" village past (113), his present disappointments. For reasons either of deference or rapt attention, the interpreter, Charu, listens for a very long time without interrupting for translation. Since there is also another (unidentified) listener, nodding in shared and intimate response to Namdeo's Marathi story, Naipaul is left to be a spectator at a show from which he is entirely excluded. And when he finally gets his translation, he curiously sustains his exclusion. He tells Namdeo that he cannot understand his apparent nostalgia for a past of so many humiliations. Why has he not simply left it behind? Namdeo answers in terms of his literary vocation: "as a poet and writer he wishes to search out his own roots," Naipaul flatly reports. "Pain has always been part of his psychology" (115).

The cultural crosscurrents here are confusing. Namdeo's involvement in his pain brings to mind a version of the sensibility that Naipaul has sweepingly dismissed as a legacy of imperialism. The lines of postcolonial genealogy have become completely crossed here. Namdeo explains, for example, that he can read if not speak English and that from his youth he was drawn to artists like Bob Dylan and Eldridge Cleaver, Leroi Jones and Allen Ginsberg—also Rimbaud, Rilke, Baudelaire, and Lorca. His list of models suggests the same porousness of postcolonial cultural boundaries conveyed by the very name Dalit Panthers (modeled on the American Black Panthers). Like Mallika's popularity, Namdeo's power to hold his Indian listeners suggests how the Western legacy of "sensibility" has taken on new coloring in Indian political and popular culture. Namdeo and Mallika hold their Marathi audience by Indianized versions of Western cultural models: they share intimate narratives of personal pain with a group in ways that allow their private stories to become compelling public testimonies.

Naipaul rejects affiliation with this rival version of postcolonial literary success. It is Naipaul who preserves and even exaggerates the impression of Otherness. His professed incomprehension seems due less to respect for differences of caste and culture than to rival artistic commitments, rival choices, even rival conceptions of humanism. Naipaul makes no reference to his larger project to identify Indian pursuits of freedom when he labels Namdeo a "prisoner" of his incomprehensible past. In the interview, he expresses pity for Namdeo because he is unable "to withdraw, to settle for ease" (116). As if sensing and also rejecting this "mature" and "sane" standard in the mind of Naipaul, Namdeo breaks out into one (English) line of humorous self-depreciation for the losses that have accompanied his own fame. Naipaul allows the inflected English to stand in this one remark, so that it oddly darts out to taunt Naipaul's own new persona, as well as his advice: "*Now I'm too much normal and gentleman*" (118).

Naipaul refuses Namdeo the last word in his story, however. The chapter ends with Naipaul authoritatively deflating Namdeo's romantic individuality by generalizing the man, the house, the wife all together into "an expression of the old internal cruelty of that poverty: people at the bottom, full of emotion, with no politics at that moment, just rejecting rejection" (119).

There is something shocking about the covert aggressiveness of this narrative transformation of Namdeo into an emblem of collective impoverishment. For all Naipaul's sympathy of tone, he is in effect erasing the vivid individual character he has himself just finished creating on the page. Our sense of Namdeo's elusive combination of success and failure, intelligence and emotion, cruelty and disappointment, sincerity and opportunism, all comes from Naipaul's own writing, but at the end, Naipaul shuts off the ambiguous expressivity of his own full Namdeo story by pushing it all into the huge, abysmal category of impoverishment. The interview ends under the control of Naipaul's assessment, but with much less acknowledgment of authorial aggression than in *An Area of Darkness*.

A similar twist of judgment shows Naipaul turning more subtly against another vivid individual figure in *India: A Million Mutinies Now*: a Brahmin ex-clerk in Madras, named Sugar, whom Naipaul telephones as a friend from his Indian trip of the 1960s. Like Namdeo, Sugar, in 1989, is ailing and diminished. He has been forced to retire from his modest clerical job and hardly has the physical strength to leave his bedsitting room. He is also helplessly at the mercy of the streams of rather prosperous people who come regularly to his "little blue sanctuary" (215), the temple he has set up in his room, where he dispenses holy counsel, domestic advice, and (so his visitors affirm) an exceptionally calm atmosphere conducive to meditation.

The first impressive point about Sugar, however, has less to do with his private sorrows or public duties than with his relation to Naipaul himself. Naipaul records how detailed a memory Sugar retains from their time together twenty-eight years before. Naipaul presents his own memory, by contrast, as remarkably porous. Here as elsewhere in the book, Naipaul seems almost to pride himself on his power to empty his mind through writing. He tells that once his Indian experiences became transferred to the page in *An Area of Darkness* details like those mentioned by Sugar—how Naipaul ate pumpkin every day in Madras in 1962, how he engaged in long, serious talks with Sugar's father—no longer crowded his mind. Naipaul seems to associate this efficiency of mental life with prosperous busyness and healthy freedom, while Sugar's kind of retentiveness is made to seem merely pitiable: "It was flattering to be remembered in this way, in these details, after so long. I felt it also spoke of a life plain to the point of tears" (216).

As with Namdeo, the condescending terms of Naipaul's pity reduce Sugar's humanity. Moreover, Naipaul does not quite make the connection between Sugar's kind of memory and the attraction others have to him as counselor and guide. Sugar's attentive and retentive perception of human detail presents another version of what one might want to call humanism, but to Naipaul here, it seems too confining and burdensome. Naipaul wants humanism to bring strength, but Sugar's gifts make him sick: "I can sit there and read your face, give full details," he says to Naipaul. "But after that I will get a headache. I will suffer for two days" (241). When the Indian subject confronts Naipaul with signs of a "gift" that enfeebles, Naipaul withdraws his own voice to the side of health. Taking on the role of counselor himself, he advises Sugar, "You will have to get rid of this gift," ignoring the point that Sugar's empathy, however debilitating, defines his vocation, his identity, and the entire foundation of his human associations. The recommendation to get rid of empathic gifts, like pity for imprisoning memories, discloses the recurrent negation in Naipaul's imagining of freedom.

Before leaving Madras, Naipaul receives from Sugar a gesture of friendship in the form of an intimate observation and question: "When I saw you in the Himalayas in 1962," he remarks, "your face was *bright*. It was one of the things that attracted me to you. Now you look troubled. Has it to do with your life? Your work?" (279). Naipaul includes this gentle challenge to the mature sanity of his persona in this whole narrative, but he also shows himself brushing it off: "I was more troubled in 1962. But I was younger. Like you." Naipaul will not enlist in the circle of Sugar's advisees, and, though he may acknowledge the shared human fate of aging, he is quick to reinstate the distance between himself—more mature, normal, and less troubled than be-fore—and Sugar: a weak man near death, "in the little space that he had made his own . . . the little space he was soon to vacate."

In these examples, as in *India: A Million Mutinies Now* as a whole, Naipaul's mobility as a traveler neither obsessed with his own past nor enfee-bled by other people's needs and woes takes on the force of an argument identifying humanism with the categories of health, strength, and freedom. Naipaul withdraws into baffled uneasiness whenever his Indian subjects show signs of being unfree, even when their forms of bondage follow recog-nizably appealing human patterns. The nostalgia in the Dalit Panther's rec-ollections of his impoverished and humiliating past, for example, has enough analogy in Western literature and life to seem rather less incomprehensibly pitiable than Naipaul implies when he calls him "the prisoner of an Indian past no one outside could truly understand" (116). While the degree and even the kind of deprivation and degradation in the Mahar community may exceed an outsider's understanding, the dynamic of nostalgia for pain that one has at the same time struggled to escape offers precisely the point where Dalit particularity might connect to wider human experience.

It is likewise less difficult than Naipaul implies to understand how the Brahmin ex-clerk Sugar may at once love and regret his burdens as holy counselor. When Naipaul simply labels him a "prisoner of his reputation" (278), he peculiarly belittles an entirely familiar and estimable role in a com-munity, excluding it from his category of human freedom. Naipaul's own mobility as a world traveler without heavy baggage of nostalgia, resentment, or any irrational attachments is left to embody the highest kind of freedom.[20] Yet Naipaul the interviewer ends up seeming strangely adrift and isolated in an abstraction of freedom that corresponds to very little, not only in the In-dian lives presented but in most actual particular lives anywhere.[21] Perhaps Naipaul is not meant to be a travel writer or interviewer, for all the energy he has put into this work. He is too irritable, too inflexible; he doesn't convey enough pleasure in the unpredictable flow of conversation with ordinary people in what he disparages as their "little" spaces. The colonial adminis-trator Sleeman displays an entirely different engagement in dialogues with Indians, despite all his interfering involvement in reforming the conditions of their lives. But Sleeman was more than a traveler in India; he enjoyed being there and wrote his book after two decades of residence.

The most dramatically unstable interviews in *India: A Million Mutinies Now* open universalizing definitions of humanism, as well as individuality, to complications beyond what Naipaul chooses to affirm in principle. In failing to meet Naipaul's standard of "freedom," yet succeeding to counterassert their own commitments, figures such as Sugar, Namdeo, and Mallika expose the weakness of Naipaul's conception of humanism. Their resistance to him establishes their individuality within communities too small, too stifling to win his regard. But their perceptions, and the hints given of responses by other Indians to them, suggest that particularity and principle need not be at odds as much as Naipaul's humanistic formulae presume. His bookish idea of "wholeness" and "wide human association" lacks the texture of actual life by comparison with Namdeo's refusal to be cowed by an important foreign visitor or Sugar's feelings of obligation and his memories (even of a brighter, homier Naipaul from the past, invisible in *An Area of Darkness*). When Naipaul allegorizes figures such as Namdeo and Sugar into emblems of Indian impoverishment or constriction, he ineffectually moves to impose power over individuals who are able to resist him with strengths developed in their own "little" lives.

It is to Naipaul's credit as a writer in *India: A Million Mutinies Now* that he does display, if only intermittently, postcolonial authors—himself as well as Namdeo—not simply floating above public situations nor simply embodying them but also striving to manipulate, control, and (in his own term) impose themselves on the world. The best of Naipaul's Indian interviews represent competing ways of imposing the self in order to elicit recognition of difference as well as commonality. There is conspicuous irony in Mallika's title, *I Want to Destroy Myself*, because her book so blatantly belongs to a familiar genre of literary self-display. Naipaul's own vacillation between self-effacement and self-assertion shows comparable, if less vulgar, ironies. As an expert in the anxious and often undignified manifestations of the troubled ego, Naipaul has the basis for more imaginative affiliation with Indian and other people than he easily acknowledges.

8

Epilogue: Pankaj Mishra and Postcolonial Cosmopolitanism

Thanks to the World Wide Web, readers from all over may now converse, even in "real time," with authors in India and elsewhere. The shorthand style and the cryptic pseudonyms of e-mail obscure identities and locations. Thus Pankaj Mishra, the young Indian journalist, literary critic, and author of a first novel, *The Romantics*, fielded random questions from Delhi on a Saturday in February 2000, in a chat room sponsored by Rediff Music Shop.[1] In the online conversation, one interlocutor who calls himself "Biblio" rather aggressively remarks that it is ironic for Mishra to call himself a critic and yet dismiss criticism of his own novel.[2] Mishra, unfazed, comes back with a tempered though far from humble reply: "Not anyone who gets to write for newspapers can call himself a critic. It takes long years of reading and reflection and writing before you can call yourself a critic." Since Mishra himself was hardly past age thirty in 2000 and had begun to publish literary criticism in Indian newspapers as a student in his early twenties, something of an assumed persona may be felt in the air of great experience and maturity in this reply. Or, it may express aspiration as much as claim to accomplishment. Mishra stands out among postcolonial critics for the wide range of literary reference he seeks for his judgments.

Most of Mishra's questioners online do address him as already a model of success whose strategies and secrets they want to know. Someone somewhere called "Spinoza" inquires directly: "WHAT IS MOST URGENT TO YOU, MR MISHRA?" Three seconds later, Mishra responds: "Dear Spinoza, the urge to express a particular experience of the world which is something all writers share." Next comes "Farooq," with a variation on the same question, in lower-case style: "Pankaj, I'm sure u are struck by a lot of ideas . . . how do you select one that finally makes a novel?" Mishra's immediate reply suggests that he has at hand certain formulations to serve interlocutors who order a credo from him: "Dear Farooq, the idea which seems most likely to yield a true impression of life." After an hour, he cheerily ends the chat: "Got to go now. Thanks everyone. I greatly enjoyed this."

The Rediff chat room with Mishra is enjoyable to read, also; everyone sounds so young and eager—Spinoza, Farooq, and the others, with monikers such as Hero, Daytripper, Ingenue, and Zeus. Even Pankaj, despite his reference to long-maturing experience, sounds more like an older brother than a formidable Author imposing himself from on high, like Naipaul in his cantankerous *Salmagundi* interview of 1979.[3]

Yet there are also intimations of a more serious and controversial aspiration in Mishra's self-definition. Although "a particular experience of the world" and "a true impression of life" are neither original nor manifestly controversial goals for a writer, there are hidden barbs in Mishra's friendly replies, recognizable to readers of the outspoken and independent work that has quickly established him as a writer to reckon with on many fronts. "A true impression of life" is what Mishra's political journalism accuses the mainstream Indian press and its favored politicians of suppressing or avoiding; "a particular experience of the world" is what he finds missing in the derivative Indian novels in English that capitalize on Rushdie's Indianization of magic realism. His own novel, *The Romantics*,[4] together with his daring reportage from Kashmir and from rural North India, seeks truth and particularity through techniques of ironic realism out of fashion in both India and the West at the turn of the millennium. His good-natured ease on the World Wide Web notwithstanding, Mishra is a dissenter and a maverick within India because he dares to affiliate his writing with aspirations and values that risk being dismissed as out of date and unpatriotic, to boot.

Mishra more specifically speaks to the concerns of this book in the way his writing in every genre explores the difficulties of achieving truth and particularity about the colonial past and the postcolonial present of the subcontinent. Like Subaltern and other left-wing historians, Mishra traces and deplores the continuities between the British colonial regime and the native elites that have ruled India since independence. Yet at the same time that he shares the revulsion of many radical intellectuals toward the greed and callousness of the new global consumer economy that has left the vast majority of the subcontinent's population in the same impoverished misery as before, Mishra's radicalism eschews neo–Marxist terminology, along with the Utopian hopes it carries. His reportage skeptically inspects all mythologies of heroism and demonology. Against the jingoistic public rhetoric that he identifies as promoting an Indian dynamic of fear and aggression, he urges closer imaginative attention to the small tragedies of individuals and communities, as they are at once caught in longstanding historical struggles and dislocated by the loss of traditional forms of solace and security. Mishra's journalism reaches across many contested boundaries in contemporary India, humanizing figures stereotyped as demons or saviors in the media and in some contemporary fiction. Mishra's kind of cosmopolitanism is not a popular form of cultural mobility in current Indian public discourse, even at a time when American clothes, music, business schools, travel, and the Internet are the increasing norm of an affluent middle class.

Mishra has been willing to risk unpopularity and controversy in the service of what he insists on as the particularity of Indian experience and true impressions of Indian life. More than the debatable or provisional accomplishment of any single one of his pieces so far, this still unfolding career affirms an important status for English writing about contemporary India that forcefully engages the most ferocious and intractable realities of the subcontinent with complex and honest uncertainty. Rather than the phantasmagoria of Rushdie, so influential in the past two decades, Mishra prefers the model of the Russian realists of the nineteenth century—Pushkin, Turgenev, Tolstoy, Chekhov—while also recognizing the huge handicap that the use of the English language poses for any Indian writer who attempts to influence a national culture the way the Russian nineteenth-century writers succeeded in doing through conscious development of a modern Russian literary language. It is difficult to predict how disabling the linguistic choice of English will be in the long run for Mishra and for other Indian writers who follow his lead. That his language may skew his relationship to his material and at the same time make him all too directly communicative to "foreign" readers is a consequence of this language choice that Mishra glances at but has not yet fully explored in his work.

The language issue for Mishra does come up in literary essays that reflect on the larger problem of self-expression for the colonial and postcolonial author. Reviewing *Between Father and Son*, the correspondence between V. S. Naipaul (in England) and his father, Seepersad (in Trinidad), during the 1950s, Mishra quotes Seepersad's fatherly encouragement to his son's still unformed literary ambition: "Only see that you have succeeded in saying exactly what you want to say—without showing off; with utter brave sincerity—and you will have achieved style because you will have been yourself" (15).[5] Mishra's persuasive rendering of Seepersad's own sincerity in these letters minimizes the Polonius effect of the father's advice. In the colonial context of the Naipaul family, a poignant irony nevertheless informs the precept "to thine own self be true," because, as Mishra explains, the arduous creation of what could be called a "self" for writing remained Seepersad's lifelong project as well as 'Vidia's.' For all his paternal generosity, a "self" to express and a style of English in which to express it were gifts that Seepersad could not send to his son in England through the mail. As I discuss in chapter 7, the "enigma" of self eventually became the central theme of V. S. Naipaul's writing career, and his most enduring contribution to colonial and postcolonial writing in English.

Seepersad Naipaul impresses Mishra for his own extraordinary self-creation: he was a "self-taught man, reading and writing in isolation": "He was struggling to keep afloat most of his life, struggling to define himself, acquire selfhood and culture, and at the same time have a job and possess that small bit of security and comfort that would make the world a less painful place for himself and his large but close-knit family of eight, thrown together by the break-up of the network of extended Hindu families and the rebuffs of wealthier relatives" (14). Mishra's review recognizes in the letters the poignancy of the father's willingness to sacrifice almost anything to spare Naipaul some of that struggle, and the equal poignancy of the student Naipaul's "fear and panic and helplessness" at sensing only a "raw unmade self" within, utterly inadequate to the confident, worldly, apparently serene sensibility he was identifying as the necessary style of the writer's self in this first encounter with imperial Britain. Faced with an absence of self, and with a remote and impossible model of style, what could the standard of sincerity mean for a youth from Trinidad at Oxford?

The influence on Mishra of V. S. Naipaul's own mature style can be felt in the review's long cumulative sentences, which backstitch and then move forward in sympathetic meditation on struggles that hold the mind back from simple declarations or assertions. Mishra introduces into his review quotations and paraphrases from later autobiographical passages by Naipaul, especially from *The Enigma of Arrival*, where Naipaul revisits the anxieties of his early English years with a fullness not yet possible psychologically or stylistically in the early letters.[6] Meditation on the identity problems of the postcolonial writer was an activity Naipaul only gradually learned to do, and that Mishra can do so precociously in part because of Naipaul's earlier stylistic achievment.

Mishra turns in other essays to related versions of struggle in authors dislocated imaginatively even while geographically at home within India. An appreciative retrospective review of the novelist R. K. Narayan lingers over the same challenge of self-creation through the process of developing an English-language style.[7] In the case of the South Indian novelist, less given than Naipaul to autobiographical narrative, Mishra relies more on speculation:

the hurdles on [Narayan's] way would have been immense: disadvantages unique to writers from limited societies, who work without a received tradition, who are the first of their kind. These writers have to overcome their intellectual upbringing before they can learn to look directly at their world and find a voice that matches their experience. The disdain for one's own language and literature taught at school and college; the forced initiation into a foreign language; the groping for knowledge through an abstract maze of other cultures and worlds—these are things that can make for a lifetime of confusions and ambivalence. (44)

As often in Naipaul's writing, the modal auxiliary—"would have been"—shifts Mishra's narration of the past into meditative speculation,[8] creating bonds between past and present in a history that becomes a continuing, on-going story. Mishra dissociates his own writing from the fixed boundaries of political and cultural fundamentalists: "who try to reject this experience alto-gether by turning to what they think is an uncontaminated past: the time be-fore foreign rule when the world was whole and everything was in its place."

The example of pioneers such as Naipaul and Narayan, plus the success of another whole generation of Indian writers in English since the 1980s, is frequently taken to indicate the lowering of hurdles for new, aspiring writers. But for Mishra, obstacles to a direct English-language voice to match Indian experience have multiplied rather than diminished during the nation's half-century of independence. Postcolonial hypersensitivity to Western response is one problem; the deterioration of Indian English as an instrument of criti-cal thought is another; widespread disillusion with the earlier Indian ideal of cosmopolitan humanism is a third.

These obstacles become explicit in a provocative essay written by Mishra on the occasion of Nirad Chaudhuri's one-hundreth birthday in 1997.[9] With more self-distancing than in the reviews of the Naipauls and of Narayan, Mishra uses the Chaudhuri centennial to bury the Bengali Renaissance ideal of a synthesis between British and Indian culture that remained Chaudhuri's lifelong commitment. Doomed to failure, in Mishra's view, by internal con-tradictions and errors, such as exaggerated regard for the British contribu-tion to Indian culture, Chaudhuri represents for Mishra in this essay the anachronistic "Last Englishman" in both India and England. Any contem-porary renewal of the Bengali ideal seems fantastical now, especially through the mediation of the English language, which Mishra here discounts as noth-ing but "the language of power and privilege" for a corrupt ruling class and for "extravagantly ballyhooed" writers who neither represent nor can com-municate with an Indian population still suffering "grievous social and psy-chological damage" from the colonial legacy. Rather than a resource for re-form, the English language in India in this essay appears a continuing form of coercion: "Forced to learn a pidgin form of English—routinely burlesqued by British travel writers—and forced, in the process, to unlearn their first languages, millions of Indians dwell in a permanent twilight zone, exiled from the world of complex perceptions and responses that proficiency in any one language would provide."[10]

"Both Indians and Englishmen have moved on," Mishra declares at the end of the Chaudhuri essay, "further away from each other and their own cul-tural ideals of the past." But moved on to what? To what community of cul-ture can an Indian writer in English such as Mishra move on? Even if he were heroically to resist the "ballyhoo" of international publicity that has attended his own publications in London and New York, and even though his own flex-ible prose does succeed in shedding what he calls Chaudhuri's "refined Victo-rianism," the felt absence of any contemporary literary community for him in

India shadows Mishra's ambitions with a sense of isolation that not even the chattiness of Rediff on the Net dissipates: "there is no shared literary culture here the way there is in England," he replies to one query in the chat: "And, yes, the fact of this dependence upon the West plays a role in thwarting the sense of community you speak of."

In a later essay about Chaudhuri, a memorial written on the occasion of the older man's death in 1999, Mishra repeats but softens his earlier critique of the Bengali ideal in order to pay tribute to Chaudhuri's singular accomplishments: his resolute candor, his perpetual "battle with all conventional pieties and received wisdom," his intellectual precision, and his "exact and vivid prose" are here recognized as characteristics to admire, especially in *The Autobiography of an Unknown Indian*, which Mishra calls a "masterpiece of descriptive and analytic writing."[11] Yet Chaudhuri's loneliness and the cost of his isolation in a final crankiness make him more a cautionary than a tutelary example. If inadequate proficiency in any language exiles millions of Indians from "the world of complex perceptions and responses," in Mishra's view, Chaudhuri's century-long cultivation of cosmopolitan culture entails another kind of exile, from contemporary India, and from modern realities more generally at the end of the twentieth century. Mishra's critical awareness of alienated isolation as a trap for the writer differentiates him from the aggressive elitism of Chaudhuri or Naipaul. He seems determined to influence rather than withdraw in distaste from India's contemporary struggles, a determination backed so far by his resistance to the lure of easier accommodation abroad.

The great nineteenth-century Russian realists, Mishra observes, achieved a literature "in whose unfamiliar reflections a nation slowly learns to recognize itself."[12] "Self-awareness," so formulated, goes beyond the personal to a more general and collective cultural goal; the writer's self-acquired culture should ultimately serve the nation by confronting it with unfamiliar reflections of itself. Tension between participation and withdrawal is acute, however, for the cosmopolitan Indian writer must call upon linguistic skills and habits that Mishra judges to be declining in India, not only in English but in any single language: "A great chasm exists today," Mishra laments, in a tone close to Chaudhuri's own melancholy, "between the shrinking minority that possesses a language—their own or English—and people who just get by, for whom the self and the world lies inaccessible beyond a bewildering linguistic fog."[13]

What might be labeled Mishra's intellectual and linguistic snobbery resembles Chaudhuri's in being directed not primarily at the still illiterate rural peasantry but even more sharply at the Indian middle class, with its crude greed and self-serving rhetoric. The increasing size and power of this class in India's Americanized global economy keep Mishra more susceptible to the dyspepsia of a grandparental generation than any thirty-year-old might like to acknowledge. In his first published book, the travel narrative *Butter Chicken in Ludhiana*, a rather fastidious young Mishra finds his only camaraderie on a raucous bus out of Simla with an outraged elderly Bengali Communist, Mr. Banerji, who after frantically failing to "stop the music" polluting the bus, is reduced to helpless mutterings to his wife about "vulgar," "obscene," "degraded" Indian culture. Mishra's narrative makes Mr. Banerji a pathetically comic figure on this bus, contorted in a physical and mental position "too painful to maintain."[14] But he is the sole passenger with whom Mishra is drawn to converse.

Although now eager to dissociate himself from certain of his own postures in the travel book published in 1995, Mishra's ambivalence toward the earlier intellectual elite in India continues in other of his writings. The narrator, Samar, in *The Romantics*, a North Indian youth (like Mishra), implictly evokes the Bengali Renaissance in his broader allusion to a pre-Gandhian nationalist vision of India's regeneration through "direct and vigorous contact with the best of what was being thought and said in the West" (75). If Samar (or Mishra) learned that Arnoldian language at Allahabad University, it was presumably not through the regular curriculum or student community, since in his representation, the Indian university in the 1980s had become virtually a war zone, with clashes between students and police and violence by clandestine forces without any authorized academic status. Poor and desperate petitioners for the Civil Service exams—"bored, cynical, criminalish undergraduates" (75)—dominated the academic population.[15] The cosmopolitan intellectual ideals and standards that had made Allahabad University famous as the "Oxford of the East" belonged to a forgotten past: "You could get details in books. As for the present, you had to figure it out for yourself. You had to know where you stood and you had to be careful."

The first-person narrative of *The Romantics* follows the ultimately ineffectual efforts of a bookish Indian youth to figure out where he can stand in the India of the late 1980s. In the end, Samar flees, like Salim in *A Bend in the River*, Naipaul's novel of 1979, which hovers very close behind *The Romantics*.[16] Naipaul has nowhere to send his Afro-Indian narrator except out onto a riverboat, away from the African town's violence. Samar, by contrast, finds refuge at the border of India, in a remote primary school for Tibetan Buddhist children in the Himalayan town of Dharamshala. But with no evidence presented of either Samar's vocation for teaching or involvement with the Tibetan community in exile, this resolution seems merely a diminished secularized version of the age-old Indian holy retreat. Samar becomes a kind of *sadhu*, though as a storyteller he more closely resembles Naipaul's bewildered Salim and, behind him, Conrad's Marlow in *Heart of Darkness*, who in storytelling posture if not belief is said to resemble a Buddha.[17]

Mishra's Samar belongs to a tradition of dislocated and disillusioned modern narrators whose reports of colonial or postcolonial futility have a wisdom made ambiguous by intimations of the narrator's own weakness. Mishra's Samar has the advantage of his youth (he is still in his twenties at the end), but that only shifts the ambiguity, since retreat to the Himalayas overlaps with the itinerary of the perpetually adolescent Western "dropouts" who pass through the novel on their vague searches for one or another kind of Eastern enlightenment. Their inchoate hopes and disappointments in the once holy city of Benares form the novel's most obvious irony. While the Himalayas retain a spiritual aura for Mishra that is now missing from noisy, decadent, dangerous Benares, Samar's withdrawal from books, human relationships, and experience itself in Dharamshala may appear more a melancholy impasse than an arrival at deeper wisdom.

Samar is a more intellectual seeker at the beginning of *The Romantics* than his Western friends or than the Western model the novel explicitly evokes, Frederic Moreau in Flaubert's *Sentimental Education*, a book (in English translation) that Samar carries around (along with Edmund Wilson's commentary) and recommends to others in the novel's first half.[18] Samar at the start is a precocious and obsessive reader, seeking wisdom in books: "With each book, I entered into what I felt to be an exalted bond with its writer, to whom I gave all the care and attentiveness I could not bring to human relationships" (62). The narrative follows Samar from Allahabad to Benares, where solitary reading in the university library remains his only activity, until complications begin with his attraction to an intriguing group of youngish Europeans and Americans who for diverse reasons have also taken up semipermanent residence in Benares. To the Westerners, Samar is exotic as an Indian "autodidact": "he wants to read everything," remarks the Englishwoman, Miss West; the Frenchwoman, Catherine, who will eventually become Samar's romantic distraction, seems equally impressed. When Samar meets Catherine, she is fully occupied by her love affair with a sitar player named Anand and with her project of making him a musical success in Paris. An Indian autodidact is another Indian "type" that interests her, if only briefly.

The Romantics ironically traces the ineffectuality of book reading to prepare a timid young Indian autodidact for the perils of French romance. Samar is not an Emma Bovary, intoxicated with romantic fantasy from books. Mishra draws more on Flaubert's later, more withering portrait of aimless provincial young men in Paris after 1848, made susceptible to sentimental obsessions by their thwarted and empty prospects. The analogy between post-1848 Paris and post-independence India is what draws Samar to Flaubert. Mishra goes further in the tradition of Flaubert by including his "hero" in the novel's irony.

The affair with Catherine occurs on an outing in the Himalayan resort area of Mussorie, when the third member of the expedition fails to show up. No hallucinations of rape follow from this little adventure, though Mishra may have *A Passage to India* in mind as an earlier ironic narrative of intercultural fiasco in the form of sexual confusion. But the spirit of Flaubert more than that of Forster presides over Samar's incurable despair after Catherine quickly turns back to her sitar player. By the end, Catherine's sitar player project has also failed, and she (like the other international visitors in Samar's friendship group) have all more or less conventionally adapted to their native cultures. The novel lingers, however, on Samar's obsession with every banal phase of despair, renewed hope, and restless fantasy. Not a minute is left for reading books, so absorbing to Samar is his commonplace interior drama. Critics of Mishra's clichéd writing in this portion of the novel bypass the Flaubertian irony: "I would be suffused by a strange sense of anticipation; the sense that there might be something, someone—a letter, a person, a telegram,—waiting inside, who or which at one stroke would change my life forever and, leaping across all the intermediate steps, transport me instantly into a world cleansed free of such exacting cares and anxieties" (143).

If Samar's romantic misadventure represents a degraded cosmopolitanism, his recovery through withdrawal follows an equally banal Indian response to the discovery of *maya*, a term that bridges Indian and European experiences of disillusion. Mishra's skepticism about the aura of sanctity still attached to traditional Indian attitudes toward withdrawal appears more directly in his sympathetic but still critical remarks on this recurrent "non-resolution" in Narayan's novels: "the point at which you see his characters finally turning away from the challenges of self-creation and individuality—which every developing nation imposes on its people—and seeking reabsorption into the passivity and sterility of old India" ("Narayan," 47). In Narayan's novels, recognition of the illusory nature of what they have desired leads characters to accept and even welcome their losses. In *The Romantics*, irony undercuts the "old" Indian solution. Samar's widower father, who at the beginning of the novel seems to have followed orthodox teaching by withdrawal for his final years to the *ashram* of Aurobindo at Pondicherry, turns out to have settled in a situation rather like a pleasant retirement community. Instead of embracing holy solitude, he is linked now in a dependent but fairly content union with a strong-minded widow, more companionable and competent than his extravagantly pious wife ever was.

Samar proves less adaptable than his father to the vicissitudes of his life. When he goes as primary school teacher to the Himalayas, he fearfully avoids any further human entanglements for a period of seven years, settling for the calm health of long solitary walks. A stable monotony seems the only life available that will be secure from the choric caution against "greed" that punctuates the novel through the repeated imprecations of an otherwise mute servant from Samar's Benares house: " 'Greed,' he would mumble, 'is the biggest evil. It eats away man, destroys families, sunders son from parents, husband from wife'" (10).

This servant, Shyam, haunts *The Romantics* with ambiguous irony, like the blind beggar in *Madame Bovary* or, even more, the perpetually dying housepainter, Radish, in Chekhov's long story, "My Life," who announces his philosophy regularly to himself: "The grub eats grass, rust eats iron, lies devour the soul. God save us miserable sinners."[19] Chekhov thus joins Flaubert and Naipaul in the roster of ironic realists who represent the impasse of decent but unexceptional youths stuck in corrupt and menacing social worlds. Just as Chekhov's "My Life" presents the disappointments of a Russian provincial youth in a town corroded by individual and collective lies, Samar seems overcome by all the varieties of greed manifest in his Indian experience. Yet the servant's moral formula does not escape the novel's irony any more than does the holy retreat that might seem to follow from it. The narrator labels the servant's formula "a clichéd proverb in Hindi," and, when it becomes the servant's sole intelligible muttering out of his ultimately ruined mind and body, its limitations as a guide to modern Indian youth seem obvious. Mishra holds back from endorsing the traditional Indian virtue of resignation to faithful poverty. The servant is described as living "the neutered life of a feudal retainer."

Samar in many ways more closely resembles Chekhov's narrator-hero than Flaubert's Frederic. The Russian Misail and the Indian Samar have in common a natural decency that disqualifies them for any of the conventional, corrupt forms of advancement in their societies. Their main, possibly only, talent seems to be a naïve sharpness of observation about the social indecencies going on around them. Misail, too, becomes diverted by romantic involvement with a charming woman who is initially fascinated by his novel choice of manual labor. In Misail's case, the romance goes as far as marriage and subservience to this woman's doomed Utopian fantasy of their joint agricultural experiment. Devastated when she eventually flees the reality of boredom and brutality in the life they attempt, Misail takes refuge with Radish and returns to lonely drudgery as a housepainter in the town. Misail's quietly devastating perception of callousness and hypocrisy in his provincial society envisions no ethical alternative. But Misail's stolid persistence in dull toil also creates a lingering ambiguity. The virtuous hero in "My Life" is doomed to melancholy, not only by the corruption and callousness of others but by the lack of a certain élan that seems a necessary if ethically suspect component of "life" in Chekhov's vision.

The Romantics likewise envisions no ethical alternative to Samar's isolated passivity. Samar's sole Indian friend, Rajesh, enters the book as an obscurely powerful leader in the semicriminal student life of Benares Hindu University. A somewhat implausible figure in the novel, Rajesh is presented as another autodidact, with literary tastes that run from Iqbal to Wordsworth and Shelley. He even carves out time from his obscure covert activities to follow Samar's recommendation to read Flaubert (and Wilson's commentary) and to affirm Samar's recognition of their Indian contemporaries in Flaubert's Paris. *The Romantics* hints, not entirely persuasively, that the mirror of Flaubert's withering irony plays some role in Rajesh's ultimate disappearance into the contemporary underworld as a contract killer for semicriminal business powers. In Mishra's post-independence India, there seems no third choice for autodidactic youths beyond contract killing or the isolated monotony of school teaching in the Himalayas.

This predicament is even more sharply focused in Mishra's personal memoir based on the same autobiographical material, published two years before *The Romantics*. In the memoir, "Edmund Wilson in Benares,"[20] there is no distracting Western circle of acquaintances. The main disturbing temptation to the bookish narrator (now explicitly Mishra himself) comes from the Indian friend, whose nihilistic choice of a criminal career we encounter here as social fact, rather than the somewhat farfetched fictional device it may seem in the novel. Instead of a capricious Frenchwoman, a charismatically cynical Indian youth becomes the most disturbing—and obscurely erotic—figure of seduction.

An even greater contrast between novel and memoir is that Mishra does not record himself at the end of the memoir abandoning active engagement with the contemporary world. In actuality, Mishra did in his twenties withdraw for many months to the mountains for a rigorous solitary program of further self-directed reading and writing. But his nonfiction writing of the 1990s—before, during, and since publication of *The Romantics*—represents the missing alternative between contract murder and holy retreat. In Rajesh's terms (in both novel and memoir), life must go on in the space between *sunyata* (the void) and *maya* (illusion);[21] Rajesh identifies the space but cannot manage to inhabit it. His choice of crime becomes emblematic of a whole spectrum of destructive and self-destructive disappearances into the void that Mishra sees drawing a generation of youth in the subcontinent. From a psychosocial perspective, there seems little difference between a contract killer serving debt collectors for industrialists and politicians and a terrorist, though Rajesh kills without any cover of political or religious justification.

Mishra relates the limitations of characters within R. K. Narayan's novels to "a kind of intellectual self-narrowing that is often the result of the colonial's bewilderment and resentful pride before the metropolitan culture that has partly formed him" ("Narayan," 47). But he also praises Narayan for "the unmediated fidelity his novels have to his constricted experience." By the standard of Narayan, as well as of Mishra's Western predecessors—Chekhov, Forster, Naipaul, and Conrad, as well as Flaubert—*The Romantics* gives disappointingly little texture to the social world that presumably drives Samar to his radical retreat. Aside from the joint brutality of students and police in a university riot, the social reality of late twentieth-century India as it drives Samar to self-exile is limited to a few stereotyped descriptions of the notorious chaos and misery of Indian train stations. One extended account of the rural poverty encountered by Samar on a visit with Rajesh to his impoverished widow mother has disturbing force but remains strangely peripheral to the story. There is nothing here to compare to the detailed, devastating, and central social images in Chekhov's fiction of provincial Russia or to Flaubert's fiction of mid-nineteenth-century Paris. Samar as observing eye keeps the novel constricted to his idiosyncratic experience of books and his baffling American and European acquaintances.

So far, Mishra's impressive powers of social description and analysis appear more richly and with fewer distractions in his nonfiction travel writing, journalistic essays, and literary reviews. Mishra's choice of journalism as an activity becomes more urgent when viewed as having to fill the space between the void and illusion, evoked perhaps overschematically in the fiction and personal memoir. Mishra's nonfiction does not, however, call attention to its own activity in these terms; this writing is not focused on personal malaise in the way that Naipaul, for example, repeatedly represents Writing (apart from any particular subject) as having constituted the solution to his problem of postcolonial identity. Mishra's nonfiction writing is absorbing because its sharp ironies and moving details are directed outward to reality, rather than inward to the desires and disappointments of the self.

Provocative examples come from his 1999 essay "The Other India," in which Mishra follows the campaign trail of candidates for the national parliament in the region of Allahabad.[22] The characteristic irony in this, as in other of his journalistic pieces—including the remarkable Kashmir reportage[23]—focuses on the disparity between official celebrations of India's democracy and the realities behind rhetorical dramas: in the case of elections, the corrupt and shifting party alliances, the crude drive of politicians in every party to assert status and dignity over the worse-than-destitute local population that is literally and figuratively pushed to the side of broken, muddy roads by bullet-proof Ambassador cars on the campaign trail.

Most of Mishra's political journalism has been published first in India, and he recognizes that the presence of a free press there is the democratic condition that allows his provocative critiques. At the same time, he embraces this journalistic freedom to go after the theatrical fakery that he sees vitiating the nation's democratic institutions. What he calls the "annual drama" of elections suppresses "the real issues" of water, electricity, food, and illiteracy, he argues (92). The "gloss" of new middle-class affluence is meanwhile covering but also hardening the fear among those who have escaped these conditions of impoverishment that they will be pulled back into them. The misery of impoverishment in India is widely known to the point of cliché; what Mishra's journalism captures with fresh detail is the prevalent compulsion in the political class to keep that reality at a distance. Particularity of observation and description in his reportage has the goal of repudiating the gloss to get at what is not so much hidden as willfully neglected or coerced into time-worn molds of pathos and fatalism.

Mishra needs literary skills to make a confusing yet mundane event such as the Allahabad parliamentary election imaginatively fresh and significant. Neither description alone nor abstract political categories can make intelligible such confusing breakdowns between caste and class as now desperately impoverished Brahmins or the Dalit leader (of the former Untouchable caste) who turns out to be owner of a large agricultural estate (98). The sharp distinction between villains and saviors blurs in accounts of the former Mafia-style gangster who is now moving to "a higher idea of himself" as protector of the Muslim population against Hindu nationalist extremists of the Bharatiya Janata Party (BJP), or of the ineffectual Congress Party candidate from Allahabad, Rita Bahuguna, a former professor at Allahabad University who is also mayor of that city and the daughter of an influential Brahmin politician there. Set against the overheated election dramas reported in the press, Mishra offers an exact and spare particularity to lay out the whole panoply of Allahabad's election roster, the legacy of historical allegiances and new political alliances, plus the peculiarity of his own inside-outside relationship to various parts of this complex community of his own past—not really a single community at all, for candidates and groups live in proximity to each other, yet entirely apart in separate and mutually suspicious enclaves. For Mishra to travel back and forth across these boundaries in his own reportage requires uncustomary curiosity, and even daring.

The case of the Congress candidate's campaign at first seems less of a challenge because Rita Bahuguna represents a constituency that naturally includes Mishra himself: the "liberal, educated people in the city—teachers, lawyers, journalist—who, though not always political, felt comfortable with her, saw her as a bulwark against the Hindu nationalists" (97). But accompanying Mrs. Bahuguna outside the familiar setting of the university (where her election address is full of its own incongruities), Mishra separates himself from his natural "liberal, educated" cohort by making adjustments of perspective that are conspicuously lacking in the candidate and her backers. Their failure not only prepares us to understand the Congress defeat by the BJP in the Allahabad election but more fully illuminates the avoidance of contemporary Indian reality in the whole election drama .

Mishra's critical notations begin with details such as Bahuguna in the car going out to the countryside, holding "the end of her sari against her nose to keep out the diesel fumes" while talking to him of conferences she has attended in European and American cities. She is herself a cosmopolitan Indian; he notices her "bookish Hindi," different from the dialect used by the BJP candidate (though he is also a former university professor). Bahaguna becomes easy in her speech only when greeting party workers and other known Congress supporters. Mishra has his eye on other, less familiar sights along this road that seem less interesting to Mrs. Bahuguna: for example, large groups of "light-eyed boys" who, he explains, belong to a community of three thousand Muslim horse-riders from Rajasthan, now mostly unemployed and illiterate, who make a living by skinning cows killed in road accidents. Although women sifting wheat in front of mud huts and children "with distended bellies" belong to the stereotyped spectacle of rural poverty in India, Mishra wants to make us apprehend this reality more sharply (98). When he gets out of the car and enters one of these huts, he meets two teenage sons of a rice farmer and fisherman, dressed in oversized polyester pants and torn shirts, which (he finds out) are their only clothes, to be stuffed with straw when winter warmth is needed.

Mishra does not presume superior intimacy with the rice farmer or his sons, nor does he offer the bareness of this life as "news." His important striking perception is the disparity between this radical impoverishment and the terms of the campaign staged by the university-educated Brahmin candidate and her backers:

> Back where the cars had stopped, a few old women stood speechlessly, their wizened, toothless faces half hidden by sari veils pulled down to nose-level, as Mrs. Bahuguna asked them about their "problems." They said nothing, and so Mrs. Bahuguna began to explain to them Sonia Gandhi's presidency of the Congress, and how women were best placed to understand other women's problems. They looked on, puzzlement appearing in eyes that held great anxiety and patience. And now an embarrassed Dal Bahadur prompted them, "Don't you know who this is? don't you remember how her father once distributed lai chana?"
>
> Lai chana! the puffed rice and chick peas that was the poor man's snack, stuffed in rusty tin containers in the gloomy one-room shops in the shanty markets we had passed. It was hard not to feel the pathos of the situation. Decades after it had been made, the old women were being asked to remember a meaningless offering from a long-dead politician, in a village which near-total destitution had taken beyond the simple deprivation of the rural poor elsewhere, beyond lack of water, electricity, primary schools, and hospitals to the earliest, most elementary form of human community, where the outside world intrudes only in the form of election-time visitors and the propaganda leaflets the ragged children had pounced upon. (98)

When Naipaul, in *An Area of Darkness*, tells of his panicky refusal of the rice offering extended to him as a symbolic tribute by a leader of his ancestral village, his overanxious revulsion toward any claim on him by traditional India dramatizes the intense ambivalence of his entire journey to discover his "roots."[24] Mishra's relationship to the poor rural women of Allahabad is entirely different; he comes from this area, needs no interpreter for the languages, the histories, and the personalities of the candidates, knows what *lai chana* is and what it is worth. He even shares the candidate's Brahmin background and cosmopolitanism and admires the university women who work around her. This intimacy, however, only sharpens his pained irony toward the Congress party leader's reliance on empty historic and symbolic claims (not even *lai chana* is being actually offered here, only invoked). In this context, the Italian-born Sonia Gandhi and Mrs. Bahuguna herself are empty icons of an Indian women's sisterhood, just as the memory of *lai chana* is an ironic relic of the Congress Party's symbolic role as provider for a unified, progressive India. Mrs. Bahuguna unsurprisingly loses this election, a failure that remains disturbing, even if deserved, since Mishra offers no reasons to regard the victorious BJP candidate and party (or any other) with enthusiasm.

In Western nonfiction prose, the traveling reporter who opens our eyes to pathos and tragedy through small, particular observations became an established figure in nineteenth-century literature and since, with notable accomplishments by writers such as Tolstoy, George Orwell, and James Agee.[25] The worth of this reportage has always been open to question from a variety of directions: within the literary tradition, its formal modesty limits its stature; the academic social scientist distrusts the lack of theory and the reliance on anecdote, impression, and rhetorical effects. These objections do not, however, diminish the enduring interest of the social witnessing accomplished by this maverick genre of nonfiction prose. Contributions to it have come from many distinct cultures, for this writing at its best is both intensely local and personal, and also cosmopolitan in its skeptical detachment from fixed class and political loyalties. Tolstoy registering in detail the lives crowded inside poor dwellings he saw while canvassing for the Moscow census in the 1880s, Orwell crawling through the coal mines while on assignment to report on the unemployed in Wigan Pier in the 1930s, Agee becoming obsessed with a single family while on a similar assignment to depict American southern tenant farmers, were in a sense bad at their jobs; their strongly individualistic imaginations obstructed their performance of limited and routine projects but ended up producing classics of nonfiction prose whose interest exceeds their local and temporal origins. Whether Mishra's future as a writer will continue in this direction or develop further within the recognized genre of fiction, he has already gone far to fulfill Seepersad Naipaul's optimism that the Indian writer in English can successfully create for himself a style to match experience. Mishra's writing in every genre brings him as an author and India as a subject within an international modern prose tradition where the writerly activities of self-creation and social analysis are intimately fused.

For the Western admirer of any such promising career, the main anxiety must be the potential damage that praise can cause to the very qualities being praised. Readers of the *New York Review of Books*, for example, are more likely than reviewers in India to recognize and enjoy Mishra's immersion in Western writers of the past, such as Chekhov and Flaubert. They are also less perturbed by provocative insinuations about Indian politics or military behavior. Even before the events of fall 2001, criticism of Mishra in India, compared to the welcome his work had received in London and New York, underlined important differences of perspective that so-called globalization has intensified, rather than erased. Excessive Western enthusiasm in itself creates hostility as well as envy in India, if only because it betokens great monetary rewards.

There is potential damage also to a writer from the way foreign praise may translate into a beckoning temptation to pack up and relocate among kindred, or at least appreciative, spirits. The contribution of South Asian writing to a kind of mobile cosmopolitanism has recently been hailed in the *New York Times* by Shashi Tharoor, another young Indian novelist who works at the United Nations and lives mainly in New York. "Addresses don't matter," Tharoor remarks, "because writers live inside their heads."[26] According to Tharoor, even though mastery of the English language belongs to no more than 2 percent of the Indian population, to the writers who choose English the language is entirely "natural" and, in addition, has the advantage of transcending the divisive Indian boundaries of region, religion, and caste. For Tharoor, Indian writers in English comfortably enter the multicultural festival of Anglophone world literature. In his version of cosmopolitanism, Indian multiplicity becomes a rich resource for Indian writers, allowing them to bring new vitality into contemporary literature in English: "secure of themselves in their heritage of diversity . . . they write free of the anxiety of audience, for theirs are narratives that appeal as easily to Americans as to Indians—and indeed to readers irrespective of ethnicity."

Mishra has been marking out a different, more contentious conception of postcolonial cosmopolitanism. The "diversity" of India, in his writing, involves mutually suspicious divisions in often violent conflict with each other. The new global culture is shown to have produced new kinds of tensions and repellent combinations, such as he remarks between prosperous Indian communities in America and extreme nationalist groups in the homeland. Mishra has been reaching for a kind of cosmopolitanism calculated to shake up Indian, and then also American, complacency by importing into Indian discourse standards and critical values acquired through wide reading in European as well as South Asian history and literature.

To sustain authority for this kind of critique, addresses do matter, especially because the critique is so explicitly directed at the self-distancing from discomfiting reality that is found among the privileged. Aijaz Ahmad, in another version of this endeavor, draws on Raymond Williams, among other Marxist cultural critics;[27] Mishra, less politically doctrinaire, turns back to Chekhov and other Western ironists to help shape a literature of social dissent for an Indian environment that is still or perhaps increasingly resistant to cosmopolitan challenge. India—any country, really—needs to have the ferment of this literary dissent within its geographical space. The difficulty of sustaining the role of dissenter and maverick in an embattled environment cannot be overestimated. Withdrawal to the mountains of books or the smooth flow of global travel always remains a powerful temptation.

NOTES

Introduction: Why Dissent Matters to Literature

1. See Said, *Culture and Imperialism* and *Orientalism*. Quotations refer within the text to the editions listed in the bibliography, by page number and abbreviated title: O for *Orientalism;* CI for *Culture and Imperialism.*

2. Timothy Peltason astutely discusses the "minimizing" effect of Said's style of concession to literature in "The Place of Reading," 12.

3. For discussion of these shifts in postcolonial criticism, see Moore-Gilbert, introduction to *Writing India*, 5–6; Kate Teltscher, a contributor to the essay collection *Writing India*, similarly reviews this history in the introduction to her book, *India Inscribed*, 16–17.

4. Said, "Restoring Intellectual Coherence," 3.

5. Guha, *Dominance without Hegemony*. Quotations refer within the text to the edition listed in the bibliography, by page number and abbreviated title (DH).

6. See Ngugi wa Thiong'o, *Decolonising the Mind.*

7. John Stuart Mill, *On Liberty*, in *Essays on Politics and Society*, vol. 18 of *Collected Works of John Stuart Mill*, 247 (hereafter cited as *Collected Works*). Quotations refer by page number within the text to the edition listed in the bibliography.

8. Moore-Gilbert, *Writing India*, 14–18; "The Bhabhal of Tongues: Reading Kipling, Reading Bhabha," in *Writing India*, 111–38. See also Hai, "On Truth and Lie in a Colonial Sense."

9. Porter, "Orientalism and Its Problems," 179–93, 182.

10. Porter, *Haunted Journeys*, 4.

11. Ibid., 9.

12. Porter, "Orientalism and Its Problems," 181. Peter Morey, in *Fictions of India*, astutely analyzes the subversive and transgressive effects of narrative form in a number of colonial literary narratives but ultimately transfers credit for these effects from individual authors to an "idealized construct" of the postcolonial reader (10, 13).

13. Pocock, introduction to *Virtue, Commerce, and History*, 5.

14. Ibid., 13.

15. Eliot, *Middlemarch*, 4.

16. Quotations from Guha, *A Rule of Property for Bengal*, refer within the text to the edition listed in the bibliography, by page number and abbreviation (RP).

17. The term *zamindar* refers to the category of big landlords who were responsible for revenue collection under Mughal rule. Their ambiguous status as proprietors of the land underlay British land policy dispute in the eighteenth century.

18. Guha recounts Francis's quarrel with Burke in *A Rule of Property for Bengal*, 81–85.

19. The complex chronology of the Permanent Settlement as it evolved from idea to partial policy to law appears in ibid., 2 and passim.

20. The preface to Guha's *Dominance without Hegemony* (ix) dates earlier versions of its contents to three essays written in 1986–1987 and published between 1988 and 1992. The title *Dominance without Hegemony* refers to Gramsci's distinction between "dominance" as the coercive force of the state and "hegemony" as the more pervasive economic, social, moral, and intellectual unity that perpetuates the relationship between dominant and subordinate groups through consent rather than coercion. Guha's title phrase contrasts the power relationships within England to those in British India: "The metropolitan state was hegemonic in character with its claim to dominance based on a power relation in which the moment of persuasion outweighed that of coercion, whereas the colonial state was non-hegemonic with persuasion outweighed by coercion in its structure of dominance. . . . The originality of the South Asian colonial state lay precisely in this difference: a historical paradox, it was an autocracy set up and sustained in the East by the foremost democracy of the Western world" (DH, xii). Among the numerous commentaries on Gramsci's concepts of "hegemony" and "counter-hegemonic" challenges by "subaltern" (i.e., subordinate) groups, explanations relevant to the issue of textual interpretation appear in Willams, *Marxism and Literature*, 108–20; Bocock, *Hegemony*, 28–40; and Gramsci, *Gramsci Reader*, 420–31.

21. Guha, *Elementary Aspects of Peasant Insurgency in Colonial India*, 13.

22. Ibid., 16–17.

23. Bhabha, "Sly Civility," in *Location of Culture*, 93–101. Quotations from this essay refer to this edition by page number within the text.

24. For contemporary usage of *aporia* in literary theory to name an "impasse" or "textual doubt, involving the mutual assertion and negation of opposing systems of logic or rhetoric," see J. Douglas Kneale's entry, "Deconstruction," in *Johns Hopkins Guide to Literary Theory and Criticism*, ed. Michael Groden and Martin Kreiswirth (Baltimore: Johns Hopkins University Press, 1994), 189; see also Mario J. Valdés, "Aporia," in *Encyclopedia of Contemporary Literary Theory*, ed. Irena R. Makaryk (Toronto: University of Toronto Press, 1993), 507, for tracing of *aporia* to the Socratic method, where "the realization of not-knowing is the beginning of concerted searching."

25. Zastoupil, "J. S. Mill and India," 52, discusses Mill's absorption of ideas about Oriental despotism from the work of his father, James Mill's *History of British India*, as well as from Saint-Simonian influences. See also Martin Moir's

introduction to J. S. Mill, *Writings on India*, vol. 30 of *Collected Works*, xlii–xliii.
For Montesquieu and the eighteenth-century stereotype of Oriental despotism,
see Teltscher, *India Inscribed*, 29–31, 113.

26. Mill's text reads:

> There are, as we have already seen, conditions of society in which a vigor-
> ous despotism is in itself the best mode of government for training the peo-
> ple in what is specifically wanting to render them capable of a higher civi-
> lization. . . . As it is already a common, and is rapidly tending to become the
> universal, condition of the more backward populations, to be either held in
> direct subjection by the more advanced, or to be under their complete polit-
> ical ascendancy; there are in this age of the world few more important
> problems, than how to organize this rule, so as to make it a good instead of
> an evil to the subject people, providing them with the best attainable pres-
> ent government, and with the conditions most favourable to future perma-
> nent improvement. But the mode of fitting the government for this pur-
> pose, is by no means so well understood as the conditions of good
> government in a people capable of governing themselves. We may even say,
> that it is not understood at all. The thing appears perfectly easy to superfi-
> cial observers. If India (for example) is not fit to govern itself, all that seems
> to them required is, that there should be a minister to govern it: and that
> this minister, like all other British ministers, should be responsible to the
> British Parliament. Unfortunately this, though the simplest mode of at-
> tempting to govern a dependency, is about the worst; and betrays in its ad-
> vocates a total want of comprehension of the conditions of good govern-
> ment. To govern a country under responsibility to the people of that
> country, and to govern one country under responsibility to the people of
> another, are two very different things. What makes the excellence of the
> first, is that freedom is preferable to despotism: but the last *is* despotism.
> The only choice the case admits, is a choice of despotisms: and it is not cer-
> tain that the despotism of twenty millions is necessarily better than that of
> a few, or of one. But it is quite certain, that the despotism of those who nei-
> ther hear, nor see, nor know anything about their subjects, has many
> chances of being worse than that of those who do.

Considerations on Representative Government, in *Essays on Politics and Society*, vol.
19 of *Collected Works*, 567–68.

27. During the tense year of parliamentary deliberation before enactment of
the new policy, Mill was its key intellectual opponent, drafting memoranda and
petitions to Parliament arguing the preferability of Company rule. See Moir, introduction to *Writings on India*, xxix–xxxlx.

28. Moir discusses the relationship between Mill's general writings on government and his writings about India in terms of Mill's "complex balance of dif-
fering political criteria" and his "personal synthesis of . . . conflicting . . . philosophies" (ibid., xlvi).

29. See J. S. Mill, *Autobiography*, in *Autobiography and Literary Essays*, vol. 1 of *Collected Works*, 28, 83. See Zastoupil, "J. S. Mill and India," 31–54, and Moir, introduction to *Writings on India*, l–liv, for comparisons between the ideas about India of John Stuart Mill and James Mill and also for emphasis on the need for further investigation of J. S. Mill's Indian writings.

30. Quotations from Thompson, *The Other Side of the Medal*, refer by page number within the text to the edition listed in the bibliography.

31. Sarkar, afterword to *The Other Side of the Medal*, 98–120.

32. Ibid., 117.

33. Forster, *A Passage to India*, 281.

34. Morey, *Fictions of India*, 62–63, subtly shows how Forster recognizes "the ineffectual nature of liberal principles," but Morey also insists on the degree to which Forster is "ensnared in the power drives of his national discourse" (73) as a result of his filtering of Indian voices through his own narrative voice.

35. Editors, "Word to Our Readers," *Dissent* 1 (Winter 1954).

36. In *Dominance without Hegemony*, 13, Guha draws on Gramscian Marxism to establish a specific revolutionary role for intellectuals whose writing can reveal the fatal contradictions of the bourgeois capitalist hegemony that is the root of imperial evil; Guha's historical model comes from Enlightenment intellectuals who anticipated the French Revolution's destruction of the ancien régime: "In much the same way, the critique of the dominant bourgeois culture arises from the real contradictions of capitalism and anticipates its dissolution."

37. Rushdie, "In Good Faith," in *Imaginary Homelands*, 395–96.

38. See, for example, the debate in the journal *Public Culture*, beginning with Breckenridge and Arjun, "Editors' Comments" 1 (spring 1989), placing Rushdie's voice within "the literature of exile, a literature whose politics has always been tied up with certain high-minded claims to cosmopolitanism" not shared by "proletarian" exiles whose "anguish and anger cannot be dismissed as atavistic or mindless." *Public Culture* 2 (fall 1989) includes essays arguing each side of the controversy and several letters objecting to the editors' apparent defense of the attack on Rushdie. Taylor, "Rushdie Controversy," identifies *The Satanic Verses* as "a profoundly Western book . . . comforting to the western liberal mind, which shares one feature with that of the Ayatollah Khomeini, the belief that there is nothing outside their world-view which needs deeper understanding. . . . To live in this difficult world, the western liberal mind will have to learn to reach out more" (38). Jussawalla, in "Resurrecting the Prophet," sees Rushdie as "someone who writes about Oriental people, their 'customs, mind, destiny and so on' from the vantage point of a successful mainstream Westernized immigrant" (109–10). A quite different point of view is expressed by Fischer and Abede, who in a letter criticize the editors for ignoring the cultural debates within the Islamic world, and thereby essentializing Islamic culture in terms of its most conservative, authoritarian extreme (123–26).

39. Rushdie, "Outside the Whale," in *Imaginary Homelands*, 98.

40. Rushdie, "In Good Faith," in *Imaginary Homelands*, 412.

41. Rushdie, *Midnight's Children*, 3.

1. Anti-Imperialist Wit in Horace Walpole's Letters

1. Walpole's full correspondence with Horace Mann runs from 1740 to 1786 and includes nearly 1,800 letters. As noted by W. S. Lewis, editor of *The Yale Edition of Horace Walpole's Correspondence* (hereafter cited as *Correspondence*), Walpole began to make copies of his letters to Horace Mann in 1754, preparing a title page for each of six volumes and an advertisement for the series. Quotations from Walpole's letters are from the Yale edition, referred to by date, volume, and page number within the text. The first separate publication of *Letters of Horace Walpole, Earl of Oxford, to Sir Horace Mann* appeared in 1833, edited by Lord Dover in 3 volumes. See *Correspondence*, 17:1–2.

2. P. J. Marshall, editor of *The Eighteenth Century*, vol. 2 of *Oxford History of the British Empire*, closes his chapter "The British in Asia: From Trade to Dominion, 1700–1765" (487–507) in the year when the Mughal emperor granted the East India Company *diwani* (revenue collecting privileges) in Bengal, allowing that dominion to become a "bridgehead" for further territorial acquisition. See also Marshall, *Bengal: The British Bridgehead*.

3. Nirad C. Chaudhuri, *Clive of India*, 2, 397–98, includes Walpole in his observation that "chronologically, British anti-imperialism was in being before the appearance of the Empire."

4. *Correspondence*, 22:176 n. 13, dates Pitt's tribute to a speech of 1757; the entry on Clive in the *Dictionary of National Biography*, ed. Leslie Stephen and Sidney Leed (Oxford: Oxford University Press, 1921; hereafter *DNB*), 4:572, cites the phrase as "heaven-born general" and places it in a speech by Pitt of 1760, when Clive had returned to England three years after his 1757 victory at Plassy.

5. See "Letter to Mr. Urban." Chaudhuri, *Clive of India*, 377, criticizes the circulation of exaggerated and scandalous rumor that, in his opinion, led to popular demonizing of Clive and the East India Company in the 1770s. Teltscher, *India Inscribed*, 157–72, discusses the circulation of rhetoric between both sides in the East India Company controversies of the 1770s and the influence of such journals as *Gentleman's Magazine* on public rhetoric and, later, on Burke's rhetoric in the Hastings trial.

6. Marshall, *The Eighteenth Century*, 493–506, explains recent shifts in historical interpretation that replace the traditional dichotomy between "alien aggressors" and native victims in eighteenth-century India with a more complicated dynamic of mutually advantageous relations between a British commercial class and their Indian counterparts, both in a position to exploit for their own profit the British presence. See also Bayly, *Indian Society and the Making of the British Empire*. Bayly's reinterpretation transfers a significant portion of the active energy of eighteenth-century British imperialism in India to Indians themselves, while also diminishing the coherence of a British national policy.

7. See Pocock, *Machiavellian Moment*. For discussion of the dynamic between the concept of classical civic virtue and the rise of commerce in eighteenth-century England, see Pocock, *Virtue, Commerce, and History*. Ayres, in *Classical Culture*, 25–26, extends Pocock's analysis of political thought to the cultural and social

sphere; he traces Walpole's ambivalent position in part to resentment against attacks on his father for corrupt commercialism. Ayres characterizes Walpole (together with Hogarth) as an "ambivalent skeptic" in relation to the discourse of classical civic virtue (166, 216 n. 1). See also Chaudhuri, *Clive of India*, 127, 370, 385, for discussion of the Roman analogy in relation to Walpole's distrust of new Indian wealth.

8. Teltscher, *India Inscribed*, 168–69, discusses English social snobbery and fear of "the East's corrupting influence" on the nation, as expressed in such popular theater as Samuel Foote's comedy *The Nabob* (1772).

9. Ferguson, *Essay on the History of Civil Society*, 223. Cited by Ayres, *Classical Culture*, 28.

10. Macaulay, review of *Letters of Horace Walpole, Earl of Oxford, to Sir Horace Mann.*

11. Macaulay's mockery of Walpole as collector acquires a different coloring from the anecdote taken from G. O. Trevelyan's biography of his uncle, *Life and Letters of Lord Macaulay* (1876), that at age four, Macaulay was taken by his father to Strawberry Hill, where he saw Walpole's collections "and ever afterwards carried the catalogue in his memory." Cited in *DNB*, 12.410.

12. William Hazlitt, reviewing *Letters from the Hon. Horace Walpole to George Montagu*, anticipates Macaulay's terms by characterizing Walpole as "the very prince of Gossips," "the slave of elegant trifles," and by declaring "the smaller the object, and the less its importance, the higher did [Walpole's] estimation and his praises of it ascend"; Hazlitt also sees Walpole's "political character" as "a heap of confusion." Cited in Sabor, ed., *Critical Heritage*, 187.

13. The Supreme Council was constituted by the bill Macaulay had promoted to renew a reformed version of the Company's charter in 1933. See *DNB*, 12:412.

14. Samuel Johnson, "Cowley," in *Lives of the English Poets.*

15. Ibid., 20–22.

16. James Boswell, in *Life of Johnson*, 1308, recorded Johnson's succinct judgment of Walpole in June 1784: "He got together a great many curious little things, and told them in an elegant manner"; cited in Sabor, *Critical Heritage*, 261. Charles Burney described the mutual lack of admiration between Johnson and Walpole: Walpole disparaged Johnson as "unwieldy and uncouth in his figure, a Jacobite, and a Christian," while Johnson "had a natural antipathy to the noble Lord as being a Whig, the son of a Whig minister, effeminate and unmanly in his appearance, dainty and affected in his taste, a Cantabridgian, and a philosopher *à la Voltaire*. The elements of fire and water cannot be more hostile to each other than this pair." From an unsigned review of Walpole's *Works*, in *Monthly Review*, September/October 1798, cited in Sabor, *Critical Heritage*, 270–71.

17. The Indian state project of decolonizing place names has now officially converted the English transcription Oudh (misspelled by Walpole as "Oude") to Awadh. I continue to use the older, British form, Oudh, for clarity when referring to colonial texts where it appears but otherwise follow current usage.

18. *Correspondence*, 23:452 n. 13, corrects Walpole's slight misquotation from Virgil's *Aeneid*, ii.65: "crimine ab uno disce omnis" (from one crime, learn all); Walpole's tag translates as "from one, learn them all."

19. Abbé Guillaume Raynal, *Histoire philosophique et politique des établissements et du commerce des Européens dans les deux Indes* (1770). My citations are from the English translation of the third edition, *A Philosophical and Political History of the Settlements and Trade of the Europeans in the East and West Indies*, and are referred to by book and page number within the text. Arthur M. Wilson, *Diderot*, 682–86, describes Diderot's main literary labor in 1776–1777 to be his contributions to the greatly enlarged third edition. Feugère, "Raynal, Diderot et quelques autres 'Historiens des deux Indes,'" established that Diderot's main interventions occurred at two points: between 1770 and 1774 and between 1774 and 1780 (350). Teltscher, *India Inscribed*, 164, notes the significance of Raynal's *History* in the Hastings trial.

20. Macaulay, review of *Letters*, 234.

21. I adopt this composite authorship for passages that accord with Raynal's assignment for Diderot to add philosophic commentary and digressions to Raynal's text. Although certain of the passages pertaining to England have been decisively identified as Diderot's, thorough and definite attribution has been made difficult by Raynal's free revision and modification of contributions by his collaborators, by the difficulty of correlating passages inserted in different places in different editions, and, in the case of the English translation, by the difficulty of correlating texts that may have been further modified by the translator. For thorough accounts of research to identify Diderot's authorship within the collaborative enterprise of Raynal's project, see, in addition to Feugère, Dieckmann, "Les contributions de Diderot à la 'Correspondance littéraire' et à l''Histoire des Deux Indes'"; Wolpe, *Raynal et sa machine de guerre: l'Histoire des deux Indes et ses perfectionnements* and "Diderot collaborateur de Raynal."

22. The book was banned by the Church in France in 1774 and burned by royal authorities in 1781, when Raynal was ordered into exile. After returning to revolutionary France, he became a moderate proponent of a constitutional monarchy modeled on the English system and was therefore sidelined by revolutionary events after 1791. See volume 9 of *New Encyclopedia Britannica*, 15th ed. (Chicago: Encyclopedia Britannica, 1998), 996.

23. Wolpe, *Raynal*, 205, cites two versions of this passage verifiably attributed to Diderot in the editions of both 1774 and 1781.

24. I am grateful to James Noggle for helpful discussion of this topic.

25. See *Correspondence*, 25:400 n. 15, for the reference to Juvenal, *Satires* vi.347: "But who is to guard the guards themselves?"

26. See Ayres, *Classical Culture*, 42; Carnall, "Burke as Modern Cicero," 81.

27. *Correspondence*, 25:400 n. 14.

28. See chapter 2, 62, 65.

29. Letter to Rev. William Cole, March 9, 1765. Cited by W. S. Lewis in the introduction to *The Castle of Otranto*, ix. Quotations from the novel refer by page number within the text to the edition listed in the bibliography.

30. Walpole, in "Preface to the Second Edition," *The Castle of Otranto*, 8–9, invokes Shakespeare (against Voltaire) as his authority for mixing foolery with "heroics" and tragedy.

31. Walpole's identification with Father Jerome is proposed by John Samson, "Politics Gothicized." Samson perceives in the novel's plot a fantasized corrective to the political fracas Walpole was presumably trying not to think about, namely the notorious "Conway incident," in which Walpole's incitement of his beloved young cousin, General Henry Seymour Conway, to oppose what Walpole saw as tyranny in the ministry of Grenville had ended by ruining (if only temporarily) Conway's political, military, and social position. In this construction, the virtuous young peasant, Theodore, who turns out to be the rightful heir to Otranto, corresponds to Conway; Manfred, the usurping tyrant, corresponds to Grenville, and Walpole is reconfigured in the figure of the friar, Father Jerome.

32. William Shakespeare, *Henry IV, Part One*, V.iii.54–55.

2. Burke's India Campaign

1. Public acknowledgment of Burke's authority is remarked by Sutherland, *The East India Company in Eighteenth-Century Politics*, 367–68; Sutherland also gives credit to Burke's colleague, and later rival, Henry Dundas, chairman of Parliament's Secret Committee, which worked in parallel with Burke's Select Committee on Indian investigations between 1782 and 1784; in the Pitt administration of 1784, Dundas prepared the East India Act, which was the more moderate (and, to Burke, inadequate) replacement for the Fox East India Bill of 1783. See Sutherland, 371–74, 382–84, 391–94.

2. Quotations from Burke's India writings and speeches come from *India: Madras and Bengal, 1774–1785,* and from *India: The Launching of the Hastings Impeachment, 1786–1788,* ed. P. J. Marshall, vols. 5 and 6 of *The Writings and Speeches of Edmund Burke*. Quotations refer to Burke's writings and to Marshall's commentary in these editions, by volume and page number within the text.

3. Carnall, in "Burke as Modern Cicero," 76, attributes the relative neglect of Burke's India writings to incongruity between his challenge to "Establishment consensus" about the history of British India and his standing as "icon of conservatism." Carnall goes so far as to associate Burke's India critique with early twentieth-century anti-imperial movements such as the India League and the Movement for Colonial Freedom.

4. O'Brien, *The Great Melody*, xxvi. Other admiring interpretations of Burke's India writings include Whelan, *Edmund Burke and India*; Bromwich's introduction to *On Empire, Liberty, and Reform: Speeches and Letters, Edmund Burke*, 1–39; and Suleri, *The Rhetoric of English India*, who credits Burke with the "first exhaustive compilation of colonial guilt to emerge from the colonization of India" (51).

5. For denigration of Burke's India critique as derivative, see Teltscher, *India Inscribed*, 157, 163–86; Musselwhite disparages Burke's style in "The Trial of Warren Hastings," 77–103; Kramnick criticizes his character and politics in *The Rage of Edmund Burke* and in "The Left and Edmund Burke."

6. See Sutherland, *East India Company*, 366. O'Brien, *The Great Melody*, 330–35, gives a lively account of this much-studied political crisis, which involved

pressure from King George III, who wanted to bring down the Fox-North Coalition for reasons not limited to India.

7. Marshall, *Impeachment of Warren Hastings*, 39–63, 70–71.

8. See Letter to Philip Francis, December 10, 1785, in *Correspondence of Edmund Burke*: "Speaking for myself, my business is not to consider what will convict Mr Hastings, (a thing we all know to be impracticable) but what will acquit and justify myself to those few persons and to those distant times, which may take a concern in these affairs and the Actors in them" (5:243).

9. O'Brien, *The Great Melody*, 257.

10. Marshall, *Madras and Bengal*, 5:194, remarks Burke's desire to impeach Hastings as early as the Select Committee investigations; Whelan, in *Edmund Burke and India*, treats the entire body of Indian writings as a coherent whole, moving back and forth among texts for quotations without regard to chronology within the period 1781–1795.

11. The sharpest turnabout in Burke's position on India was between his opposition to the censure of Clive and to the Regulatory Bill of 1773 and his harsh critique of the East India Company, which began in his work for the Select Committee reports of 1781–1782.

12. My attention to rhetoric and imaginative forms in Burke's political writing most closely resembles the approach of Reid in *Edmund Burke and the Practice of Political Writing*: "Seen in this way, the question of Burke's consistency cannot be resolved simply by comparing the positions he stated at various points in his career, or even by exposing an underlying pattern (or patchwork) of ideas. It is an ideological question, a question of tone, manner and feeling as well as of concept, and hence a question which involves the full range of meanings and representations embodied in his work" (216). Reid acknowledges, however, that his book gives only "cursory attention" to Burke's Irish and Indian writings (14).

13. Letter to William Eden, May 17, 1784, *Correspondence of Edmund Burke*, 5:151. I thank Timothy Peltason for alerting me to Burke's allusion to a remark attributed to Caligula in Suetonius, *The Lives of the Caesars*, translated and included in *Bartlett's Familiar Quotations*, 16th ed., ed. Justin Kaplan (Boston: Little, Brown, 1992): "Would that the Roman people had a single neck [to cut off their head]" [*Utinam populus Romanus cervicem haberet*] (103).

14. Letter to William Baker, June 22, 1784, *Correspondence of Edmund Burke*, 5:154–55.

15. I thank Marshall for his expert consultation on the textual problems of those speeches not published by Burke himself.

16. Lock, *Edmund Burke*, vol. 1, *1730–1784*, 542–43.

17. Marshall, *Madras and Bengal*, 5:460; O'Brien, *The Great Melody*, 337.

18. The Wazir of Oudh was son and grandson of the Begums, whose reduction to beggary by revenue demands against their inherited property by way of the Wazir formed a principal episode of pathos in the "Speech on Fox's East India Bill," again in the "Almas Ali Khan speech," and in the Hastings impeachment trial, where their plight was a high point of Richard Brinsley Sheridan's oratory.

19. See Whelan, *Edmund Burke and India*, 143. For a fuller account of Almas Ali Khan's complex relations with Hastings, see Barnett, *North India between Empires*, 166, 171–72, 224–29.

20. Nandakumar was the Bengali Brahmin tried and executed for bribery in 1775 by the new Supreme Court under Justice Elijah Impey. Charges of "judicial murder" in the sentence and of conspiracy between Hastings and Impey created one of the major scandals of eighteenth-century British India, resulting in an impeachment trial against Impey (who was acquitted) and more than a century of controversy about the case, from Burke's Select Committee reports to James Fitzjames Stephen's defense of Impey in *The Story of Nuncomar and the Impeachment of Sir Elijah Impey*. See Marshall, *Impeachment of Warren Hastings*, 136–42.

21. Cited by Marshall, *Madras and Bengal*, 5:455, n. 5, from Parliamentary Register, xiv.21.

22. Scott, *Letter to the Right Honourable Edmund Burke*, 2.

23. The unusual word "flagitious" links Burke to the English translation of Diderot/Raynal, cited in chapter 1, 39.

24. See chapter 1, 41. Knapp, in *Personification and the Sublime*, 87–89, suggestively explores the relationship between the sublime and "self-reflexive absurdity."

25. I thank Yoon Sun Lee for helpful suggestions on this point.

26. The published version of the "Speech on Fox's India Bill" appeared January 22, 1784, two months after its delivery. Marshall, *Madras and Bengal*, 5:380, remarks that no manuscript of the spoken version survives. Reid, *Edmund Burke and the Practice of Political Writing*, 118–36, interestingly discusses the discursive differences between Burke's speeches (as preserved in transcripts) and their published, edited versions. Burke did sometimes preserve interruptions from the floor in his published texts, as in the "Speech on Fox's India Bill," in an account of the reduction to poverty of the Wazir's mother: "This antient matron, born to better things [a laugh from certain young gentlemen]—I see no cause for this mirth" (*Madras and Bengal*, 5:419).

27. The politics of Burke's defense of the East India Company in 1773 are discussed by all of Burke's interpreters and biographers. See, for example, O'Brien, *The Great Melody*, 258–70; Lock, *Edmund Burke*, 1:337–39.

28. My interpretation of this passage differs from that of Suleri, *Rhetoric of English India*, 26–27, who reads it as evidence of Burke's "insistence on the difficulty of representing India at all in the English language." Rather than perceiving intimations of the "central representational unavailability" of India in this passage, as Suleri does, I see Burke more specifically referring to the difficulty of criticizing one's own nation.

29. Musselwhite, "The Trial of Warren Hastings," 99, using the language of the Hastings impeachment trial as the Burkean norm, contrasts Burke's style unfavorably to Hastings's more "pragmatic, analytical and philological" manner. While objecting to Musselwhite's denigration of Burke, Suleri in her own way similarly underrates the analytic strength of the Fox Bill speech through her ro-

mantic model of rhetorical disempowerment in Burke's writing (*Rhetoric of English India*, 66).

30. Burke's idealization of ancient India has been criticized by many commentators, starting with James Mill, *History of British India*, 232. Guha, in *Rule of Property for Bengal*, 108–14, argues that a "physiocratic" conception of agricultural prosperity led Philip Francis (and Burke in turn) to a mythic image of an English-style Indian gentry supposedly being destroyed by Hastings's land revenue policies. See my discussion in the introduction, 12–14.

31. See, for example, Bayly, *Indian Society and the Making of the British Empire*, 45–48 and passim.

32. Suleri, *Rhetoric of English India*, 28.

33. Quotations from Burke, *A Philosophical Enquiry into the Origin of Our Ideas of the Sublime and Beautiful*, refer by page number within the text to the edition cited in the bibliography.

34. Hertz, in *End of the Line*, 40–53, uses examples from Hume and Kant to explore a range of meanings of the sublime in eighteenth-century discourse that includes a conception of invigorating arousal of the mind.

35. Reid, *Edmund Burke and the Practice of Political Writing*, 95–117, offers valuable discussion of Burke's rhetorical performances in relation to his parliamentary audience.

36. Scott, *Letter to the Right Honourable Edmund Burke*, 13.

37. Burke does propose reparation for extortion in the form of debt cancellation in "Speech on the Nabob of Arcot's Debts," *Madras and Bengal*, 5:523, where he also argues for English government funds to revive the agricultural desolation in the Carnatic caused, in his view, by Company policy. These proposals were rejected by Dundas and the Pitt administration in their bill of 1784.

38. Burke's longstanding emphasis on "public justice," specifically to impress other European nations, appears earlier in his Indian speeches, as in his (defeated) 1781 motion against secret hearings. See "Speech on Secret Committee" (1781), *Madras and Bengal*, 5:134–39.

39. Marshall, *Launching of the Hastings Impeachment*, 6:264–66, discusses the textual problems of the impeachment "Opening," including emendations by a variety of editors working from a variety of transcript versions. Marshall's text for the Oxford edition attempts "to get back to the original transcription," reinstating a grammatical looseness that nineteenth-century editors took the liberty of correcting.

40. A more famous Burkean image of a veil—"a politic well-wrought veil"— appears in relation to the illegality of the 1688 Revolution, which Burke similarly recommends not re-viewing, in *Reflections on the Revolution in France*, 17. I am indebted to David Bromwich, Luther T. Tyler, Yoon Sun Lee, and Judith Kates for discussion of the "veil" image in Burke's writings and for (inconclusive) speculation about his echoes of veil imagery in Exodus 31 and elsewhere in Scripture. Common circulation in the eighteenth century of the metaphor of the veil in relation to British crimes in India is suggested by an anonymous letter

from an "Officer who lately served in Bengal," in *Gentleman's Magazine* 42 (February 1772): 69: "For the sake of my country, and the honour of the English name, I sincerely wish that a thick veil could be drawn over the methods of acquiring fortunes in India for some years past (especially the last seven years), as well as over the monstrous and unconstitutional powers, with which our nabobs in that country have been permitted to invest themselves."

41. For interpretation of the peroration as "a kind of prayer," see O'Brien, *The Great Melody*, 377.

42. Letter to Philip Francis, December 10, 1785, *Correspondence of Edmund Burke*, 5:241.

43. Marshall, *Impeachment of Warren Hastings*, 64–69, explains how Burke's refusal to adapt his presentation to judicial restrictions established by the so-called "law lords" led to the dismissal of much of his eloquence as evidence when challenged by the defense.

44. *Gazetteer*, February 18, 1788. Cited by Marshall, *Launching of the Hastings Impeachment*, 6:460.

45. Burke argues specifically against British imposition of English law in India as "arbitrary" and tyrannical in "Speech on Bengal Judicature Bill" (1781), *Madras and Bengal*, 5:140–42.

3. William Henry Sleeman and the Suttee Romance

1. Among the many studies of *sati* and colonialism, see especially Chatterjee, "Colonialism, Nationalism, and Colonized Women"; Spivak, "Can the Subaltern Speak?"; Mani, *Contentious Traditions*; Brantlinger, *Rule of Darkness*, 85–91. British histories of India all include discussions of "suttee," starting with James Mill's *History of British India* in 1816 and continuing well into the twentieth century. See, for example, Thompson and Garratt, *Rise and Fulfillment of British Rule in India*, 287–31. Political, social, and economic analyses begin to appear in the 1950s. See especially Ballhatchet, *Social Policy and Social Change in Western India*; Stokes, *English Utilitarians and India*. Numerous "eye-witness" accounts appear in Poynder, "Human Sacrifices in India," and in Peggs, *The Suttees' Cry to Britain: Extracts from Essays Published in India and Parliamentary Papers* (hereafter cited as *Suttees' Cry*).

2. The Anglo-Indian transliteration "suttee," for the ritual, derives from transliteration of the Sanskrit *sati*, for the woman who performs it. See Yule and Burnell, "Suttee," in *Hobson-Jobson*, 878. I use the Anglo-Indian "suttee," when referring specifically to colonial discourse, but otherwise shift to *sati*, since the earlier Anglicized term now carries colonial resonance.

3. The most far-reaching work on establishing an alternate philosophical as well as practical basis for thinking about women's human rights in a global context is being done by Amartya Sen and Martha Nussbaum. See, for example, Sen, "Capability and Well-Being"; Nussbaum, *Sex and Social Justice* and *Women and Human Development*. See also Sunder Rajan, "The Subject of Sati."

4. Sunder Rajan, "The Subject of Sati," 6.

5. See Mani, *Contentious Traditions*, 11–41.

6. Sleeman, *Rambles and Recollections of an Indian Official*. Quotations refer within the text to the edition listed in the bibliography, by volume and page number.

7. Said, *Orientalism*, 154–55, 195–97.

8. Said, *Orientalism*, 3–24 and passim. Mani, *Contentious Traditions*, 184, follows the method of deconstructing apparent exceptions, making an exception herself only of a *sati* account by a woman, Ann Chaffin, who then comes to represent what Mani generalizes into a more humane female style as differentiated from the predominant male discourse. See 185–87.

9. Said, in *Orientalism*, 9, 14, 23, frequently affirms the principle of a "dialectic" between individual texts and collective formations, but his own emphasis typically returns to the side of exposing the collective formation.

10. Thompson, *Suttee: A Historical and Philosophical Enquiry into the Hindu Rite of Widow-burning* (1928).

11. From the "Asiatic Observer" (Calcutta), October 1824; cited in Peggs, *Suttees' Cry*, 81–82.

12. See Stokes, *English Utilitarians and India*, 28–31; Hutchins, *Illusion of Permanence*, 6–13.

13. See chapter 2, n.30, 201.

14. James Mill, *History of British India*, 183, quoting Ward, "View of the History, Literature and Religion of the Hindoos" (1811).

15. Ibid., 177.

16. Eliot, *Middlemarch*, 536. Brantlinger, *Rule of Darkness*, 91, remarks the allusion to suttee as a comment on Victorian marriage and widowhood in Thackeray's *The Newcomes*.

17. Mani, in *Contentious Traditions*, 158–90, interprets eyewitness accounts of certain last-minute escapes from the pyre and subsequent expressions of fear of disgrace and poverty as evidence that the widows had more complex inner lives than colonial accounts acknowledge; although her conclusion may be accurate, the textual evidence of inner conflict is necessarily meager in these brief rescue interviews.

18. Mani, *Contentious Traditions*, 189–90 and passim, faults the British suttee discourse for ignoring material and social circumstances in favor of religious models, but even though the missionary influence strongly inflects the religious emphasis in many accounts, the archive also includes frequent emphasis on coercion driven by social and economic motives.

19. Peggs, *Suttees' Cry*, 64.

20. Ballhatchet, *Social Policy*, 275.

21. The paradoxical effect of regulation is reported in Poynder, "Human Sacrifices in India," 30–60, and in Peggs, *Suttees Cry*, 51–52. See also Thompson, *Suttee*, 62–66, 71, 74; Thompson and Garratt, *Rise and Fulfillment*, 287; Smith, *Oxford History of India*, 648; Ballhatchet, *Social Policy*, 275. Spivak, "Can the Subaltern Speak?," 300, emphasizes the economic consequences of inheritance rules in Bengal.

22. Analysis of census data appears in Poynder, "Human Sacrifices in India," 188–96; Peggs, *Suttees' Cry*, 66, 71; Thompson and Garratt, *Rise and Fulfillment*, 288, 326; Thompson, *Suttee*, 21, 29, 68; Ballhatchet, *Social Policy*, 276–78, 291.

23. John Stuart Mill, *The Subjection of Women* (1869), in *Essays on Equality, Law and Education*, vol. 21 of *Collected Works*, 303 note.

24. Thompson and Garratt, *Rise and Fulfillment*, 180–81; Madhavananda and Majumdar, eds., *Great Women of India*, 358–61; Smith, *Oxford History of India*, 490.

25. The leading Hindu reform theologian was Raja Rammohun Roy, whose writings on widow burning are reprinted in *The English Works of Raja Rammohun Roy*, 87–138; see 57–74 for his controversies with Christian missionaries. Spivak analyses the ideology of the Brahminic tradition ("Can the Subaltern Speak?," 302–3); Mani, *Contentious Traditions*, 67–80, discusses the complex relationship of Rammohun Roy to Brahminic traditions.

26. Peggs, *Suttees' Cry*, 3; see also 50, 81.

27. J. S. Mill, *Subjection of Women*, vol. 21 of *Collected Works*, 264–65.

28. See Holcombe, *Wives and Property*.

29. Holcombe explains Common Law distinctions between "real" and "personal" property and the testamentary restrictions and liberties allowed to men regarding their estates (ibid., 20–24). The widow had a right to a life interest in one-third of her husband's lands (although evasions were in practice possible), but no testamentary claim on personal property: "By the fourteenth century . . . it became possible for a man to leave to his surviving wife and children no share at all in his personal property, including that which had come to him from his wife. This freedom of testation survived well into the twentieth century" (24).

30. Wollstonecraft, *Vindication of the Rights of Woman*, 119.

31. See Hutchins, *The Illusion of Permanence*, xi, 60–61, 66, 70–78.

32. Macaulay, "Minute on Indian Education," February 2, 1835, in *Prose and Poetry*, 728.

33. Cited in Thompson, *Suttee*, 131.

34. Brantlinger, *Rule of Darkness*, 209–10; his chapter "The Well at Cawnpore: Literary Representations of the Indian Mutiny," 199–224, presents an excellent analysis of the British Mutiny literature.

35. Alexander Hamilton, in vol. 1 of *A New Account of the East Indies*, 2 vols. (London, 1744), 280, cited in Yule and Burnell, *Hobson-Jobson*, 882.

36. See Spear, *The Nabobs*, 62–63.

37. The monitory example of Antony is introduced by Trevelyan, *The Competition Wallah*, 202. Cited by Hutchins, *Illusion of Permanence*, 29. Cleopatra's death, from the perspective of *sati*, forms an interesting subject in itself.

38. Hamilton, vol. 2, 6–7, cited in Yule and Burnell, *Hobson-Jobson*, 882. See also Thompson and Garratt, *Rise and Fulfillment*, 43; Philip Woodruff (pseudonym for Philip Mason), *Founders of Modern India*, vol. 1 of *Men Who Ruled India*, 74.

39. Verne, *Around the World in Eighty Days*, 45–46.

40. Sleeman, "Suttee on the Nerbudda," in *Rambles and Recollections*, 1:24–40.

41. *DNB*, 18:373.

42. Woodruff (Mason), *Founders of Modern India*, 254.

43. Mani, *Contentious Traditions*, 172–74, discusses the problematic nature of so-called "voluntary" *sati*.

44. Coomaraswamy, "Status of Indian Women," in *The Dance of Siva*, 91–92. Cited by Thompson as an epigraph to *Suttee*.

45. See Thompson, *Suttee*, 138; for post–World War I disillusionment with the ideal of heroic self-sacrifice, see also Fussell, *The Great War and Modern Memory*, 21–24, 153–54.

46. Clifford, *The Predicament of Culture*, 41–51.

47. Spivak, "Can the Subaltern Speak?," 297, 307, generalizes that in accounts of *sati*, "one never encounters the testimony of the woman's voice-consciousness"; Mani, *Contentious Traditions*, 162–80, does include interesting brief examples of reported speech from the aftermath of rescue scenes in order to demonstrate more "agency" among victimized widows than Spivak and others acknowledge, but none of these dialogues involves a determined resolve later carried out.

48. Spear, *The Nabobs*, 129–41, discusses increasing British racism and withdrawal from social intercourse with Indians (especially Hindus) in the "reformed" administration of the first half of the nineteenth century.

49. See Sabin, *Dialect of the Tribe*, 16–17.

50. The credo appears, in virtually the same words, on 2:174 of Sleeman, *Rambles and Recollections*.

51. Kakar, *Intimate Relations*, 43–63.

52. Said, *Orientalism*, 93.

4. Victorian Oblivion and The Moonstone

1. *The Moonstone* was serialized in *All the Year Round* for the first eight months of 1868; public excitement in anticipation of the installments is described by Davis, *Life of Wilkie Collins*, 257.

2. Reed, "English Imperialism and the Unacknowledged Crime of *The Moonstone*," 288 and passim. See also Lonoff, *Wilkie Collins and His Victorian Readers*, 178–79; Thomas, *Dreams of Authority*, 205–9; Heller, *Dead Secrets*, 143–48; Nayder, *Wilkie Collins*, 115–25.

3. Roy, "The Fabulous Imperialist Semiotic of Wilkie Collins's *The Moonstone*," 657–81.

4. Ibid., 676; for analogy to Conan Doyle, "The Great Agra Treasure," see 678–79 n. 10. Roy's argument, that the novel presents "a *mythos* entirely consonant with arguments for empire" (657), adds the topic of imperialism to the more general argument by Miller in *Novel and the Police*, 36 and 33–57 passim, that *The Moonstone* "restricts its scope to a socially approved enterprise."

5. My emphasis runs contrary to Miller, in *The Novel and the Police*, who contends that the novel affirms "the policing power inscribed in ordinary practices and institutions" (46–47).

6. Seeley, *Expansion of England*. Quotations refer by page number within the text to the edition cited in the bibliography.

7. Roy, "Fabulous Imperialist Semiotic," 676.

8. Thomas, *Dreams of Authority*, 212, interestingly discusses Jennings's reading experiment as anticipating the methods of psychoanalysis.

9. Collins, *The Moonstone*. Quotations refer by page number within the text to the edition cited in the bibliography.

10. Brantlinger, "The Nineteenth-Century Novel and Empire," 562. Brantlinger also invokes what he calls Seeley's "misleading dictum" in *Rule of Darkness*, 7. Other analogous uses of Seeley's famous sentence appear in Said, *Culture and Imperialism*, 9; Perera, *Reaches of Empire*, 1. See Sabin, "Literary Reading in Interdisciplinary Study."

11. Cited by Lonoff, *Wilkie Collins and His Victorian Readers*, 66, 248 n. 86, from an unpublished letter to Edward Smyth Pigott. Lonoff presents thorough and astute assessment of Collins's relationship to the Victorian reading public. I am indebted to her research.

12. "Preface to the Revised Edition," May 1871, reprinted in *The Moonstone*, 29–30.

13. Lonoff, *Wilkie Collins and His Victorian Readers*, 171, 260 n. 2, cites William Winter, *Old Friends: Being Literary Recollections of Other Days* (New York: Moffat, Yard, 1909), 112–13, and Mary Anderson de Navarro, *A Few Memories* (New York: Harper, 1896), 141–42.

14. Lonoff, *Wilkie Collins and His Victorian Readers*, 171–73.

15. Frequently cited letter of September 24, 1858, from Dickens to W. H. Wills, subeditor of *Household Words* and *All the Year Round*, in *Letters of Charles Dickens*: "I wish you to look well to Wilkie's article . . . and not leave anything in it that may be sweepingly and unnecessarily offensive to the middle class. He has always a tendency to overdo that" (8:669).

16. William Shakespeare, *A Midsummer Night's Dream*, V.i.423–26.

17. Reed, "English Imperialism," 284. See also Roy, "Fabulous Imperialist Semiotic," 671.

18. Good accounts of Collins's Indian research in history and contemporary events appear in Lonoff, *Wilkie Collins and His Victorian Readers*, 176–80, and in Sandra Kemp's notes for *The Moonstone*, 473–75. Collins's sources include J. Talboys Wheeler, vol. 1 of *The History of India* (London: Trubner, 1867); Theodore Hook, *The Life of General Sir David Baird, Bart.* (London: Bentley, 1833); *Encyclopedia Britannica*, 8th ed. (1860); C. W. King, *The Natural History of Precious Stones and Gems, and of the Precious Metals* (London: Bell and Daldy, 1865).

19. The relevance of the 1848–1849 Anglo-Sikh wars and victory in the Punjab to Collins's Indian framework has been widely remarked. See Reed, "English Imperialism," 287; Lonoff, *Wilkie Collins and His Victorian Readers*, 176; Roy, "Fabulous Imperialist Semiotic," 658.

20. Collins, "The Great (Forgotten) Invasion." Teltscher, *India Inscribed*, 246–55, discusses celebration of the British victory at Seringapatam in painting and historiography.

21. See Hook, *Life of General Sir David Baird*, 1:217. Cited by Nayder, *Wilkie Collins*, 119. See also Kemp, notes for *The Moonstone*, 474 n. 9; Lonoff, *Wilkie Collins and His Victorian Readers*, 177.

22. Hook, *Life of General Sir David Baird*, 1:200–201. Cited by Kemp, notes for *The Moonstone*, 475 n. 10.

23. George Elers, cited by Kemp, notes for *The Moonstone*, 474 n. 4. Among the treasures looted from the palace of Tipu Sultan after his defeat at Seringapatam was the musical organ enclosed in the representation of a royal tiger in the act of devouring a prostrate British soldier. A photograph of this object, known as "Tippoo's Tiger," appears on the jacket cover of this book. For historical accounts of "Tippoo's Tiger" in the court of Tipu Sultan and its later history as a popular exhibition item in London, see Archer, *Tippoo's Tiger*, and Buddle, *Tigers Round the Throne*.

24. See chapter 2, 65.

25. See Lonoff, *Wilkie Collins and His Victorian Readers*, 176–77; Roy, "Fabulous Imperialist Semiotic," 678 n. 8.

26. As with *sati* for suttee and Awadh for Oudh, changes in the transliteration of Indian words and names cause difficulties in choice of spelling. Except when referring to earlier texts, I follow modern English spellings (for example, Tipu for "Tippoo," Mohammedan for "Mahometan," Mahmud of Ghazni for "Mahmoud of Ghazmi").

27. Teltscher, *India Inscribed*, 111–28, discusses commonplace justification for British rule because of the Mughal empire's disintegration. Bayly, *Indian Society and the Making of the British Empire*, calls into question this interpretive tradition (81–82) and, more specifically, reinterprets Tipu Sultan's significant political and economic threat to British power (97–99).

28. Geraldine Jewsbury, in an unsigned review of *The Moonstone*, *Athenaeum*, July 25, 1868, 106, reprinted in Page, ed., *Wilkie Collins: The Critical Heritage*, 170, praises the "solemn and pathetic human interest" of the epilogue.

29. I am indebted to Roy, "Fabulous Imperialist Semiotic," 679 n. 13, for directing me to the parliamentary debate over Ellenborough's venture. Smith, *Oxford History of India*, 605–6, describes the episode with the further comment that the gates were later ascertained not to be the lost originals.

30. Macaulay, "The Gates of Somnauth," 348, 339.

31. Ibid., 330, 323.

32. Ibid., 331; Smith, *Oxford History of India*, 606, identifies the gates taken by Ellenborough as coming from Mahmud of Ghazni's tomb, not from a mosque as Macaulay charges, with the effect of heightening a religious insult to Mohammedans.

33. Macaulay, "The Gates of Somnauth," 337, 325.

34. Reed, "English Imperialism," 289; Thomas, *Dreams of Authority*, finds the novel's affirmation in its model of a "cooperative hermeneutic drama" (210).

35. I agree with Lonoff, *Wilkie Collins and His Victorian Readers*, in judging Collins a "rebellious Victorian" whose "social criticism . . . is most expressive when it is least blatant" (230).

36. See Clarke, *The Secret Life of Wilkie Collins*, 54–57. Collins's first book was a memoir of his father, *Memoirs of the Life of William Collins, Esq. R.A. with Selections from His Journals and Correspondence*, 2 vols. (London: Longman, Brown, Green and Longmans, 1848).

37. For sexual interpretations of the theft of Rachel's jewel, see, among others, Thomas, *Dreams of Authority*, 203–19; Lawson, "Wilkie Collins and *The Moonstone*"; Rycroft, "A Detective Story."

38. See Lonoff, *Wilkie Collins and His Victorian Readers*, 191 and 265 n. 61.

39. Lonoff, *Wilkie Collins and His Victorian Readers*, 32, cites an unpublished letter by Collins to his mother, written in France in 1845, in which he notes his surprise that a "kitchen maid" from an earlier visit had sent regards to him: "Fancy the astonishment of a thoroughbred Englishman at hearing that a kitchen-maid named Virginia (!) whom he scarcely recollected and whom he never feed [*sic*] with money, had sent him her kindest remembrances." Collins's own attentiveness to women of lower social classes led him to his notoriously unconventional dual household, with a "morganatic" marriage to a fisherman's daughter in one and a widow who later served as his housekeeper in the other. See Clarke, *Secret Life*, 125–33.

40. See the introduction, 23.

41. Roy, "Fabulous Imperialist Semiotic," 673. Nayder, *Wilkie Collins*, 122–23, observes the "idealized colonial relationship" in Jennings's devotion to Franklin.

42. Dickens's indebtedness to *The Moonstone* in *The Mystery of Edwin Drood* (1870) has been frequently noted. See Cardwell, introduction to *The Mystery of Edwin Drood*, viii–ix. Thomas, *Dreams of Authority*, 219–37, uses Freudian terms to analyze the "dialectical relationship between the personal and the political" in both novels; his emphasis on the hero-villain Jasper's "self-repression" and unintelligible dream focuses on the combined obsession and repression of criminality in the imperialist psyche.

43. Macaulay, "Minute on Indian Education," 729.

44. Neville's "infatuation" is for Miss Rosebud, the quintessence of English innocence.

45. Miller, *Novel and the Police*, 41, ignores Jennings's crucial role when he asserts that Cuff's departure turns the investigation over to "prominent members of the community" (41).

46. J. S. Mill was instrumental in the Jamaica Committee's call for Eyre's criminal conviction. Nayder, *Wilkie Collins*, 102–7, discusses Collins's ambivalent response to the Jamaican crisis, as represented in the novel *Armadale* (1866).

47. Letter to Angela Burdett-Coutts, October 4, 1857, *Letters of Charles Dickens*, 8:459. Dickens's sentence continues: "and that I begged them to do me the favor to observe that I was there for that purpose and no other, and was now proceeding, with all convenient dispatch and merciful swiftness of execution, to blot it out of mankind and raze it off the face of the earth." Brantlinger, *Rule of Darkness*, 207, cites the letter as part of the racist frenzy of British Mutiny discourse.

48. Conrad, *Heart of Darkness*, 51.

49. Collins, "Sermon for Sepoys." Brantlinger, *Rule of Darkness*, 206, neglects to mention this article, citing Collins in relation to the Mutiny only as coauthor with Dickens of a Christmas story published in *Household Words* a few months earlier: "The Perils of Certain English Prisoners," reprinted as a work by Dickens in volume 13 of *Works* (New York: Bigelow, Brown, n.d.), 207–68. Brantlinger, 295 n. 19, mentions *The Moonstone* only in passing as reflecting the Mutiny "perhaps in an anti-imperialist way"; his chapter "The Well at Cawnpore: Literary Representations of the Indian Mutiny of 1857" serves the purpose of presenting the majority discourse, rather than deviations or exceptions to it. Collins's ambivalent attitude toward his collaboration with Dickens on "The Perils" is discussed by Davis, *Life of Wilkie Collins* (208); he characterizes Collins's contribution (chapter 2) as comic, with the effect of making a "burlesque out of Dickens' philipic against the Sepoys." Davis dates the assignment and composition of "Sermon for Sepoys" to the weeks before "The Perils" and traces the origin of the story to Dickens's dissatisfaction with Collins's article, publication of which was delayed until March 1858 (three months after "The Perils" appeared).

50. Collins, "Sermon for Sepoys," 244.

51. See Lonoff, *Wilkie Collins and His Victorian Readers*, 51; Clarke, *Secret Life*, 125.

52. Thomas, *Dreams of Authority*, 206–7, conflates the idea of Jennings's "self-possession," in the sense of keeping secrets, and "repression," in the Freudian sense of emotions closed off from consciousness. For discussion of Jennings's "self-suppression," see also Heller, *Dead Secrets*, 142.

Prologue to Part II

1. Orwell, *Road to Wigan Pier*, 177.

2. Among the Bengali writers of the nineteenth century involved in this advocacy as both creative writers and critics, Michael Madhusudan Dutt, Bankimchandra Chatterjee, and Rabindranath Tagore are included in the anthology *Picador Book of Modern Indian Literature*, ed. Amit Chaudhuri. These writers are also discussed by Nirad C. Chaudhuri in *Autobiography of an Unknown Indian*, 188–89, as I remark further in chapter 5, 123–24.

3. Macaulay's case for the civilization conveyed through English writing, presented in his "Minute on Indian Education," was famously influential on the decision in the late 1830s to establish English as the language for Indian higher education.

4. M. K. Gandhi, "To the Students" (Ahmedabad: Navajivan, 1949), 14–22; reprinted as "Benares University Speech," in *The Gandhi Reader: A Source Book of His Life and Writings*, ed. Homer A. Jack, 129–36. Quotations refer by page number within the text to this edition, listed in the bibliography. Jack's headnote explains that "Gandhi's frankness in criticizing both British and Indian shortcomings led to such an uproar in the audience that he was unable to finish his speech" (128).

5. Publishing details of *My Experiments with Truth* are included in Jack, *The Gandhi Reader*, vi, 3.

6. Wolpert, in *A New History of India*, 368–70, succinctly describes the language and regional threats to the federation of independent India in the 1950s. The establishment of Urdu as the national language of Pakistan, along with the continuing predominance of English as the language of government, higher education, and the judicial system, is succinctly described by Craig Baxter et al. in *Government and Politics in South Asia*, 166–68; Tariq Rahman, in *Language, Education, and Culture*, 65–70, explains in further detail the complexity and conflicts of multilingual Pakistan, including the threat to Pakistani national unity in the 1950s posed by the predominance of the Bengali language in East Pakistan (later Bangladesh).

7. Amit Chaudhuri's *Picador Book of Modern Indian Literature* seeks to redress the skewed perception on the part of English-only readers of Indian modern literature by featuring English translations of Indian vernacular writers. It is noticeable, however, that of the writers born since 1925, the anthology includes only seven selections originally written in the vernacular, as compared to fourteen written originally in English; only two living writers of Hindi are included: Nirmal Verma (b. 1929) and Krishna Sobti (b. 1925). Chaudhuri acknowledges in his introduction that his selection was limited by the paucity of good translations as well as by space (xxxi–xxxiv). Meenakshi Mukherjee discusses the limitations of publicity and marketing of the increasing number and quality of translations into English from Indian languages, in "Divided by a Common Language," in *The Perishable Empire*, 187–203.

8. Fanon, *Black Skin, White Masks*; Memmi, *The Colonizer and the Colonized*; Ngugi wa Thiong'o, *Decolonising the Mind*.

9. Goonatilake, *Crippled Minds*; Nandy, *The Intimate Enemy*; Jha, *The Imprisoned Mind*; Chatterjee, *Nationalist Thought and the Colonial World*; Viswanathan, *Masks of Conquest*.

10. The distorting imposition of Western postcolonial studies on the Indian situation is a major theme of Ahmad, *In Theory*.

5. The Beast in Nirad Chaudhuri's Garden

1. Nirad C. Chaudhuri, *The Autobiography of an Unknown Indian*. Quotations refer by page number within the text to the edition listed in the bibliography.

2. Notable counterparts to Chaudhuri in his devotion to the fruits of a colonial literary education appear in both Anglophone and Francophone Africa and the Caribbean; the best-known parallel in Chaudhuri's generation is the Trinidadian writer and political leader C. L. R. James, whose Marxist political activism and leadership have sustained his reputation for resistance despite his open indebtedness to Western literary influences. For a good introduction to James's writings, see *The C. L. R. James Reader*, ed. Anna Grimshaw (Oxford: Blackwell, 1992). Said, in "Third World Intellectuals and Metropolitan Culture," writes appreciatively about James's accomplishment as a prewar anticolonial intellectual who "stood stubbornly for the Western heritage, at the same time that he belonged also to the insur-

rectionary anti-imperialist moment" (36). Chaudhuri's antirevolutionary politics, by contrast, have cost him regard from postcolonial cultural critics.

3. Rushdie, *Imaginary Homelands*, 67.

4. Ibid., 12.

5. See Verghese, "Nirad C. Chaudhuri"; Walsh, *Growing Up in British India*; Philip, *Perceiving India through the Works of Nirad C. Chaudhuri, Narayan and Ved Mehta*.

6. Nirad C. Chaudhuri, "India's Kulturkampf."

7. Mukherjee compares Chaudhuri's English style and themes to the Bengali writing he had published during his youth in Calcutta, but resumed only thirty years later, in the mid-1960s; Mukherjee sees consistency in Chaudhuri's wit and provocative iconoclasm in both languages but observes his pleasure in bawdy and the "crude energy" of popular culture in his Bengali writing. See " 'We say Desh': The Other Nirad Babu," in *The Perishable Empire*, 117–33.

8. William Walsh astutely describes the "late-Victorian flavour" of Chaudhuri's *Autobiography* in *Indian Literature in English*, 45.

9. *The Golden Treasury of the Best Songs and Lyrical Poems in the English Language*, selected and arranged with notes by Francis Turner Palgrave, first appeared in 1861 and was reissued regularly as a textbook for use throughout the English-speaking world, even after Palgrave's death in 1897. The shorter *Children's Treasury of Lyrical Poetry*, with a preface dedicating the book to the "dear English and English-speaking children, all the world over," was first published in 1876. Palgrave's policy of excluding living poets left Tennyson out of the early editions, but twelve poems by Tennyson were added to the 1892 edition of the *Children's Treasury*. Chaudhuri's recollections of reading Tennyson in Palgrave probably refer to this edition.

10. The commentators who criticize Chaudhuri by the standard of objectivity include Iyengar, *Indian Writing in English*, 600; Verghese, *Nirad C. Chaudhuri*, 31; Sudesh Mishra, "The Two Chaudhuris."

11. Nirad C. Chaudhuri, *Thy Hand, Great Anarch!*, 918. Previous to this long-delayed continuation of his autobiographical narrative, Chaudhuri published an account of his first trip to England, *A Passage to England* (1959).

12. See chapter 4, 106.

13. Chaudhuri, *Thy Hand, Great Anarch!* (1987), 957.

14. Joyce, *Ulysses*, 28, 47–150: "and on a heath beneath winking stars a fox, red reek of rapine in his fur, with merciless bright eyes scraped in the earth, listened, scraped up the earth, listened, scraped and scraped." Webster's dirge is suggested as a possible source for Joyce's image by William Schutte, cited by Thornton, *Allusions in "Ulysses,"* 31. Schutte traces the scavenging wolf to Webster's *Duchess of Malfi* (IV.ii. 332–34) as well as to *The White Devil*, where the lyric of the dirge appears (V.iv. 97–98). Thornton explains the proverbial superstition that wolves dug up murdered bodies.

15. McCutchion, review of *Indian Writing in English*, by K. R. Srinivasa Iyengar, *Quest* (1962), reprinted in McCutchion, *Indian Writing in English*, 59–61.

16. Desani, in *All about H. Hatterr* (1948), experimented with a parodic English style for an Indo-English novel. His book was composed, published, and noticed in England in the 1940s but did not at that time reach or influence Indian writers. T. S. Eliot's praise is cited by Anthony Burgess, in his introduction to the 1986 reprint of *All about H. Hatterr*, 8.

17. *The Woman in White* was a popular international success from the time of its publication in 1860. Collins's interest for Indian readers was heightened by the Indian elements in *The Moonstone* (1868).

6. *The Politics of Cultural Freedom*

1. Seth, *A Suitable Boy*, 1112.

2. Coleman presents a judicious history of the Congress for Cultural Freedom in *The Liberal Conspiracy*; Lasch's abbreviated history, "The Cultural Cold War," in *The Agony of the American Left*, 63-114, presents a harsher critique.

3. See Jeffreys-Jones, *The CIA and American Democracy*. Between March and September 1967, articles reporting and analyzing the "scandal" of CIA financing appeared in every serious Anglo-American journal of opinion; notable examples include Chomsky, "The Responsibility of Intellectuals," *New York Review of Books*, February 23, 1967; Epstein, "The CIA and the Intellectuals," *New York Review of Books*, April 20, 1967; Kopkind, "CIA: The Great Corruptor," *New Statesman*, February 24, 1967; Coser, "The CIA—Enemy or Promise," *Dissent*, May/June 1967; *Dissent*, September/October 1967, also reprinted an earlier article by Harrington criticizing the American Committee for Cultural Freedom, "Liberalism: A Moral Crisis," in order to register the early date of *Dissent*'s warnings about government involvement in the Congress for Cultural Freedom.

4. See Muggeridge (writing in his role as former president of the British Committee for Cultural Freedom), "Books," *Esquire*, September 1967.

5. See Coleman, *The Liberal Conspiracy*, 48-50.

6. By comparison with the harsh contempt of the younger generation of New Left critics, such as Kopkind, Chomsky, and Lasch, a tone of rueful sympathy marks the writers of *Dissent*, such as Coser, Harrington, and Howe, who had been struggling for decades with the difficulty of formulating an independent anti-Stalinist radical position; they are willing to grant their former colleagues and friends complexities and "generous" impulses gone awry in the Congress for Cultural Freedom.

7. Coleman, *The Liberal Conspiracy*, 149.

8. Kristol, *Reflections of a Neoconservative*. See also Shils, "Remembering the Congress for Cultural Freedom." Coleman, *The Liberal Conspiracy*, 152-53, describes Shils's role as chief Congress advisor to Indian programs.

9. Coleman, *The Liberal Conspiracy*, 77.

10. For discussion of the slow awakening in the postwar period from long-standing American ignorance and indifference to India, see Isaacs, *Scratches on Our Minds*, 283-91 and passim.

11. Burnham, "Parakeets and Parchesi." See also Orwell, "Reflections on Gandhi."

12. *Quest*, no. 17 (April–May 1958), features a change in subtitle from "A Bimonthly of Arts and Ideas" to "A Quarterly of Inquiry, Criticism, and Ideas" and announces the shift of editorship from Nissim Ezekial to Abu Sayeed Ayyub and Amlan Datta. Nirad C. Chaudhuri and Sudhin Datta, from the original group of advisory editors, remain, but Laxmanshastri Joshi replaces D. G. Nadkarni. The new editors explain that the new title signals a shift of orientation from "arts" to "ideas," with more emphasis on "cultural freedom" as it pertains to the Cold War (10). This narrowing of political focus, however, does not in actuality change the proportion of the journal given to literature for the remainder of the 1950s.

13. Natarajan, *American Shadow over India*, 195, 204–9, 251. In his preface, Natarajan ironically thanks the U.S. Information Service for "its generous, if unwitting cooperation" (xvi), since his sources are largely U.S. publications such as the *New York Times* and *Newsweek* (some sent by his anonymous American correspondent).

14. Natarajan, *American Shadow*, xi.

15. See Passin, "The Jeevan-Dani." See also Jha, "Three Gandhian Gurus: Jayaprakash Narayan, Vinoba Bhave, and Morajio Desai," in *The Imprisoned Mind*, 130–50.

16. Masani, in his essay "Bhoodan in Action," cites this phrasing as recollected speech by Narayan: "'Bhoodan,' Jayaprakash would say, 'is thus a great mass movement of conversion and the creation of a new climate of thought and values of life. It brings about a living and immediate revolution in the minds of men and their mutual relationships. It attacks and corrects here and now the system of exploitation and inequality. It teaches men to share what they have with their fellowmen.'" Masani is actually quoting from a published article by Narayan: "Jeevandan," first published in *Janata* (1954), reprinted in Narayan, *Socialism, Sarvodaya and Democracy*, 123–25. Quotations from *Encounter* are identified by volume, date, and page number within the text.

17. See chapter 5 n. 6, 213.

18. Quotations from *Quest* are identified within the text by volume, date, and page number until April 1958, and by number and date thereafter, when the new quarterly format identifies issues only by date and number.

19. Irele, "African Letters."

20. See chapter 5, 132.

21. A taste for Joyce seems to have been a mark of sophistication in India of the 1950s, as indicated by the campaign of Vikram Seth's young English instructor in *A Suitable Boy* to have Joyce included in the English curriculum of "Brahmpur" University.

22. Cited by Wald in *The New York Intellectuals*, 272.

23. Narayan's later activities exceed the scope of this chapter, but it is worth remarking that, like Chaudhuri, though with very different politics, he outlived the Congress for Cultural Freedom to remain one of India's most indomitable

dissenters. He returned to politics in the 1970s and was arrested and imprisoned at age seventy-three for organizing mass nonviolent protest against Indira Gandhi's policies in the Emergency. For an account of Narayan's political activities in the 1970s, see Wolpert, *A New History of India*, 394–410.

24. In his June 1958 profile of Narayan in *Encounter*, Passin more reverently endorses and echoes Hallam Tennyson's idealization of self-sacrificing Indian spirituality: "There is nothing that stirs Indians to such enthusiasm as the spectacle of a man in the fullness of life making an act of renunciation" (46).

25. For discussion of the limited successes of and the practical obstacles to the Bhoodan movement, see Linton, *Fragments of a Vision*, 255–59. In addition to noting the large proportion of uncultivatable land among the four-and-one-half-million acres gifted during the 1950s, Linton observes the lack of appeal to educated classes of the movement's religious image (and poorly edited written material). The Bhoodan goal had been to redistribute fifty million acres of gifted cultivatable land to landless peasants. The resistance of large landholders to the Congress Party's legal measures for land distribution in the 1950s forms a major plot line in Seth's *A Suitable Boy*.

26. For a strong statement against "enlightenment rationalism" as mere mimicry of colonial discourse, see Chakrabarty, "Postcoloniality and the Artifice of History."

27. Warnings against the authoritarian dangers in religious revivalism continued under the new editorship of *Quest*, as in the inaugural editorial by Ayyub and Datta, which notes that "the medievalist-authoritarian trend in our culture makes us very susceptible to totalitarian influences" (*Quest*, no. 17 [April–June 1958]: 11). The tragic terrorist attacks of September 11, 2001, in New York and Washington, D.C., brought to American public attention the fateful consequences of America's opportunistic and shortsighted support of another authoritarian religious movement for the purposes of anti-Communist warfare in Afghanistan in the 1980s. Writing before the American crisis, Pankaj Mishra, in "The Birth of a Nation," discusses this history in the context of the ongoing struggles in Kashmir (37).

28. Chakrabarty, "Postcoloniality," 5, 8, interprets the self-deprecating emphasis on "lack" in Indian writing as colonialized mimicry of Western stereotypes of the East. Imagery of loss and "nothingness" in Western literature of the twentieth century, however, is not focused principally on the East. Joshi's deconstruction of nationalist myth making in 1957 can be understood as an Indian version of a worldwide modern sentiment and, more particularly, as a search for language to articulate difficulties and conflicts within postcolonial India. Insofar as Joshi's encounter with nothingness participates in Western discourse, the affiliation is as persuasively to anticolonial modernists, such as the Joyce of *Dubliners*, as to Orientalist discourse.

29. *Encounter* announced its separation from the Congress for Cultural Freedom in a postscript in 23 (July 1964): 96; the journal continued as an independent publication until 1990.

30. Jussawalla, "Resurrecting the Prophet." Jussawalla makes the same complaint about Rushdie in "Decolonizing the Decolonizers" and *Family Quarrels*, 103–23.

7. Individuality as a Problem in Naipaul's Indian Narratives

1. Said, "Intellectuals in the Post-Colonial World," 53.

2. I agree with Suleri's argument in *Rhetoric of English India* that "the need for angry critiques" of Naipaul's work is now "obsolete" (158) and with her complex interpretation of his writing's troubled internal dynamics (149–73). Gorra, *After Empire*, 93–96, also perceptively presents Naipaul's unresolved pursuit of individuality in his fiction and other writing.

3. Nixon, *London Calling*, comments on Naipaul's "jealous individualism" and "insurmountable suspicion of group identities" (85).

4. "A Conversation" with Robert Boyers and Bharati Mukherjee, *Salamagundi*, 5.

5. Jameson, "Third-World Literature in the Era of Multinational Capitalism," 85.

6. For influential critique of Jameson's essay, see Ahmad, "Jameson's Rhetoric of Otherness and the National Allegory," *Social Text* 17 (fall 1987): 3–25, reprinted in Ahmad, *In Theory*, 95–122. Ahmad wrote not in defense of Westernized individualists such as Naipaul, but as an Indian Marxist sensitive to the blurring of class divisions and the false homogenization of very different national situations in the Western category of "third world." See also Sabin, "Lu Xun."

7. Naipaul, *India: A Million Mutinies Now*. Quotations refer by page number within the text to the edition listed in the bibliography. The interviews for this book took place during a trip in 1989. The trip that was the basis for *An Area of Darkness* took place in 1961–1962.

8. For discussion of William Henry Sleeman as interviewer, see chapter 3, 81–83. Henry Mayhew was a Victorian journalist whose newspaper interviews with the poor in London became the four-volume classic *London Labour and the London Poor* (London: Griffin, Bohn, 1861–1862); Orwell's *Road to Wigan Pier* began with an assignment from the Left Book Club to report on the condition of the unemployed in the coal mining area of Wigan during the Depression. His interviews became the basis of a more far-ranging book that in its second half shifts to an extended autobiographical narrative and meditation on imperialism and socialism.

9. See Clifford, *The Predicament of Culture*, cited in chapter 3, 81.

10. See, for example, Studs Terkel, *Division Street: America* (New York: Pantheon, 1967), a sampling of attitudes toward the civil rights movement among Chicagoans in the late 1960s, and *Race* (New York: Pantheon, 1974), a compendium of American black and white voices.

11. Xinxin Zhang and Sang Ye, *Chinese Lives* (New York: Pantheon, 1987).

12. Nixon, *London Calling*, 168–72, presents a contrary evaluation, praising

India: A Million Mutinies Now for its "startling freshness" due to Naipaul's new role as "professional listener."

13. Naipaul, *The Enigma of Arrival*. Quotations refer within the text to the edition cited in the bibliography, by page number and abbreviated title (EA). Suleri, *Rhetoric of English India*, 165–73, offers a subtle and appreciative reading of the autobiographical chapter "The Journey" (EA, 97–179).

14. Naipaul, *An Area of Darkness*; quotations refer by page number within the text to the edition cited in the bibliography.

15. For the parallel between India and medieval Europe, see Metcalf, *Ideologies of the Raj*, 72–80.

16. Nixon, *London Calling*, traces Naipaul's fear of disappearing into the "quicksands of oblivion" to his perception of his father's disappointments as a writer (12).

17. Nixon, *London Calling*, discusses Naipaul's obsession with sight as the source of authority (80–87).

18. Kanga, review of *India: A Million Mutinies Now*.

19. Miller, review of *India: A Million Mutinies Now*, 11.

20. Ezekial observes and criticizes Naipaul's restrictive conceptions of freedom and escape in "Naipaul's India and Mine," 74: "That temperament is not universal, not even widely distributed, that choice is not open to all, the escape for most is not from the community but into it. To forget this is to be wholly subjective, wholly self-righteous, to think first and last of one's own expectations, one's extreme discomfort." Cited by Nixon, *London Calling*, 85.

21. Nixon, *London Calling*, remarks that even in *India: A Million Mutinies Now*, Naipaul "invariably perceives community or collective endeavor of any kind as a noose, strangling all hope of solitude and individuality" (172).

8. Epilogue: Pankaj Mishra

1. "Pankaj Mishra Chat" [February 5, 2000], Rediff on the Net, referred to within the text in future citations as Rediff.

2. In an "unedited" portion of Rediff, posted as an appendix, "Biblio" identifies himself as Nigel Leask, fellow and professor at Queen's College, Cambridge University. Mishra's novel received very good reviews in the United States, especially in the *New York Review of Books* (February 24, 2000), the *New York Times* (March 21, 2000), and the *Washington Post* (March 5, 2000). In England, more critical judgments appeared in *The Economist* (March 18, 2000), *New Statesman* (February 14, 2000), and *The Observer* (February 13, 2000). In India, the *Hindustan Times* (January 6, 2000) offered a mixed review. For summary of many reviews, see "The Complete Review: *The Romantics*, by Pankaj Mishra."

3. See chapter 7, 157.

4. Mishra, *The Romantics: A Novel*. Quotations refer by page number within the text to the edition listed in the bibliography.

5. Cited in Mishra, "House of Mr. Naipaul." Quotations from this essay are identified by page number within the text.

6. Mishra invokes *Enigma of Arrival*'s fuller representation of Naipaul's early years in England in "House of Mr. Naipaul," 15. See also chapter 7, 160–61.

7. Mishra, "The Great Narayan." Quotations from this essay are identified by page number within the text .

8. The modal auxiliary is one of several syntactical techniques used by Naipaul to reconstruct the experience of actual figures from history or his own earlier life in what he calls "an imaginative exercise" in *A Way in the World*, 74. Naipaul thus imagines Christopher Columbus's landfall in Trinidad: "He would have kept well clear of the Point. . . . A few hours on from that, he would have had his first glimpse of the South American continent. He would have taken it for another island" (73); in another chapter, the black Trinidadian acquaintance of his youth, later murdered in East Africa: "He would always have been too old for the better schools, and he would never have had the clear vision of a way ahead that had been given to me. . . . He would have always had to feel his way" (363). Other details from Mishra's own "imaginative exercise," in relation to the Naipaul family, include Seepersad's coercion of his mother to stay in Trinidad rather than repatriate to India: "She, if not Seepersad, would have had some regret about that"(14); about Naipaul's novel, *A House for Mr Biswas*: "It is . . . a valuable historical record of what would have been an intellectually neglected part of the world."

9. Mishra, "The Last Englishman."

10. Ibid.

11. Mishra, "The Art of Inquisition."

12. Mishra, "Little Inkling."

13. Ibid.

14. Mishra, *Butter Chicken in Ludhiana*, 24.

15. Mishra describes the decline of Allahabad University similarly in "The Other India," 93.

16. The influence of Naipaul's *A Bend in the River* on *The Romantics* can be felt most strongly in the narrative description of cultural isolation and insecurity in the opening pages of both novels.

17. For the comparison of Marlow to "a meditating Buddha," see Conrad, *Heart of Darkness*, 76.

18. Flaubert, *Sentimental Education*; Edmund Wilson, "Flaubert's Politics."

19. Chekhov, "My Life," 71 and passim. Mishra remarks the importance to him of Chekhov in Rediff.

20. Mishra, "Edmund Wilson in Benares."

21. Mishra, *Romantics*, 169, and "Edmund Wilson in Benares," *Picador Book*, 362–63.

22. Mishra, "The Other India." Quotations refer by page number within the text to the article listed in the bibliography.

23. Mishra's controversial trio of articles about Kashmir appeared first in *The Hindu* as: "Paradise Lost," August 27, 2000; "Destroyed Lives," September 3, 2000; "Peace or a Piece of Land," September 10, 2000. The articles were published shortly after in the *New York Review of Books* as "Death in Kashmir," "The

Birth of a Nation," "Kashmir: The Unending War." A sample of Indian criticism of Mishra's Kashmir reportage (and a reply to it by him) appears at *Outlook* [online] www.outlookindia.com.

24. Naipaul, *An Area of Darkness*, 266–71. See my discussion of this episode in chapter 7, 164–65.

25. See, for example, Tolstoy, *What Then Must We Do?*; Orwell, *Road to Wigan Pier*; Agee and Evans, *Let Us Now Praise Famous Men*.

26. Tharoor, "A Bedeviling Question in the Cadence of English."

27. See Ahmad, *In Theory*, 48–49.

BIBLIOGRAPHY

Primary Texts

Agee, James, and Walker Evans. *Let Us Now Praise Famous Men: Three Tenant Families.* Boston: Houghton Mifflin, 1941.

Bailur, M. G. "Bhoodan and Sarvodaya: A Critique of an Ideology." *Quest* 1 (August 1955): 5–10.

Burke, Edmund. *The Correspondence of Edmund Burke.* Vol. 5. Edited by Holden Furber (with the assistance of P. J. Marshall). Cambridge: Cambridge University Press, 1965.

———. *India: The Launching of the Hastings Impeachment, 1786–1788.* Edited by P. J. Marshall. Vol. 6, *The Writings and Speeches of Edmund Burke*, edited by Paul Langford. Oxford: Clarendon, 1991.

———. *India: Madras and Bengal, 1774–1785.* Edited by P. J. Marshall. Vol. 5, *The Writings and Speeches of Edmund Burke*, edited by Paul Langford. Oxford: Clarendon, 1981.

———. *A Philosophical Enquiry into the Origin of Our Ideas of the Sublime and Beautiful.* 1757. Edited by James T. Boulton. London: Routledge and Paul, 1958.

———. *Reflections on the Revolution in France.* Edited by J. G. A. Pocock. Indianapolis, Ind.: Hackett, 1987.

Burnham, James. "Parakeets and Parchesi: An Indian Memorandum." *Partisan Review* 18, no. 5 (1951): 557–68.

Chaudhuri, Nirad C. *The Autobiography of an Unknown Indian.* London: Macmillan, 1951. Reprint, Reading, Mass.: Addison-Wesley, 1989.

———. *Clive of India: A Political and Psychological Essay.* London: Barrie and Jenkins, 1975.

———. *The Continent of Circe: Being an Essay on the People of India.* New York: Oxford University Press, 1966.

———. "The Finest Story about India." *Encounter* 8 (April 1957): 47–53.

———. "India's Kulturkampf." *Quest* 1 (June–July 1954): 12–20.

———. "Passage to and from India." *Encounter* 2 (June 1954): 19–24.

———. *A Passage to England.* New York: St. Martin's, 1959.

———. *Thy Hand, Great Anarch! India: 1921–1952.* Reading, Mass.: Addison-Wesley, 1987.

Chekhov, Anton. "My Life." In *The Chorus Girl and Other Stories*. 1921. Translated by Constance Garnett. New York: Ecco, 1985.

Collins, Wilkie. "The Great (Forgotten) Invasion." *Household Words*, March 12, 1859, 337–41. Reprint, in *My Miscellanies*. Vol. 1. London: Sampson, Low, Son, 1863.

———. *The Moonstone*. 1868. Edited by J. I. M. Stewart. London: Penguin, 1998.

———. "A Sermon for Sepoys." *Household Words*, February 27, 1858, 244–47.

———. *The Woman in White*. 1860. Edited by Harvey Peter Sucksmith. Oxford: Oxford University Press, 1980.

Conrad, Joseph. *Heart of Darkness*. 1902. Edited by Robert Kimbrough. New York: Norton, 1988.

Coomaraswamy, Ananda. *The Dance of Siva: Fourteen Indian Essays*. New York: Sunwise Turn, 1918.

Dickens, Charles. *Letters of Charles Dickens*. Vol. 8. Edited by Graham Storey and Kathleen Tillotson. Oxford: Clarendon, 1995.

———. *The Mystery of Edwin Drood*. 1870. Edited by Margaret Cardwell. Oxford: Oxford University Press, 1982.

Desani, Govindas V. *All about H. Hatterr: A Novel*. 1948. New Paltz, N.Y.: McPherson, 1986.

Eliot, George. *Middlemarch*. 1872. Edited by David Carroll. Oxford: Clarendon, 1986.

Ezekial, Nissim. Editorial. *Quest* 1 (August 1955): 2–3.

———. "James T. Farrell." *Quest* 1 (June–July 1956): 33–34.

———. "Naipaul's India and Mine." In *New Writing in India*. Edited by Adil Jussawalla. Baltimore: Penguin, 1974.

Farrell, James. Letter. *Quest* 2 (August–September 1956): 65–66.

———. Letter. *Quest* 2 (December–January 1956–1957): 57–59.

Ferguson, Adam. *Essay on the History of Civil Society*. 1767. Edited by Duncan Forbes. Edinburgh: Edinburgh University Press, 1966.

Flaubert, Gustave. *L'Education sentimentale*. 1869. Paris: Gallimard, 1965.

———. *Sentimental Education*. Translated by Robert Baldick. Harmondsworth, U.K.: Penguin, 1964.

Forster, E. M. *A Passage to India*. 1924. San Diego: Harcourt Brace Jovanovich, 1984.

Gandhi, M. K. "Benares University Speech." In *The Gandhi Reader: A Source Book of His Life and Writings*, edited by Homer A. Jack. Bloomington: Indiana University Press, 1956.

———. *My Experiments with Truth*. Translated by Mahadev Desai. Ahmedabad, India: Navajivan, 1927–1929.

Haldar, M. K. "What Shall We Celebrate? 1857 and Indian Nationalism." *Quest* 3 (October–November 1957): 8–14.

Hazlitt, William. Review of *Letters from the Hon. Horace Walpole to George Montagu, Esq. Edinburgh Review* 31 (December 1818): 80–93.

James, Henry. *What Maisie Knew*. 1897. Edited by Paul Theroux. New York: Viking Penguin, 1985.

Johnson, Samuel. "Cowley." In vol. 1 of *Lives of the English Poets*, edited by George Birkbeck Hill, 1–69. Oxford: Clarendon, 1905.

Joshi, R. B. "A Day in Bithur." *Quest* 3 (August–September 1957): 38–41.

Joyce, James. *A Portrait of the Artist as a Young Man*. New York: Viking Penguin, 1964.

———. *Ulysses*. Edited by Hans Walter Gabler. New York: Garland, 1996.

"Letter to Mr. Urban." *Gentleman's Magazine* 41 (September 1771): 402–4.

"Letter Written by an Officer Who Lately Served in Bengal." *Gentleman's Magazine* 42 (February 1772): 69.

Macaulay, Thomas Babington. "The Gates of Somnauth." In vol. 9 of *The Complete Writings of Lord Macaulay*, edited by Lady Trevelyan. New York: Knight, 1898.

———. "Minute on Indian Education." In *Prose and Poetry*, edited by G. M. Young. Cambridge, Mass.: Harvard University Press, 1967.

———. Review of *Letters of Horace Walpole, Earl of Oxford, to Sir Horace Mann, British Envoy at the Court of Tuscany*, edited by Lord Dover. *Edinburgh Review* 58 (October 1833): 227–58.

Mill, James. *The History of British India*. Edited and abridged by William Thomas. Chicago: University of Chicago Press, 1975.

Mill, John Stuart. *Autobiography and Literary Essays*. Vol. 1, *Collected Works of John Stuart Mill*, edited by J. M. Robson and Jack Stillinger. Toronto: University of Toronto Press, 1981.

———. *Essays on Equality, Law and Education*. Vol. 21, *Collected Works of John Stuart Mill*, edited by J. M. Robson. Toronto: University of Toronto Press, 1984.

———. *Essays on Politics and Society*. Vols. 18 and 19, *Collected Works of John Stuart Mill*, edited by J. M. Robson. Toronto: University of Toronto Press, 1977.

———. *Writings on India*. Vol. 30, *Collected Works of John Stuart Mill*, edited by J. M. Robson, Martin Moir, and Zawahir Moir. Toronto: University of Toronto Press, 1990.

Mishra, Pankaj. "The Art of Inquisition." *Outlook*, August 16, 1999. Online. Available: http://outlookIndia.com. Accessed July 12, 2001.

———. "The Birth of a Nation." *New York Review of Books*, October 5, 2000, 32–37.

———. *Butter Chicken in Ludhiana: Travels in Small Town India*. New Delhi: Penguin, 1995.

———. "Death in Kashmir." *New York Review of Books*, September 21, 2000, 36–42.

———. "Edmund Wilson in Benares." *New York Review of Books*, April 9, 1998. Reprint, in *Picador Book of Modern Indian Literature*, edited by Amit Chaudhuri, 356–72. London: Picador, 2001.

———. "The Great Narayan." *New York Review of Books*, February 22, 2001, 44–47.

———. "House of Mr. Naipaul." *New York Review of Books*, January 20, 2000, 14–17.

———. "Kashmir: The Unending War." *New York Review of Books*, October 19, 2000, 23–28.

———. "The Last Englishman." *Prospect*, November 1997. Online. Available: http://prospect-magazine.co.uk/highlights/last_englishman/index.htm. Accessed May 10, 2001.

———. "Little Inkling." *Outlook*, November 15, 1999. Online. Available: http://outlookIndia.com. Accessed July 12, 2001.

———. "A New Nuclear India?" *New York Review of Books*, June 25, 1998, 55–64.

———."The Other India." *New York Review of Books*, December 16, 1999, 91–100.

———. "Pankaj Mishra Chat [February 5, 2000]." Rediff on the Net. Online. Available: http://rediff.com.chat/pankchat.htm. Accessed May 10, 2001.

———. *The Romantics: A Novel*. New York: Random House, 2000.

Naipaul, V. S. *An Area of Darkness*. London: Deutsch, 1964.

———. *A Bend in the River*. New York: Knopf, 1979.

———. *Between Father and Son: Family Letters*. Edited by Gillon Aitken. New York: Knopf, 2000.

———. "A Conversation" with Robert Boyers and Bharati Mukherjee. *Salmagundi* 54 (fall 1981): 4–22.

———. *The Enigma of Arrival: A Novel*. New York: Knopf, 1987.

———. *India: A Million Mutinies Now*. London: Heinemann, 1990.

———. *India: A Wounded Civilization*. New York: Knopf, 1977.

———. *A Way in the World: A Novel*. New York: Knopf, 1994.

Narayan, Jayaprakash. *Socialism, Sarvodaya, and Democracy*. Edited by Bimla Prasad. New York: Asia, 1964.

Nehru, Jawaharlal. *Toward Freedom: The Autobiography of Jawaharlal Nehru*. Boston: Beacon, 1941.

Orwell, George. "Reflections on Gandhi." *Partisan Review* 16, no. 1 (1949): 85–92.

———. *The Road to Wigan Pier*. London: Gollancz, 1937.

Palgrave, Francis Turner, ed. *The Children's Treasury of Lyrical Poetry*. London: Macmillan, 1892.

———, ed. *Palgrave's Golden Treasury*. 2d series. London: Macmillan, 1890.

Passin, Herbert. "The Jeevan-Dani: A Profile of Jayaprakash Narayan." *Encounter* 10 (June 1958): 46–55.

———. "Journey among the Saints." *Encounter* 4 (February 1955): 71–74.

Peggs, J. *The Suttees' Cry to Britain: Extracts from Essays Published in India and Parliamentary Papers*. London: Seely, 1827.

Poynder, John. "Human Sacrifices in India." Speech to Proprietors of East India Stock, March 21, 28, 1827. London: Hatchard, 1827.

Rammohun Roy, Raja. *The English Works of Raja Rammohun Roy*. Edited by K. Nag and D. Burman. Calcutta: Sadharan Brahmo Samaj, 1945.

Raynal, Abbé Guillaume. *A Philosophical and Political History of the Settlements and Trade of the Europeans in the East and West Indies*. 6 vols. Translated by J. Justamond. Edinburgh: Mundell and Son for Bell and Bradfute, 1804.

Rushdie, Salman. *Imaginary Homelands: Essays and Criticism, 1981–1991*. London: Granta, 1991.

———. *Midnight's Children*. New York: Penguin, 1980.

———. The Satanic Verses. New York: Viking, 1989.

Scott, Major John. *A Letter to the Right Honourable Edmund Burke, Paymaster General of Her Majesty's Forces*. London: Printed for J. Stockdale, 1783.

Seeley, J. R. *The Expansion of England*. Cambridge: Cambridge University Press; Boston: Roberts Brothers, 1883.

Seth, Vikram. *A Suitable Boy*. New York: HarperCollins, 1993.

Shah, A. B. "Religion and Indian Democracy: The Strategy of Freedom." *Quest* 1 (December–January 1955–1956): 25–30.

Sleeman, William Henry. *Rambles and Recollections of an Indian Official*. 2 vols. London: Hatchard, 1844.

Stephen, James Fitzjames. *The Story of Nuncomar and the Impeachment of Sir Elijah Impey*. London: Macmillan, 1885.

Tennyson, Hallam. "A Dynasty of Saints." *Encounter* 3 (December 1954): 3–8.

Tharoor, Shashi. "A Bedeviling Question in the Cadence of English." *New York Times*, July 30, 2001, B1–B2.

Thompson, Edward. *The Other Side of the Medal*. 1925. Reprint edited by Mulk Raj Anand. New Delhi: Sterling, 1989.

Tolstoy, Leo. *What Then Must We Do?* 1887. Translated and edited by Aylmer Maude. Vol. 14, Tolstoy Centenary Edition. Oxford: Oxford University Press, 1925.

Trevelyan, G. O. *The Competition Wallah*. London: Macmillan, 1866.

Verne, Jules. *Around the World in Eighty Days*. 1873. Translated by George Makepeace Towle. New York: Bantam, 1984.

Vijayatunga, J. "Pondicherry Journal: Record of a Critical Mood." *Quest* 1 (October–November 1955): 17–22.

Walpole, Horace. *The Castle of Otranto*. Edited by W. S. Lewis. London: Oxford University Press, 1964.

———. *The Yale Edition of Horace Walpole's Correspondence*. 48 vols. Edited by W. S. Lewis. New Haven, Conn.: Yale University Press, 1937–1983.

Wollstonecraft, Mary. *A Vindication of the Rights of Woman*. In vol. 5 of *The Works of Mary Wollstonecraft*, edited by Janet Todd and Marilyn Butler. New York: New York University Press, 1989.

Secondary Texts

Ahmad, Aijaz. *In Theory: Classes, Nations, Literatures*. London: Verso, 1992.

Archer, Mildred. *Tippoo's Tiger*. London: Her Majesty's Stationery Office, 1959.

Ayres, Philip. *Classical Culture and the Idea of Rome in Eighteenth-Century England*. Cambridge: Cambridge University Press, 1997.

Ballhatchet, Kenneth. *Social Policy and Social Change in Western India: 1817–30*. London: Oxford University Press, 1957.

Barnett, Richard B. *North India between Empires: Awadh, the Mughals, and the British, 1720–1801*. Berkeley: University of California Press, 1980.

Baxter, Craig, et al. *Government and Politics in South Asia*. 4th ed. Boulder, Colo.: Westview, 1987.

Bayly, C. A. *Indian Society and the Making of the British Empire*. New Cambridge History of India, no. 2.1. Cambridge: Cambridge University Press, 1988.

Bhabha, Homi K. *The Location of Culture*. London: Routledge, 1994.

Bocock, Robert. *Hegemony*. Key Ideas Series. London: Tavistock, 1986.

Brantlinger, Patrick. "The Nineteenth-Century Novel and Empire." In *Columbia History of the British Novel*, edited by John J. Richetti et al., 560–78. New York: Columbia University Press, 1994.

———. *Rule of Darkness: British Literature and Imperialism: 1830–1914*. Ithaca, N.Y.: Cornell University Press, 1988.

Breckenridge, Carol A., and Appadurai Arjun. "Editors' Comments: On Fictionalizing the Real." *Public Culture* 1 (spring 1989): i–v.

Bromwich, David. Introduction to *On Empire, Liberty, and Reform: Speeches and Letters, Edmund Burke*, edited by David Bromwich. New Haven, Conn.: Yale University Press, 2000.

Buddle, Anne. *Tigers Round the Throne: The Court of Tipu Sultan (1750–1799)*. London: Zamana Gallery, 1990.

Cardwell, Margaret. Introduction to *The Mystery of Edwin Drood*, by Charles Dickens. Oxford: Oxford University Press, 1982.

Carnall, Geoffrey. "Burke as Modern Cicero." In *The Impeachment of Warren Hastings: Papers from a Bicentenary Commemoration*, edited by Geoffrey Carnall and Colin Nicholson. Edinburgh: Edinburgh University Press, 1989.

Chakrabarty, Dipesh. "Postcoloniality and the Artifice of History: Who Speaks for 'Indian' Pasts?" *Representations* 37 (winter 1992): 1–26.

Chatterjee, Partha. "Colonialism, Nationalism, and Colonized Women: The Contest in India." *American Ethnologist* 16 (November 1989): 622–33.

———. *Nationalist Thought and the Colonial World: A Derivative Discourse?* London: Zed, 1986.

Chaudhuri, Amit. Introduction to *The Picador Book of Modern Indian Literature*, edited by Amit Chaudhuri. London: Picador, 2001.

Chomsky, Noam. "The Responsibility of Intellectuals." *New York Review of Books*, February 23, 1967, 16–25.

Clarke, William M. *The Secret Life of Wilkie Collins*. London: Allen, 1981.

Clifford, James. *The Predicament of Culture: Twentieth-Century Ethnography, Literature, and Art*. Cambridge, Mass.: Harvard University Press, 1988.

Coleman, Peter. *The Liberal Conspiracy: The Congress for Cultural Freedom and the Struggle for the Mind of Post-War Europe*. New York: Free Press, 1989.

"The Complete Review: *The Romantics*, by Pankaj Mishra." Online. Available: http://complete-review-com/reviews/mishrap/romantics.htm. Accessed July 12, 2001.

Coser, Lewis. "The CIA—Enemy or Promise." *Dissent* 14 (May–June 1967): 274–83.

Couto, Maria. "Midnight's Children and Parents: The Search for Indo-British Identity." *Encounter* 58 (February 1982): 61–66.

Crane, Ralph. *Inventing India: A History of India in English-Language Fiction*. Basingstoke, U.K.: Macmillan, 1992.

Davis, Nuel Pharr. *The Life of Wilkie Collins*. Urbana: University of Illinois Press, 1956.

Dieckmann, Herbert. "Les contributions de Diderot à la 'Correspondance litté-raire' et à l' 'Histoire des Deux Indes.'" *Revue d'histoire littéraire de la France* 51 (1951): 417–40.

Editors. "A Word to Our Readers." *Dissent* 1 (winter 1954): 3–4.

Epstein, Jason. "The CIA and the Intellectuals." *New York Review of Books*, April 20, 1967, 16–21.

Fanon, Frantz. *Black Skin, White Masks*. Translated by Charles Lam Markmann. New York: Grove, 1967.

Feugère, Anatole. "Raynal, Diderot et quelques autres 'Historiens des deux Indes.'" *Revue d'histoire littéraire de la France* 20 (1913): 343–78.

Fischer, Michael, and Mehda Abede. Letter. *Public Culture* 2 (fall 1989): 123–26.

Fussell, Paul. *The Great War and Modern Memory*. New York: Oxford University Press, 1975.

Goonatilake, Susantha. *Crippled Minds: An Exploration into Colonial Culture*. New Delhi: Vikas, 1982.

Gorra, Michael. *After Empire: Scott, Naipaul, Rushdie*. Chicago: University of Chicago Press, 1997.

Gramsci, Antonio. *A Gramsci Reader: Selected Writings 1916–1935*. Edited by David Forgacs. London: Lawrence and Wishart, 1988.

Guha, Ranajit. *Dominance without Hegemony: History and Power in Colonial India*. Cambridge, Mass.: Harvard University Press, 1997.

———. *Elementary Aspects of Peasant Insurgency in Colonial India*. Delhi: Oxford University Press, 1983.

———. *A Rule of Property for Bengal: An Essay on the Idea of Permanent Settle-ment*. 1963. Reprint, Durham, N.C.: Duke University Press, 1996.

Hai, Ambreen. "On Truth and Lie in a Colonial Sense: Kipling's Tales of Tale-Telling." *ELH* 64 (summer 1997): 599–625.

Harrington, Michael. "Liberalism: A Moral Crisis." *Dissent* 2 (September–Octo-ber 1967): 13–22.

Heller, Tamar. *Dead Secrets: Wilkie Collins and the Female Gothic*. New Haven, Conn.: Yale University Press, 1992.

Hertz, Neil. *The End of the Line: Essays on Psychoanalysis and the Sublime*. New York: Columbia University Press, 1985.

Holcombe, Lee. *Wives and Property: Reform of the Married Women's Property Law in Nineteenth-Century England*. Toronto: University of Toronto Press, 1983.

Hutchins, Francis G. *The Illusion of Permanence: British Imperialism in India*. Princeton, N.J.: Princeton University Press, 1967.

Irele, Abiola. "African Letters: The Making of a Tradition." *Yale Journal of Criti-cism* 5 (fall 1991): 69–100.

Isaacs, Harold R. *Scratches on Our Minds: American Images of China and India*. 1958. Reprint, Westport, Conn.: Greenwood, 1973.

Iyengar, K. R. S. *Indian Writing in English*. New Delhi: Sterling, 1987.

Jameson, Fredric. "Third-World Literature in the Era of Multinational Capital-ism." *Social Text* 15 (fall 1986): 65–88.

Jeffreys-Jones, Rhodri. *The CIA and American Democracy*. New Haven, Conn.: Yale University Press, 1989.

Jha, Akhileshwar. *The Imprisoned Mind*. New Delhi: Ambika, 1980.

———. *Intellectuals at the Crossroads*. New Delhi: Vikas, 1977.

Jussawalla, Feroza F. "Decolonizing the Decolonizers." *North Dakota Quarterly* 55, no. 3 (1987): 175–89.

———. *Family Quarrels: Towards a Criticism of Indian Writing in English*. New York: Lang, 1985.

———. "Resurrecting the Prophet: The Case of Salman, the Otherwise." *Public Culture* 2 (fall 1989): 106–16.

Kakar, Sudhir. *Intimate Relations: Exploring Indian Sexuality*. Chicago: Univer-sity of Chicago Press, 1989.

Kanga, Firdaus. Review of *India: A Million Mutinies Now*, by V. S. Naipaul. *Times Literary Supplement*, October 5, 1990, 1059.

Kemp, Sandra. Notes to *The Moonstone*, by Wilkie Collins. London: Penguin, 1998.

Knapp, Steven. *Personification and the Sublime: Milton to Coleridge*. Cambridge, Mass.: Harvard University Press, 1985.

Kopkind, Andrew. "CIA: The Great Corruptor." *New Statesman*, February 24, 1967, 249–50.

Kramnick, Isaac. "The Left and Edmund Burke." *Political Theory* 2, no. 2 (1983): 189–214.

———. *The Rage of Edmund Burke*. New York: Basic, 1977.

Kristol, Irving. *Reflections of a Neoconservative: Looking Back, Looking Ahead*. New York: Basic, 1983.

Lasch, Christopher. *The Agony of the American Left*. London: Deutsch, 1970.

Lawson, Lewis A. "Wilkie Collins and *The Moonstone*." *American Imago* 20 (spring 1963): 61–79.

Lewis, W. S. Introduction to *The Castle of Otranto*, by Horace Walpole. London: Oxford University Press, 1964.

Linton, Erica. *Fragments of a Vision*. New Delhi: Prithvi Raj, 1972.

Lock, F. P. *Edmund Burke*. Vol. 1, *1730–1784*. Oxford: Clarendon; New York: Ox-ford University Press, 1998.

Lonoff, Sue. *Wilkie Collins and His Victorian Readers: A Study in the Rhetoric of Authorship*. New York: AMS, 1982.

Macdonald, Dwight. "No Miracle in Milan." *Encounter* 5 (December 1955): 68–74.

Madhavananda, Swami, and Ramesh Chandra Majumdar, eds. *Great Women of India*. The Holy Mother Birth Centenary Memorial. Mayavati, India: Advaita Ashrama, 1953.

Mani, Lata. *Contentious Traditions: The Debate on* Sati *in Colonial India*. Berkeley: University of California Press, 1998.

Marshall, P. J. *Bengal: The British Bridgehead*. New Cambridge History of India, no. 2.2. Cambridge: Cambridge University Press, 1987.

———. *The Impeachment of Warren Hastings*. London: Oxford University Press, 1965.

———, ed. *The Eighteenth Century*. Vol. 2, *The Oxford History of the British Empire*. London: Oxford University Press, 1998.

Masani, Minoo. "Bhoodan in Action." *Encounter* 3 (December 1954): 8–13.

Mason, Philip [Philip Woodruff]. *The Founders of Modern India*. Vol. 1 of *The Men Who Ruled India*. New York: St. Martin's, 1954.

———. *The Guardians*. Vol. 2 of *The Men Who Ruled India*. New York: St. Martin's, 1954.

McCutchion, David. *Indian Writing in English: Critical Essays*. Calcutta: Writer's Workshop, 1973.

———. "Report on the *Quest* Seminar: Belief and Literature." *Quest*, no. 21 (April–June 1959): 47–52.

Memmi, Albert. *The Colonizer and the Colonized*. Translated by Howard Greenfeld. New York: Orion, 1965.

Metcalf, Thomas R. *Ideologies of the Raj*. New Cambridge History of India, no. 3.4. Cambridge: Cambridge University Press, 1994.

Miller, D. A. *The Novel and the Police*. Berkeley: University of California Press, 1988.

Miller, Karl. Review of *India: A Million Mutinies Now*, by V. S. Naipaul. *London Review of Books*, September 27, 1990, 11–13.

Mishra, Sudesh. "The Two Chaudhuris: Historical Witness and Pseudo-Historian." *Journal of Commonwealth Literature* 23, no. 1 (1988): 7–15.

Moir, Martin. Introduction to *Writings on India*, by John Stuart Mill, vii–liv. Vol. 30, *Collected Works of John Stuart Mill*, edited by J. M. Robson, Martin Moir, and Zawahir Moir. Toronto: University of Toronto Press, 1990.

Moore-Gilbert, Bart. "The Bhabhal of Tongues: Reading Kipling, Reading Bhabha." In *Writing India, 1757–1900: The Literature of British India*, edited by Bart Moore-Gilbert, 111–38. Manchester: Manchester University Press, 1996.

———. "Writing India, Reorienting Colonial Discourse Analysis." Introduction to *Writing India, 1757–1990: The Literature of British India*, edited by Bart Moore-Gilbert. Manchester: Manchester University Press, 1996.

Morey, Peter. *Fictions of India: Narrative and Power*. Edinburgh: Edinburgh University Press, 2000.

Muggeridge, Malcolm. "Books." *Esquire* 68 (September 1967): 12–16.

Mukherjee, Meenakshi. *The Perishable Empire: Essays on Indian Writing in English*. New Delhi: Oxford University Press, 2000.

Musselwhite, David. "The Trial of Warren Hastings." In *Literature, Politics, and Theory: Papers from the Essex Conference, 1976–84*, edited by Francis Barker et al. London: Methuen, 1986.

Nandy, Ashis. *The Intimate Enemy: Loss and Recovery of Self under Colonialism*. Delhi: Oxford University Press, 1983.

Natarajan, L. *American Shadow over India*. Bombay: People's Publishing House, 1952.

Nayder, Lillian. *Wilkie Collins*. Twayne English Author Series, no. 544. New York: Twayne; London: Prentice Hall, 1997.

Ngugi wa Thiong'o. *Decolonising the Mind: The Politics of Language in African Literature*. Portsmouth: Heinemann, 1986.

Nixon, Rob. *London Calling: V. S. Naipaul, Postcolonial Mandarin*. New York: Oxford University Press, 1992.

Nussbaum, Martha C. *Sex and Social Justice*. New York: Oxford University Press, 1999.

——. *Women and Human Development: The Capabilities Approach*. Cambridge: Cambridge University Press, 2000.

O'Brien, Conor Cruise. *The Great Melody: A Thematic Biography and Commented Anthology of Edmund Burke*. Chicago: University of Chicago Press, 1992.

Page, Norman, ed. *Wilkie Collins: The Critical Heritage*. London: Routledge & Kegan Paul, 1974.

Panikkar, K. M. *Asia and Western Dominance*. New York: Day, 1954.

Peltason, Timothy. "The Place of Reading: Graduate Education and the Literature Classroom." *ADE Bulletin* 13 (spring 1996): 9–12.

Perera, Suvendrini. *Reaches of Empire: The English Novel from Edgeworth to Dickens*. New York: Columbia University Press, 1991.

Philip, David Scott. *Perceiving India through the Works of Nirad C. Chaudhuri, Narayan and Ved Mehta*. New York: Envoy, 1986.

Pocock, J. G. A. *The Machiavellian Moment*. Princeton, N.J.: Princeton University Press, 1975.

——. *Virtue, Commerce, and History: Essays on Political Thought and History, Chiefly in the Eighteenth Century*. Cambridge: Cambridge University Press, 1985.

Porter, Dennis. *Haunted Journeys: Desire and Transgression in European Travel Writing*. Princeton, N.J.: Princeton University Press, 1991.

——. "Orientalism and Its Problems." In *The Politics of Theory: Proceedings of the Essex Conference on the Sociology of Literature, July 1982*, edited by Francis Barker, Peter Hulme, Margaret Iversen, and Diane Loxley. Colchester, U.K.: University of Essex, 1983.

Rahman, Tariq. *Language, Education, and Culture*. Karachi: Oxford University Press, 1999.

Reed, John. "English Imperialism and the Unacknowledged Crime of *The Moonstone*." *Clio* 2 (June 1973): 281–90.

Reid, Christopher. *Edmund Burke and the Practice of Political Writing*. Dublin: Gill and Macmillan; New York: St. Martin's, 1985.

Roy, Ashish. "The Fabulous Imperialist Semiotic of Wilkie Collins's *The Moonstone*." *New Literary History* 24 (summer 1993): 657–81.

Rycroft, Charles. "A Detective Story: Psychoanalytic Observations." *Psychoanalytic Quarterly* 20 (1957): 229–45.

Sabin, Margery. *The Dialect of the Tribe: Speech and Community in Modern Fiction*. New York: Oxford University Press, 1987.

————. "Literary Reading in Interdisciplinary Study." *Profession* 95 (1995): 14–17.

————. "Lu Xun: Revolution and the Individual Talent." *Raritan Quarterly* 9 (summer 1989): 41–67.

Sabor, Peter, ed. *Horace Walpole: The Critical Heritage*. London: Routledge & Kegan Paul, 1987.

Said, Edward W. *Culture and Imperialism*. New York: Knopf, 1993.

————. "Intellectuals in the Post-Colonial World." *Salmagundi* 70–71 (spring–summer 1986): 44–64.

————. *Orientalism*. New York: Pantheon, 1978.

————. "Restoring Intellectual Coherence." *MLA Newsletter* (spring 1999): 3–4.

————. "Third World Intellectuals and Metropolitan Culture." *Raritan Quarterly* 9 (winter 1990): 27–50.

Samson, John. "Politics Gothicized: The Conway Incident and *The Castle of Otranto*." *Eighteenth Century Life* 10, n.s. 3 (October 1986): 145–58.

Sarkar, Sumit. Afterword to *The Other Side of the Medal*, edited by Mulk Raj Anand. New Delhi: Sterling, 1989.

Sen, Amartya. "Capability and Well-Being." In *The Quality of Life*, edited by Martha Nussbaum and Amartya Sen, 30–53. Oxford: Clarendon; New York: Oxford University Press, 1993.

Shils, Edward. "Remembering the Congress for Cultural Freedom." *Encounter* 75 (September 1990): 53–65.

Smith, Vincent A. *The Oxford History of India*. 4th ed. Edited by Percival Spear. Delhi: Oxford University Press, 1981.

Spear, Percival. *The Nabobs: A Study of the Social Life of the English in Eighteenth-Century India*. London: Oxford University Press, 1963.

Spender, Spender. "Notes from a Diary." *Encounter* 5 (December 1955): 54–55.

Spivak, Gayatri Chakravorty. "Can the Subaltern Speak?" In *Marxism and the Interpretation of Culture*, edited by Cary Nelson and Lawrence Grossberg, 271–308. Urbana: University of Illinois Press, 1988.

Stokes, Eric. *The English Utilitarians and India*. Oxford: Clarendon, 1959.

Suleri, Sara. *The Rhetoric of English India*. Chicago: University of Chicago Press, 1992.

Sunder Rajan, Rajeswari. "The Subject of Sati: Pain and Death in the Contemporary Discourse on Sati." *Yale Journal of Criticism* 3, no. 2 (1990): 1–23.

Sutherland, Lucy. *The East India Company in Eighteenth-Century Politics*. Oxford: Clarendon, 1952.

Taylor, Charles. "The Rushdie Controversy." *Public Culture* 2 (fall 1989): 118–22.

Teltscher, Kate. *India Inscribed: European and British Writing on India, 1600–1800*. Delhi: Oxford University Press, 1995.

Thomas, Ronald R. *Dreams of Authority: Freud and the Fictions of the Unconscious*. Ithaca, N.Y.: Cornell University Press, 1990.

Thompson, Edward. *Suttee: A Historical and Philosophical Enquiry into the Hindu Rite of Widow-burning*. London: Allen and Unwin, 1928.

Thompson, Edward J., and G. T. Garratt. *Rise and Fulfillment of British Rule in India*. London: Macmillan, 1935.

Thornton, Weldon. *Allusions in "Ulysses."* Chapel Hill: University of North Carolina Press, 1961.

Verghese, Paul C. *Nirad C. Chaudhuri*. Indian Writers Series, no. 2. London: Arnold-Heinemann India, 1973.

———. "Nirad C. Chaudhuri: An Assessment." In *Perspectives on Indian Prose in English*, edited by M. K. Naik, 200–212. New Delhi: Abhinav, 1982.

Viswanathan, Gauri. *Masks of Conquest: Literary Study and British Rule in India*. New York: Columbia University Press, 1989.

Wald, Alan M. *The New York Intellectuals: The Rise and Decline of the Anti-Stalinist Left from the 1930s to the 1980s*. Chapel Hill: University of North Carolina Press, 1987.

Walsh, Judith E. *Growing Up in British India: Indian Autobiographers on Childhood and Education under the Raj*. New York: Homes & Meier, 1983.

Walsh, William. *Indian Literature in English*. London: Longman, 1990.

Whelan, Frederick G. *Edmund Burke and India: Political Morality and Empire*. Pittsburgh: University of Pittsburgh Press, 1996.

Williams, Raymond. *Marxism and Literature*. Oxford: Oxford University Press, 1977.

Wilson, Arthur M. *Diderot*. New York: Oxford University Press, 1972.

Wilson, Edmund. "Flaubert's Politics." In *The Triple Thinkers: Ten Essays on Literature*. 100–121. New York: Harcourt Brace, 1938.

Wolpe, Hans. "Diderot collaborateur de Raynal." *Revue d'histoire littéraire de la France* 60 (1960): 531–62.

———. *Raynal et sa machine de guerre: l'Histoire des deux Indes et ses perfectionnements*. Stanford, Calif.: Stanford University Press, 1957.

Wolpert, Stanley. *A New History of India*. 6th ed. New York: Oxford University Press, 2000.

Yule, Henry, and A. C. Burnell. *Hobson-Jobson*. Edited by William Crooke. 1903. Rev. ed., Delhi: Munshiram Manoharlal, 1968.

Zastoupil, Lynn. "J. S. Mill and India." *Victorian Studies* 32 (fall 1988): 31–54.

INDEX